ROUTLEDGE LIBRARY EDITIONS:
PHILOSOPHY OF LANGUAGE

Volume 3

LANGUAGE, MIND AND VALUE

LANGUAGE, MIND AND VALUE
Philosophical Essays

J. N. FINDLAY

LONDON AND NEW YORK

First published in 1963 by George Allen & Unwin Ltd

This edition first published in 2017
by Routledge
2 Park Square, Milton Park, Abingdon, Oxon OX14 4RN

and by Routledge
711 Third Avenue, New York, NY 10017

Routledge is an imprint of the Taylor & Francis Group, an informa business

© 1963 George Allen & Unwin Ltd

All rights reserved. No part of this book may be reprinted or reproduced or utilised in any form or by any electronic, mechanical, or other means, now known or hereafter invented, including photocopying and recording, or in any information storage or retrieval system, without permission in writing from the publishers.

Trademark notice: Product or corporate names may be trademarks or registered trademarks, and are used only for identification and explanation without intent to infringe.

British Library Cataloguing in Publication Data
A catalogue record for this book is available from the British Library

ISBN: 978-1-138-68428-7 (Set)
ISBN: 978-1-315-52145-9 (Set) (ebk)
ISBN: 978-1-138-69099-8 (Volume 3) (hbk)
ISBN: 978-1-315-53593-7 (Volume 3) (ebk)

Publisher's Note
The publisher has gone to great lengths to ensure the quality of this reprint but points out that some imperfections in the original copies may be apparent.

Disclaimer
The publisher has made every effort to trace copyright holders and would welcome correspondence from those they have been unable to trace.

LANGUAGE
MIND
AND VALUE

PHILOSOPHICAL ESSAYS

BY

J. N. FINDLAY

M.A., PH.D., F.B.A.

Professor of Philosophy in the University of London
(King's College)

Καὶ ὡς ἀληθῶς τὸ ἀγαθὸν καὶ
δέον συνδεῖν καὶ συνέχειν οὐδὲν οἴονται

London
GEORGE ALLEN & UNWIN LTD

FIRST PUBLISHED 1963

*This book is copyright under the Berne Convention.
Apart from any fair dealing for the purposes of private
study, research, criticism or review, as permitted under
the Copyright Act 1956, no portion may be reproduced
by any process without written permission. Enquiry
should be made to the publishers*

© *George Allen & Unwin Ltd, 1963*

PRINTED IN GREAT BRITAIN
in 11 *on* 12 *point Fournier type*
BY UNWIN BROTHERS LIMITED
WOKING AND LONDON

PREFACE

THE articles collected in this volume were written over the last twenty years: I have selected them for republication because they seem to me to make some points that are still worth making, and because they have in some cases interested and influenced others. The opening articles, 'Some Reactions to Recent Cambridge Philosophy' (1940–1) and 'Time: a Treatment of Some Puzzles' (1941), represent the impact of Wittgenstein on my thought, after I had spent some time attending his courses in 1939, and had brooded over the *Blue Book*, *Brown Book* and what had then been written of the *Philosophical Investigations*. They have seemed to me worth re-publishing because they reflect sides of Wittgenstein's teaching not usually stressed: his deep love for the philosophical puzzles he tried to liquidate, as well as his valuable doctrine (mainly used by him to excuse his own *penchant* for solipsism) that the special notations of philosophers serve to bring out important likenesses and differences (or to suppress these or falsely suggest their presence), in other words to 'illuminate' or 'mislead'. In this last doctrine Wittgenstein seems to me to have suggested that 'truth' in philosophy is no mere question of correctness or incorrectness, but for the most part a question of *goodness* and *badness* in speaking, a view which seems to me of incalculable importance, and which has inspired *all* the articles in this volume, including the somewhat homiletic 'Values in Speaking' (my inaugural address at Newcastle). I hope that I have also testified indirectly to Wittgenstein's personal inspiration, to the liberating intellectual light he seemed to diffuse. I do not now think that this personal influence was a wholly good thing, as it made one blind to the unquestioned background, the unfinished performance and the unclear tendency of some of his thinking.

The articles which follow represent my gradual return to an orbit more natural to myself, but, I think, more sensitive to the many pulls which render a philosophical orbit 'reasonable'. I have included my review (1955) of Wittgenstein's *Philosophical Investigations* to indicate the extent of my disengagement, and the later articles include a tribute to G. E. Moore, a philosopher whom I rank above any other British thinker in the present century. I have also included a lecture on Hegel largely because it contains points—those comparing dialectic to 'metalinguistic comment'—which seem to me to supplement what I said about the dialectic in my book *Hegel: A Re-Examination* (1958). My interest in Hegel is in no sense new: he was the first philosopher to whom I devoted myself, and my interest in him (though not in his commentators or followers) has persisted throughout several revolutions of outlook. I have also tried to give renewed circulation to an important idea of Husserl in the article 'Some Reflections on Meaning' (1959).

Of the remaining articles in the volume two, 'Goedelian Sentences' (1942) and 'The Notion of Infinity' (1953) reflect an interest in symbolic logic and mathematical philosophy which the endless proliferation of these subjects, the bracketless notation of the Polish logicians, and my own limited capacity, have at length finally stifled. The articles 'Linguistic Approach to Psychophysics' (1950) and 'The Logic of *Bewusstseinslagen*' (1955) express my interest in the philosophy of mind and my great admiration for the work of the Würzburg psychologists. The articles 'Morality by Convention' (1944), 'The Justification of Attitudes' (1954) and 'The Methodology of Normative Ethics' (1961) express my basic belief that the supreme heads of goodness and badness form an ordered family, linked together and arranged by something that may be called a 'logic', and not having the sheer arbitrariness that some modern theories have given them. These convictions are the theme of my *Values and Intentions* (1961): the article 'The Methodology of Normative Ethics' should throw light on the method pursued in that work.

The volume also includes an excursion into theology, 'Can God's Existence be Disproved?' (1948). I still think that it makes a valid point: that if it is *possible*, in some logical and not merely epistemological sense, that there is no God, then God's existence is not merely doubtful but *impossible*, since nothing *capable* of non-existence could be a God at all. Kant, who at times suggested that the existence of anything was a synthetic and *a posteriori* matter (though perhaps establishable only by a non-sensuous intuition) should have seen that his views constituted a *disproof* of the existence of God, not left Him a flawless ideal to which some noumenal reality *might* correspond. Professor Hartshorne has, however, convinced me that my argument permits a ready

PREFACE

inversion, and that one can very well argue that if God's existence is in any way *possible*, then it is also *certain* and *necessary* that God exists, a position which should give some comfort to the shade of Anselm. The notion of God, like the notion of the class of all classes not members of themselves, has plainly unique logical properties, and I do not now think that my article finally *decides* how we should cope with such uniqueness.

I wish to thank the Editor of the *Australasian Journal of Philosophy* for permission to reprint articles I and II, the Editor of *Mind* for permission to reprint articles III, IV, V and IX, the Editor of *Philosophy* for permission to reprint articles VI and XI, the Secretary of the Aristotelian Society for permission to reprint articles VII and VIII, the Editor of the *Philosophical Quarterly* for permission to reprint article X, the Editor of the *Indian Journal of Philosophy* for permission to reprint article XII, and the Editor of the *Journal of Philosophy* for permission to reprint article XV.

J. N. FINDLAY

King's College
London
June 1962

CONTENTS

PREFACE *page* 7

I SOME REACTIONS TO RECENT CAMBRIDGE PHILOSOPHY (1940–1) 13

II TIME: A TREATMENT OF SOME PUZZLES (1941) 39

III GOEDELIAN SENTENCES: A NON-NUMERICAL APPROACH (1942) 57

IV MORALITY BY CONVENTION (1944) 66

V CAN GOD'S EXISTENCE BE DISPROVED? (1948) 96

VI VALUES IN SPEAKING (1950) 105

VII LINGUISTIC APPROACH TO PSYCHO-PHYSICS (1950) 128

VIII THE NOTION OF INFINITY (1953) 146

IX THE JUSTIFICATION OF ATTITUDES (1954) 165

X THE LOGIC OF 'BEWUSSTSEINSLAGEN' (1955) 182

XI REVIEW OF WITTGENSTEIN'S 'PHILOSOPHICAL INVESTIGATIONS' (1955) 197

XII SOME REFLECTIONS ON MEANING (1959) 208

XIII THE CONTEMPORARY RELEVANCE OF HEGEL (1959) 217

XIV SOME NEGLECTED ISSUES IN THE PHILOSOPHY OF G. E. MOORE (1960) 232

XV THE METHODOLOGY OF NORMATIVE ETHICS (1961) 248

INDEX 257

I

SOME REACTIONS TO
RECENT CAMBRIDGE PHILOSOPHY[1]

(1940–1)

I

I wish in this paper to set down what I have managed to understand of the general features and trend of recent philosophy in Cambridge, that is, of the later doctrines of Wittgenstein and of those who have come under his influence. I do so more to clear up my own mind than to produce illumination in others: it is impossible to listen to a series of very perplexing, very ill-expressed but immensely exciting statements, obviously coming from a mind of supreme integrity, without wishing to react to them comprehensively, and see what one can do about them or with them in one's own thinking. After listening to Wittgenstein one becomes alive to an infinity of unsuspected weaknesses and stupidities in the thinking of practically all philosophers: the result is that it is impossible to persist in one's previous ways of thinking and talking on any question whatsoever. If one's philosophical existence is to go on at all—whether it *should* go on may of course be debated—one must necessarily come to some terms with an influence so valuably subversive.

It is by attempting to explain to myself what the Cambridge people are saying, in a paper such as this, and by attempting, further, to go with them as far as I can, that I hope in the long run to come to terms with them. I must emphasize, however, that nothing I say can claim to be a faithful representation of anyone's views or to mirror the historical connections that have led to their development. Only someone who had lived in Cambridge continuously since 1929, when

[1] Published in the *Australasian Journal of Psychology and Philosophy*, December 1940 and April 1941.

LANGUAGE, MIND AND VALUE

philosophy began to move in a new direction, could hope to have a proper understanding of the turns thought has taken there in the last decade, and of the precise place where it stands at present. In an air heavy with allusions to phases of thought and controversy now superseded, the interested outsider can at best succeed in overhearing fragments of a fine conversation which must have lost much in being torn from their context. But these fragments, whether distorted or otherwise, prove, when one goes away with them, to be far more valuable and memorable than many other systems perfectly stated and accurately understood. One turns them over in one's mind repeatedly, one finds oneself using them in unexpected connections, one has, in short, been deeply changed by them. These remarks will, I think, excuse my giving this account, whether accurate or otherwise, of recent philosophy at Cambridge.

The most important fact about recent Cambridge philosophy is that it is a philosophy of *language*: it is an attempt to throw light on the linguistic framework by which we measure everything, and through which we deal with everything. Its attitude to that linguistic framework is twofold: on the one hand it draws us *apart* from our language and makes us look on it more simply and more externally than we are accustomed to do, on the other hand it makes us *return* to our ordinary ways of saying things with a deepened consciousness of their import and value. Now as regards the first proceeding it is certainly not possible to *dispense* with words in discussing our use of words, but it is at least possible to talk about words without superstition, just as we talk about other things in our natural environment. The typical attitude of philosophers has been to *stare* at words rather than to use them or to see how they are used, and, seen in that glazed stare, words invariably become magical, mysterious and 'profound'. Their laws begin to seem less escapable than other human conventions, they tantalize us with prospects of new and inaccessible worlds, like the worlds reflected in mirrors, and they tie us up in tangles which we cannot even begin to unloosen. The typical philosopher does not even *know* that he is staring at the words in his language: he looks *through* them upon various beautiful, rather symmetrical and also rather puzzling patterns, much as, in migraine or fatigued vision, we see various odd assemblages of lines, cubes and pyramids, normally seen through, marching strangely across the sky. If we relax this glassy, philosophic stare we begin to see words simply as counters used in a game, or as tools or materials employed in a certain work,

SOME REACTIONS TO RECENT CAMBRIDGE PHILOSOPHY

and this homely vision is at once far more illuminating, and also far more charming, than the abstract metaphysical vision in which we were previously absorbed. For we realize at once the bewildering variety of ways in which words *are* used, and, what is more, the astonishing variety of the ways in which they *could* be used. The verbal framework loses its mystery: its symmetries and orders cease to seem cosmic, as also do its puzzles and perplexities. We see how we can change or resolve either by altering the ways in which we talk about things. But at the same time we are also brought back, with new understanding, to the various forms of language that we previously used. We see the legitimacy, the value, the purpose of saying certain things in certain ways, the reason why certain men struggle to retain old forms of utterance, and why others feel impelled to alter theirs in the most startling and revolutionary manner. We see the reason for those various forms of picturesque and exaggerated language that have been called metaphysical, how far they take us and where they break down: we also see the value of all the various precise technical jargons and symbolisms, which have assisted us greatly in dealing with certain subject-matters, despite their nonsensical claim that they alone correspond to 'real' alignments and arrangements. And we see, above all, the value of ordinary language, which, despite its lack of precision at certain points, and its inability to give answers to certain questions, remains by far the most pliable of linguistic instruments, and the most faithful to 'experience', correcting the rigidities and misleading suggestions of one use of words by the flexibilities and varied associations of alternative uses. If our faith in the absolute character of certain verbal structures is taken away, we are nevertheless reinforced in our feeling of their permanent value. Nor need we yield to the depreciatory force of such phrases as 'merely verbal', 'only a matter of terminology' and so forth, as if, in a world not merely natural but cultural, there were anything of greater value and dignity, anything more deserving of serious study, than words and their uses.

The primary emphasis of modern Cambridge philosophy is on the *use* of words. This means that, if we wish to understand words, signs, sentences and other forms of symbolism, we must consider how people *operate* with them, in what ways they think it obligatory or legitimate or improper to combine them, what moves in discourse they think themselves entitled to make with them, in what situations they would think it proper to apply them, or what they are looking forward to when they utter them. We must also consider the all-important question as to how people *teach* the use of a given word to others, and how they were themselves taught the use of such words in the first instance. (If we always considered this latter question we should, for example, never fall into such philosophical absurdities as that the word 'I' properly applies to an immaterial subject, or that words like 'anger', 'love', 'perplexity' properly apply to purely private feelings which inhabit our own breasts.) There may seem to be nothing very new about these interests or these emphases: they are to some degree the commonplaces of any reflective treatment of language as a human, social phenomenon. Grammarians and philologists have always treated language in this way. But the treatment in question has never made much headway in philosophy because it always had to contend with another tacitly presumed, not always clearly formulated theory of language, which was all the more insidious in that its positions seemed to be suggested and confirmed by the forms of language iself. This theory of language, the typical theory of philosophers, completely stultifies our understanding of its subject-matter, because it has every appearance of explaining what it merely reiterates unexplained. While it says nothing false, it also says nothing that is not nugatory and tautologous, and it is profoundly misleading because it suggests and claims that it is really being very helpful.

The theory or mode of diction in question is the one which bases itself on the unquestionable fact that words are the *expression* of *thoughts*, on the one hand, and that they *mean things*, on the other. Now our ordinary language does talk about itself in quite definite ways, and it clearly is correct English to say, in many perfectly definite circumstances, that a word or combination of words is *expressing* a thought in someone's mind or head, and that it *means* something in the world of our common experience. But even at the level of ordinary language we have a tendency to be misled by our own ways of talking about our talk, into forming a picture of our language which is neither true nor false, since it cannot be interpreted. The picture in question is one that conceives of our thoughts as invisible, ghostly acts, which accompany our speech but can in certain circumstances dispense with it, and which have their own peculiar ghostly structure which is mirrored, more or less adequately, in the verbal structures of our language. It is, of course, the official theory of linguistic expression sponsored by Aristotle when he speaks of the $\pi\alpha\theta\acute{\eta}\mu\alpha\tau\alpha$ in the soul of which spoken words are the tokens: from Aristotle it has passed down to those numberless thinkers and schools of thinkers who have

SOME REACTIONS TO RECENT CAMBRIDGE PHILOSOPHY

been content to copy his errors. It runs riot, for instance, over the pages of idealist logicians where *the* judgement, a versatile Atlas, is said to be capable of the most varied feats of sustaining, supporting, referring, connecting or holding things together. It is suggested, further, by most of those discussions where it is questioned whether a certain verbal form does or does not correspond to a 'genuine distinction of thought', a question legitimate enough and capable of a plain answer, but not by the intuitive methods employed by most of those who ask it. As a theory it appears to have solid support, for is it not clear that we often see things or surmise things we have no time to put in words or illustrate by pictures? And is it not equally clear that the words and pictures we *do* use often fall short of the packed intensity of significance of quite transitory perceptions? Again, is it not perfectly plain that we often utter words 'automatically', unintelligently, and does this not show that there is something *more* to thinking than mere manipulation of signs or pictures? Like other ghostly manifestations, the ghostly acts of thinking have even shown themselves to scientific observers, who have henceforth been hounded by those of their fraternity who have not been able to elicit similar effects. The theory has further led to elaborate researches into the varieties of mental act and their relations to each other, researches sometimes conducted empirically and sometimes by *a priori* intuition; it has led to a vast assemblage of insoluble questions such as 'Is pleasure a referential attitude?' 'Is disbelief a peculiar experience, or merely belief in something negative?' 'What is the status of images in memory?' and so on.

If we have a tendency to build up an unhelpful picture of the 'thoughts' which underlie language, we have no less a tendency to build up an unhelpful picture of the 'things' to which language refers. The simplest and most arresting relation of words to things is the relation of the *name* to the object to which it is given: I point to a given object and utter the name 'Charles'. The supposition then lies ready to hand that I am *always* doing something of this sort whenever I talk, and that every word in my utterance *stands* for something, either in my physical or in some other environment. It is certainly correct, if obvious, to say that 'John' means John, 'beauty' means beauty, 'and' means and, and 'or' means or: but these elementary tautologies of semantics readily give rise to a picture, according to which all words correspond to 'real analogues' or 'objects', and such that words which do not appear to name anything nevertheless name certain 'imponderables', such as redness, inherence or disjunction, which are somehow 'present to the mind' of the man who uses them. We are then led on into an exciting but difficult investigation of the ultimate varieties of 'object' in the universe and their relations to each other. And if a belief in imponderable *objects* has never been as widespread as a belief in ghostly *acts* of thinking, the prevalence of the latter rendering the former to some extent superfluous, the two theories are nevertheless so much alike that there is only a verbal nuance between them.

The two approaches to language we have mentioned, which have been characteristic of philosophers at all times, are both highly unhelpful because they attempt to throw light on language by postulating the existence of entities which are mere projections, in another medium, of linguistic symbols and rules. If a man is in the frame of mind and body in which he would say 'It is raining' with appropriate behaviour and an appropriate air of intelligence, we rightly say that he knows or supposes or believes that it is raining: this is all very well as long as we do not think that the thought he is 'experiencing' is a ghostly analogue of his words, and that it explains why he says what he says and not something else. Again it is very proper to say of the same man that he is considering a certain proposition, as long as we do not imagine that there is some ethereal original before him to which his words correspond and which likewise explains why he says what he says and not something else. Thought along these lines would readily lead us to an epistemology like that of Meinong or Husserl, where we wonderingly discover a point to point correspondence between thinking and objectivity, such and such an experiential feature being the mental modification which 'presents' such and such an objective feature. All such harmonies are in reality trivial: they arise because 'thoughts' and 'meanings' are alike reflections of linguistic structure. And if 'thoughts' and 'meanings' are merely such reflections, they can no more explain linguistic structure than can the dormitive virtue of opium explain why those who have taken opium go to sleep.

These points would be clear, as regards 'thoughts', if we consider the process by which we were taught to say, of ourselves and other people, that we were thinking this or that. No one at any time directed us to look into our own bosoms and discover there certain mysterious goings on, nor would there be any way of teaching anyone to describe events so private and so inaccessible. But it often happened that, when

SOME REACTIONS TO RECENT CAMBRIDGE PHILOSOPHY

we or someone else made some statement about objects or happenings in our common world, e.g. that the train was moving, that the postman was late, etc., we were told, especially if our statement was inaccurate, that we (or they) had *thought* what was said. We were then taught to extend this use to cases in which a person behaved in such a way that he seemed *ready* to make a certain statement, if an appropriate occasion were present, e.g. we learnt to say of a man who tilted a teapot into a cup that he thought there was tea in it. There were also many occasions on which we ourselves were ready to utter some statement S in response to a given situation, and chose instead, as a result of our training in the use of the verb 'to think', to say 'I think that S' and not simply S. There was, in most cases, practically no difference when we said the former and when we said the latter, but our mode of diction created the impression, both in ourselves and in others, that we were *observing* something very queer and private going on in ourselves. This impression was accentuated when we began to run through and relive, with a new subjective interest, our own reactions of the last few minutes: in this process we verbalized reactions previously unverbalized, and we did so in such forms as 'Then it occurred to me that S_1', 'Then I suddenly felt that S_2' and not in the direct forms S_1 and S_2. The impression then became irresistible that we were observing certain curious things called 'thoughts', and there is in fact no reason why we should not say we are observing them, provided we do not think observation of thoughts is like observation of houses and trees. But the essential point emerges that we were not taught to use the term 'thought' of private happenings in our breasts, but of those complex states of persons which issued in certain phrases and sentences, or which we had reason to believe would have issued in such phrases and sentences if circumstances had been favourable. There is therefore no light that can be shed on the structure of phrases by examining the structure of thoughts, since all thoughts, even our own, are only approached by way of phrases.

Why, however, do we so emphatically *distinguish* a thought from its expression, and regard the former as so much *more* than the latter (or the possibility of the latter)? The answer is plain: a man who is having (as we say) a certain thought is not bound to the one phrase in which he has chosen to express himself, he may say it in other equivalent or roughly equivalent phrases, he may say it 'better' in some phrase not conventionally equivalent, he may say it in other

19

LANGUAGE, MIND AND VALUE

languages, and, furthermore, he may say it without phrases at all, in gestures, in facial expressions, or in appropriate responses. Lastly, but not most importantly, as philosophers have supposed, he may utter it in 'mental pictures', or in those indescribable, felt adjustments, those 'moods of soul', which are even less tangible than mental pictures. A man, in short, who is thinking a certain thought, is ready to utter a certain phrase, but he is also ready to utter other phrases, to execute certain gestures, to adjust himself to certain situations, and to have certain images or experience certain 'conscious attitudes'. It is because a thought is virtual in such a multitude of ways, and actual, at any moment, in so few of them, that we tend to say that it is 'something more' than its actual or virtual expressions. And there is no reason why we should not say this provided we do not think we are talking about some mysterious *source* of all the expressions in question, and provided we do not think that even God or His angels could get at thoughts in any other way than through what we are pleased to call their expressions. And it is also plain that, in our use of the word 'thought', no one of its many expressions is regarded as essential. We may have thoughts we do not utter, thoughts we do not allow to register on our faces, thoughts that do not affect our practical responses, and thoughts unaccompanied by images or 'moods of soul'. Hence we are tempted to think that we can think with nothing at all, purely and nakedly, but this unfortunately is the one thing we cannot do. Thought is possible without any *given* expression, but thought without *any* expression is nothing at all.

But while linguistic expression is not the sole nor the most important aspect of thought, it is the aspect through which we *talk* about thought; it is by virtue of its connection with a certain linguistic expression that every other expression is said to express a given thought. A man who hesitates before he crosses a stream may be said to be wondering whether the stones before him are wobbly, because we think he would say 'Perhaps those stones are wobbly', 'I wonder if those stones are wobbly', if there were any occasion for saying so. In the same way a man who is having certain images or experiencing certain indescribable internal adjustments may also be said to be wondering whether certain stones are wobbly because he too would say this if asked. It is harder to say whether an *animal* which hesitates, shows signs of confusion, etc., is or is not wondering whether the stones are wobbly, because we can scarcely give an answer to the question 'Would this animal say "Perhaps these stones are wobbly" if it were endowed with

20

SOME REACTIONS TO RECENT CAMBRIDGE PHILOSOPHY

speech?' We cannot say whether animals think or not, or what kinds of thought they think, because we have no clear use of the word 'thought' in connection with creatures that *never* speak. We *may*, if we like, say of an animal that behaves as we should behave when we are prepared to say something, that it is thinking that thing, but we may, if we like, refuse to say this. What we say will depend on conventions that have not, as yet, been laid down. The point, however, emerges that certain verbal expressions are, as it were, the *key-forms* of all that range of behaviour which, as we say, expresses a certain thought; it is through its verbal form that a thought is marked off and pinned down. This view contrasts sharply with the typical philosophical opinion according to which certain private mental images, or private conscious attitudes and feelings, are the key-forms of thinking, are, in fact, thinking itself, while other forms of thought are only its 'outward expressions'. It is perfectly plain that such images and attitudes are not what anyone normally calls thinking, that we were never taught to use the word of them, that we have in fact no proper language to describe them, and that, finally, they are not indispensable to thinking. In ever so many cases we should rightly say (since usage is the only test in these matters) that someone thought so and so, even though he experienced neither images nor conscious attitudes. There are ever so many cases of intelligent utterance, of appropriate behaviour, of demonstable understanding, in which the whole development of images and conscious attitudes is foreshortened and forestalled. We think the floor will hold us by treading firmly on it, we believe and know many propositions by the unhesitating 'Yes' with which we answer obvious questions, we see a man is a liar by ignoring him, and so on. To deny that we think in such situations because we have no peculiar inward feelings is simply to abuse language: it is an abuse born of the philosophical habit of staring at words and mistaking the mild dizziness which ensues for the thought behind the words. And it is equally clear that there is not one standard experience of 'wondering if', 'suddenly perceiving that', 'doubting whether' and so on; there are innumerable experiences, of very varying richness and intensity, which may all be described by these words since they all issue in utterances and behaviour of a certain sort. Having images and experiencing 'moods of soul' are in fact only called 'thinking' because they involve a readiness to utter certain phrases and sentences, and to behave in a manner which 'goes with' such an utterance. And where this readiness is not really present, we may report the presence of 'thoughts' which were not there at all. How often are we not deluded in our belief that we have grasped a meaning, seen a point, or have hold of something clear and important? How often in dreams have we not made 'discoveries' which proved themselves, on waking, to be utterly nugatory? Here as elsewhere the proof of the pudding is in the eating, and we can only be sure that we really had a flash of insight, a clear conviction, a genuine understanding of something, if we can talk and act appropriately. We can *say* without hesitation that we thought this or that a moment ago, but the proof that we really did so is for us as circuitous and indirect as it is for other people.

We have shown reason to think that thought-structure is nothing but the dispositional shadow of speech-structure; it would be even easier to show that there is nothing in the realm of logical meanings which is not likewise a shadow of speech-structure. There is no way of acquainting a man with universals, logical constants, etc., but by showing him how to use certain symbols correctly in certain concrete situations. When a man says 'blue' wherever I say 'blue', or 'not' wherever I say 'not', then I have succeeded in teaching him what I mean by 'blue' or 'not'. I may say, if I like, that I have introduced him to certain subsistent objects, that he is now intuitively acquainted with certain universals or logical constants: only I must not imagine that I have made him see anything as he might have seen a house or a tree. There is therefore nothing with regard to the realm of logical meanings which can throw light on linguistic structure: we only say a man means such and such a logical entity when he uses such and such a linguistic form correctly.

II

Having disposed of a wrong philosophy of language, according to which it is to be understood in terms of ghostly processes within us, or ghostly meanings hanging before us, we may attempt to develop our notion of a correct philosophy of language, which concerns itself primarily with the way in which words are *used*. Now the essential feature of the linguistic philosophy we are studying is that it makes the basic use of words anticipatory and prognostic: they stand for certain situations which will (or might) reveal themselves in the future, and which will when they occur, 'justify' or 'satisfy' a given

SOME REACTIONS TO RECENT CAMBRIDGE PHILOSOPHY

verbal utterance. Language is essentially a performance whose rules allow us to utter words when the situations they stand for are *not present*, as well as when they *are* present. They also allow us to utter words which are *not* satisfied by the situations which follow as well as words that *are* satisfied by them. In other words, language is more than a game of tying tags to situations which are already there: it is essentially a game which forestalls situations, and which may therefore fit or fail to fit those situations, and so achieve verification or falsification. A game of tying tags to objects according to fixed rules has *some* of the features of speaking, and may therefore incline us to call it 'speaking', but it ought nevertheless not to be called 'speaking', since it does not anticipate, and is incapable of error or falsity. A man who ties tags to situations as they occur may possibly make a slip in his tag-tying, a slip which 'doesn't count' and 'has to be taken back', but he cannot, as an essential part of his game, do anything with a tag which does not fit the situation before him. Whereas, in the language game, a statement which does not fit the facts is just as much a statement, and just as much a part of the game, as one that does. There can be no language where there is no error, and there can be no error where there is not a 'leap in the dark' which is subsequently 'justified by sight'.

We may next emphasize the fact that the kind of situation which the use of words anticipates is always a *palpable*, an *observable* situation: it is the sort of situation whose reality one can establish by looking, touching, smelling or otherwise exploring with the senses. When we speak, we mean something because there will (or could) arise a situation which will cause us to say: 'That is what I meant', 'Now you see such and such is really the case', and so on. If, however, there were no situation which ever arose (or could arise) which caused us to say any of these things, then, it is plain, our performance would not be one of speaking. We might conceivably be playing some other game, which might have an importance all its own, but we certainly should not be *saying* anything in the ordinary sense of the word. For words do not mean by virtue of some mysterious internal property: they only do so because the man who utters them is prepared in some situation, actual or conceivable, to apply them to something. If, no matter what situation turns up, he still refuses to say that this is what he meant, if he persists in saying that he means 'something different' or 'something more', we may rightly question whether he means anything at all. A man who says he is going some-

23

LANGUAGE, MIND AND VALUE

where, but denies that he is going there by foot, or by bicycle, or by car, or by carriage, or by train, or by boat, or by plane, would likewise make us feel doubtful as to whether he is really going anywhere, or whether he knows what 'going' means. Now some have suggested that certain highly obscure philosophical sentences are really not part of the language-game at all, because there is no observable situation, or group of situations, which could ever satisfy them: they have called such sentences 'metaphysical' and spoken depreciatingly of those who uttered them. We may, however, doubt very seriously whether *all* these obscure utterances are pseudo-references which no situation could satisfy, and whether *all* who are called metaphysicians are really attempting the silly enterprise attributed to them.

The third feature of speech that requires to be stressed is the fact that it is essentially a game that involves a number of players: one cannot talk unless one talks to someone, and that someone different from oneself. This does not mean that there are not situations in which one utters words, whether overtly or inwardly, without there being anyone to listen to them, but such a performance is only speech because one is behaving *as if* there were someone else present, or because one is for the time acting *as if* one were two persons, and so on. The situation is not, properly speaking, one of speech, but we may stretch the word 'speech' to cover it, on account of its analogies with speaking. Granted that there is a fully developed social activity called 'speaking', it is permissible to say that certain activities, which lack essential features of speaking, are nevertheless a 'sort of' speaking. The soul's inward dialogue with itself, which Plato identified with thinking, is only a dialogue because it is occasionally uttered and heard, just as a book is only a book because it is sometimes opened and read.

From the fact that all speech involves a number of persons we deduce the important consequences that the situations which speech anticipates and prognosticates, and which give it its meaning, must be such situations as could (in principle at least) be shown to all the persons we are addressing, and by whom we hope to be understood. They must be situations which are *public*, at least to a small band of speakers and auditors; they must form a world which is *common* to us and the people to whom we are talking. This means that we *cannot* talk, in the proper sense of talking, about something accessible to ourselves, but never, in any conceivable set of circumstances, accessible to the people to whom we are talking. Nor, for the same reason, can we talk about something only accessible to other people, but never, by any manner of means, to ourselves. This statement may seem to *restrict* our talking, and to prohibit us from referring to our own sensations, images, dreams, feelings and inner experiences, or to those of other people. No restrictions are, however, involved: there is nothing that we *can* talk of that we may not talk of. Now we certainly *do* talk to each other about our own and other people's sensations and feelings, and we have further established quite definite and understandable uses for unconventional subjective terms like sense-datum, after-image, etc. It follows, therefore, not that we can talk to each other about inaccessibly private events, but that the events we are talking about, in so far as we can talk about them, are not inaccessibly private.

There are, in fact, definite sets of public tests by means of which we can decide whether a man really dreamt what he says he dreamt, whether he really sees a blue-green after-image, whether he really feels pleased and so on. We can ask him whether he is quite sure he has (or had) the experience he describes, we can inquire into further details concerning it in order to see whether they harmonize with his original statement, we can carefully test his use of words in other, public situations, we can investigate his veracity, his intelligence, his suggestibility and so forth. We can also put other people in situations similar to his, and see whether they report the same sort of things he reports. If all or a very large proportion of these tests have a positive outcome, then we may regard it as established, in the only sense in which it ever could be established, that he had the experiences he claimed to have. Hence there is nothing we cannot say about our inner experiences and those of other people, provided we remember that a thing is effable precisely to the extent that it is ostensible, and that beyond the limits of the effable there can only be either silence or unmeaning noise.

The impropriety of talking about feelings, experiences, presences, visions, inner voices, etc., in phrases unintelligible to one's auditors and governed by one's own private grammar, has always been recognized by polite people: what should further be recognized is that such utterances are not really speech at all, since they lack some of the essential characteristics of speaking. We only have speaking where there are *conventions*, and conventions imply that a number of people have access to certain situations in which they agree in using certain symbolic combinations. These publicly accessible situations constitute

25

the 'reality' which is relative to a given language and a given community of speakers. A man may have a private language of his own, in the sense of having a certain *cipher* which an appropriate key will transform into publicly intelligible terms, but he has not even a private language if neither the situations referred to by the cipher, nor the key which governs its use, could be communicated to anyone. There may be a certain pleasant game which some people play when they become lost in a trance and talk (as they say) to themselves about their own experiences, but, whatever that game is, it certainly is not language, since it lacks some of its essential features. What then should we do if we found ourselves simultaneously among two communities of speakers, inhabiting different 'planes of being', and lacking all knowledge of each other, so that we could not show anything we could show to the one set of beings to the other set? What then would be reality and what dream? The problem immediately resolves itself, when we consider that it could not be stated in the language with which we addressed either group of speakers.

The theory of language we have been attempting to outline was at one time condensed in the formula: 'The meaning of any sentence is the way in which it is verified', and this formula was interpreted psychologistically: what a sentence meant was a set of possible *experiences* of the person who used it. The formula so interpreted was no doubt illuminating at the time, but it is open to such disastrous misinterpretations and abuses that it is far better to discard it. The stress on *experiences* is, in the first place, unfortunate: it suggests that language is a kind of soliloquy, governed by a private grammar, in which a person predicts his own inner states. But we have seen that such a game, if it exists at all, can only be called language by courtesy, if the soliloquiser occasionally deigns to give other people some key to his utterances. For the 'experiences' of the formula we ought to substitute observable situations of different kinds, which are all public in principle, though often accessible only to a single person, e.g. the view one gets from a window, the noise one hears at a certain place or time, the reading of a thermometer, etc. 'Experiences' certainly have a place in our language, but they have to be defined and described by the kind of public object *of* which they are, and the kind of public reaction they would involve towards such an object: it is nonsense to suggest that we always mean things which are approached so indirectly. Again the formula involves a definite, if illuminating, abuse of language, even if it is *not* interpreted psycho-

SOME REACTIONS TO RECENT CAMBRIDGE PHILOSOPHY

logistically. For we *do not* say that a man who uses the word 'table *means* by it the observable situation that would justify him in applying it: we say that he means a *table* by it, and, if someone is not satisfied with this statement, we say he means a board supported by legs and used for eating, writing, etc. We must be clear, if we use the formula suggested, that we *are* abusing language: that we are not meaning by 'meaning' what is conventionally meant by it. But we may claim that what a sentence means, in the ordinary sense of 'meaning', is of little philosophical interest, whereas what it means, in our novel sense of 'meaning', throws an immense degree of light on it.

It will be objected at this point by certain philosophers that the theory of language we are sketching simply skates over all the fundamental philosophical problems, and is plausible only because it ignores these. 'How do you know', the familiar protest will ring, 'that we *can* communicate with other persons, that we *do* share a common public environment with them, that we *can* show them what we mean by our symbols, that they *do* see the same qualities, relations, objects, etc., as we see, or even that they *really exist* and are not phantoms in a dream?' The only answer to this questionnaire is to ask the questioner what he himself means by 'communication', 'having a common environment', 'showing what he means by something', 'seeing the same qualities as other people', or the 'real existence of persons'. For all these phrases have established and well-recognized uses in common speech, and, if we conform with these uses, there is no doubt that we sometimes talk with other people, who are real and not phantoms, that these people *do* see the same objects and qualities as we do, and that it is possible to make them understand what we are saying. There are definite procedures we can adopt to see whether a certain appearance is a real person or a phantom; there are also definite procedures we can adopt in order to teach him how we use words and to ascertain how he uses them. If we carry out these procedures we can establish the reality of a plurality of persons and of communication between them in the only sense that has ever been given to these phrases. To say, after applying such procedures, that we still doubt whether other people exist, or whether we can communicate with them, is to use 'doubt' in a novel and perplexing way. There may of course be *other* procedures by which one could establish something one calls 'communication' and the 'reality of persons', but these would plainly *not* be the 'communication' and 'reality of persons' one normally talks of, and it is not at all plain what they would be. It is

LANGUAGE, MIND AND VALUE

plain, further, that solipsism is not a philosophy that can be uttered in language: it is not, in fact, a philosophy at all. It is not merely impolite, but absurd, for me to address people in order to persuade them that I alone exist. The only significant solipsism would be that of a man really left alone on a dying planet, and he would only be able to say 'I alone exist' because he had once conversed with persons, and was still a social being.

III

We now pass on to show how the theory of language we are considering enables us to deal with the activities of philosophers and with many of the traditional problems of philosophy. Here the illumination derived from the theory is certainly extraordinary: it is as if no one previously had begun to diagnose the philosophical condition, or to prescribe its remedy. By comparison no one previously seems to have had an inkling of what philosophers are really doing in their queer, hopeless, passionate disputes, disputes in which there are neither agreed premises nor rules of argument, and which terminate, with approximately equal frequency, in an impasse, a truism or a paradox. There is all the difference between knowing what philosophers are doing in terms of *such* a theory and knowing what they are doing in terms of their *own* theory, as there would be between knowing what erotic behaviour meant in biological terms and listening to the language of lovers. The effect of the theory is to show us, on the one hand, how confused are many philosophical inquiries, how they spring from a misunderstanding or abuse of linguistic forms, leading to questions which have no answers since they are not properly questions at all, and also to show how there *is* a genuine sense and meaning in some of the most confused of these inquiries. We may also derive from the theory of language in question a new conception of the task of the philosopher which is quite as lofty in its way as the traditional Platonic or Hegelian picture.

Now what have most philosophers supposed themselves to be doing when they faced problems, propounded solutions, or engaged in controversy with each other? They have thought of themselves as men trying to fill in some puzzling gap in their knowledge with unexpected links or connections, or as men trying to explain some unusual effect by postulating the presence of hidden factors or agencies, or as men trying to find proofs for certain plausible but complex

28

theorems, or, alternatively, as hard-headed, sceptical men denying the existence of forces, agencies, media which less rigorous minds had accepted. They have tried to go beyond the veil, to be spectators of all time and existence, to explore the realm of essence, but, whatever they have thought about their problems and questions, they have never thought of them as having a verbal origin; nor have they supposed that, in suggesting solutions for those problems, they were merely suggesting that our usage in regard to certain terms and forms should be altered or supplemented. Verbal difficulties they might admit in plenty, but these were only initial hindrances, to be cleared away before one proceeded with the genuine business of philosophy. Now the philosophy of language we are studying maintains precisely that philosophy has no true resemblance to science or mathematics, that it is not trying to augment our knowledge of reality or to demonstrate new theorems of an abstract, self-evident character, but that its whole endeavour is directed to altering the way in which we *talk* about things. And this endeavour it may carry on confusedly, believing that it is doing something else, and so fail altogether to shed light on the situation, perhaps even making it more obscure and complex. It may, on the other hand, carry on its endeavour consciously and aptly, so as to find linguistic projections which 'do justice', as we say, to unrecognized likenesses and kinships, and give ease to a mind vexed by the 'rigidity', the 'vagueness', the 'inconsistency', the 'confusion', or any other defect of our common diction.

These points will be clearer if we pass from generalities to a consideration of a number of typical philosophical puzzles. We may first look, for our purpose, at the group of problems clustering around the words 'identity' and 'same', such problems as whether the *same* individual thing could conceivably have had different properties from those it actually has, whether the *same* individual thing can persist through time, and have different properties at different times, whether the *same* quality can be present as a characteristic in many different objects, whether different people can see or think of the *same* objects, or live through the *same* feelings and experiences, whether the *same* place can be occupied by different objects at different times, and so on. In all these cases there are some people who maintain very passionately that the same thing *can* fulfil the roles we have just enumerated, whereas there are others who maintain, with equal vehemence, that it cannot be the same, but only a *like* or *similar* thing, which enters into the various situations men-

LANGUAGE, MIND AND VALUE

tioned. To some it is plain that Socrates sitting and Socrates walking may be 'literally the same' person, whereas others are open to the queer suspicion that the one is *not* the same individual as the other, but a *new* individual which has replaced or superseded its predecessor. These suspicions seem particularly acute when it is Socrates's *mind*, rather than Socrates's body, which is under discussion. Again it seems sense to some to say that Socrates might, in some conceivable set of circumstances, have gone to Megara instead of to his death, or have married some other woman than Xanthippe, whereas to others it is plain that anyone who differed from the historical Socrates in the tiniest particular, or had any relation which the historical Socrates did not have, would not have been Socrates, but a totally different person. In the same way some say that the same universals are 'present' in a variety of contexts, whereas others maintain that the characteristics of particulars are as particular as they are. And while many maintain that we can share a common realm of objects, and fewer that we do or could 'literally' share each other's thoughts, sensations and feelings, others are quite sure that this is utterly impossible.

In all these problems concerning identity it is important that we should not allow ourselves to ask any questions or propound any solutions, before we have asked ourselves how the word 'same' is normally used, and how we ourselves propose to use it in situations where ordinary usage is indefinite. It is important to emphasize that 'identity' means nothing more or less than what we choose it to mean, and that there is no sense of 'same' which corresponds more closely with the 'nature of things' than any other. As regards the identity of concrete individual things, the tests for the use of the word 'same' are also the tests for the use of the proper names of those individual things: if it is correct to use a name N in a given situation, and also correct to use it in another situation, we say we are dealing with the same object or entity in both cases. Thus there is a range of observable situations, differing very considerably from each other, and involving a complex context of other observable situations, in which we think it correct to use the name 'Stalin': these are the situations we should call 'Stalin sitting', or 'Stalin walking', or 'Stalin signing a death warrant', or 'Stalin entering the Japanese capital', also the very different situations we should call 'Stalin mentioned in a newspaper', or 'Stalin appearing in a photograph', or 'Stalin reported as having occurred in someone's dream', and so on. In all these situations, actual or hypothetical, it would be correct, according to the accepted con-

30

SOME REACTIONS TO RECENT CAMBRIDGE PHILOSOPHY

ventions of our language, to say that we were dealing with one and the same individual, whom we might further describe as a Georgian peasant, the general secretary of the Russian Communist Party, and so on. Now what, for instance, is a man doing who raises doubts as to whether Stalin in various successive historical situations is 'really' one and the same individual, whether he may not in reality be a series of individuals (called 'events' or whatever) which vanish and supersede each other? He is really proposing that we should abandon our very convenient, reasonably unambiguous use of 'same' for a new use according to which a man is only the same entity for a couple of minutes together, a use which promises no special advantages, and would be very hard to carry out in practice. And why is he doing this? In part he is doing this because he is the victim of a confusion. For there genuinely are situations in which we feel tempted to say 'This is the same man I saw yesterday' and yet, on closer examination, we have to admit that this is not a correct statement, but that a new man has replaced the old one. If Stalin genuinely has a series of doubles who replace him on various occasions, then there is sense in wondering whether the man who is bowing to us from the rostrum is the same man who signed the German–Soviet pact. One might find, if one observed more closely or collected further evidence, and made use of accepted tests of identity, that he was not really the same man, but only someone closely similar. Now because there are such genuine cases in which it really is not clear whether this, which looks like that, is the same or different, we are forthwith seduced into saying, quite senselessly, that there might be some doubt as to the identity of a person or a thing even in a case where we assume that every test for identity has been or will be satisfied. But though there is all this confusion in our doubt as to the persistent identity of Stalin, there is also this amount of illumination in the whole suggested change of usage. Our use of the terms 'same' and 'different' suggests that there is a hard and fast line to be drawn between cases in which it is proper to say 'This is the same as that' and cases in which it is proper to say 'This is different from that'. Now there is no such clear line to be drawn, and there are many cases, actual and hypothetical, in which we simply could not say whether this was or was not the same as that. If a person resembling Stalin externally, and connected with him unbrokenly, sometimes exhibited the traits of a Russian Marxist and sometimes the traits of a quietistic Buddhist philosopher, we might be at a loss to say whether he was or was not the same person.

31

LANGUAGE, MIND AND VALUE

Nor would there be any way of solving our perplexity except by legislating *ad hoc* for this peculiar case. And even where it is clear that some object is the same object we saw some time ago, it is nevertheless valuable to stress its resemblance to cases where, as we say, we have an unbroken series of distinct objects following and replacing each other: the paradox of Heraclitus, that we cannot step into the same river twice, emphasizes an analogy that ordinary language ignores, and is accordingly 'profound' and 'wise'. But profundity and wisdom are not a sufficient reason for subverting all our established conventions with regard to the use of the terms 'same' and 'different'. Very similar considerations could be brought up in connection with the problem of accidental properties and 'external relations' referred to above. Would anyone otherwise like Stalin, but lacking one of his qualities or relationships, be the *same* person or someone else? Is it nonsensical to say that Stalin might not have had some property he in fact has, or not have stood in some relation in which he in fact stands? The answer to this is that, as our present usage goes, it *would* be possible for an actual A and a hypothetical B to differ in *some* respects, referred to as 'unimportant' or 'unessential', without forfeiting their right to be called 'identical'. But it is not clear at what point precisely we should give up saying that A and B were the same, and prefer to start saying that they were different, or rather it is clear that there is a considerable zone of hesitation within which we should not know what to say. It certainly would not be more convenient to adopt any other usage, but it would at least enable us to satisfy our desire for *situations nettes*, and our dislike of fumbling indecision, as well as our liking for broad and simple rulings, if we laid down that the *smallest* difference in A and B, whether of quality or relation, was sufficient to make them different; this would make everything inwardly unmodifiable and rigidly related to everything else. (We might also have laid it down, if we wished, that *any* amount of actual or possible difference is compatible with 'fundamental identity', a ruling at the base of the Indian self-philosophy, which affords indefinite linguistic satisfaction to some people.) When we go from these questions to questions as to the identity of the qualities present in various instances, or of the pains felt by different people, or of the regions pervaded by happenings at various times, we are passing from cases in which there is some degree of uniformity of usage to cases in which everything is wavering and uncertain. Here we are delivered from oppressive perplexity, and acquire a charter of freedom, when we see that we may

SOME REACTIONS TO RECENT CAMBRIDGE PHILOSOPHY

say precisely what pleases us, provided we realize the advantages and disadvantages as regards intricacy or simplicity, or illuminating or misleading associations, which are connected with any proposed usage.

Having shown how the philosophy of language we are considering enables us to deal with the abstract metaphysical puzzles connected with a logical category like identity, we may next consider its relevance to a totally different group of puzzles, those which concern the reality of an external world, and of the relations of states of consciousness to this world. Since the time of Descartes one of the principal occupations of philosophers has been to try to make us doubt whether material objects really exist, whether we are not dreaming when we seem to see them, whether they do not secretly vanish when we turn our backs on them, and so on; also to arouse less fundamental doubts as to whether material objects are really coloured, odorous, sonorous, extended and so forth. Since the time of Descartes philosophers have also stressed the irrefragable certainty of our knowledge of the 'subject' and its 'acts', and of the perceptual appearances of things to subjects. And they have either tried to prove the reality of an external world, and then tried to connect it with the realm of subjective happenings, or, alternatively, have held that there was no external world, but that tables, chairs, tigers, trees, etc., were merely ideas in our own or someone else's minds. Now in order to show how these puzzles arise, and thereby to resolve them, we must consider how such terms as 'matter', 'reality', 'mind' are used in ordinary language, or in forms of diction that keep passable terms with ordinary language.

We have seen that our language, by its very nature as a language, is concerned with objects such as tigers and trees, that can be observed by many people in many ways, and that can be successfully shown by one person to another so as to establish conformity of usage. This possibility of observation by many, and ostension to many, is an actuality in the only sense that has ever been given to it. And the objects revealed in this way are 'physical', 'material' or 'external' in the sense that would be given to these words in any diction not too far removed from ordinary language. Now a very important feature of our statements concerning physical things is that they are all, by their very nature, *corrigible*: if I say 'That is a tiger', 'This is a tree', I can never, by the rules of the game I am playing, incorrigibly establish that what I am saying really is the case, since it is not possible to exhaust the tests to which my statement might be subjected. Thus the

C

33

LANGUAGE, MIND AND VALUE

mere fact that I *see* a tiger does not complete the 'proof' that there really is one, for I can also hear it or feel it or smell it. Even when I have done this it is still open to me to dissect it, to subject it to chemical tests and so forth. And it plainly would not be a real material tiger if other people could not see, hear, feel or smell it; I am therefore able to confirm its reality over and over again by the simple expedient of trying to show it to someone else. And it plainly would not be a real material tiger if it vanished periodically, or became miraculously changed into other forms: every time it does not do this, therefore, it proves its real and material character. And finally it is characteristic of all real tigers that they leave behind them when they perish an endless train of records, effects, memories which would enable anyone sufficiently informed and intelligent to infer that they once existed. If the majority of such records, effects, and memories were mysteriously blotted out, like the records of departing embassies, we should have grave reason to doubt whether we were dealing with a real material tiger. But nevertheless, though the possible proofs of a thing's materiality are inexhaustible, there is a point fixed by good sense and common usage at which it is correct to say that we *know* there is (or was) a tiger present: it is no longer a matter of hypothesis, supposition or surmise, but of knowledge. It is logically possible we may be mistaken is nothing to the point: we so use the word 'know' that we know many things concerning which it is logically possible we may be mistaken.

We are now in a position to see where and why philosophical scepticism as to the existence of material objects arises and leads to the 'view' that all our experience is only an orderly dream, and so on. There is undoubtedly a good sense in doubting whether the material objects which seem to be before us really are there, and really have their apparent properties: even when we *think* we know they are there and what they are like, we may nevertheless find ourselves completely mistaken. But because all material-object statements are subject to correction, it is easy to slip over into the quite different thesis that even if we were sure that all tests for the reality of a material object were going to be fulfilled, it would *still* be doubtful whether we were not dreaming, subject to an hallucination, deceived by an evil genius, and so forth. It is also possible to hold that, because any finite amount of evidence for a thing's materiality would not preclude the logical possibility of its ultimate refutation, we cannot therefore *know* that there are material objects, that it is merely an act of faith, a

34

SOME REACTIONS TO RECENT CAMBRIDGE PHILOSOPHY

leap in the dark, and what not. Now the former of these positions is essentially absurd, since it is only possible to doubt something if one knows what observable situations would make that statement true or false, and also surmises that some of those observable situations will refute the statement. To doubt something without being able to say what situation would resolve one's doubt, is merely to assume a pose of doubting without any concrete content whatsoever. But the second position, of maintaining that we do not know that there are tigers, trees, etc., because *all* the tests for these things have not been carried out, is only reprehensible inasmuch as it involves an exaggerated and unnatural use of language. For it is good English to say that we know there are trees, that we have *sufficient* evidence to assert that there are such things without a trace of hesitation.

On all grounds, then, no sense has been given to scepticism as to the existence of material objects: there is therefore no reason why we should have recourse to those idealistic paraphrases of our ordinary ways of talking, which think they have explained a great deal when they tell us that trees and tigers are only ideas in someone's mind. Idealism as a theory of the world says nothing that materialism does not also say: only it uses the words 'idea', 'mind', etc., in so eccentrically wide a way as to leave them no clear significance whatsoever. Very similar criticisms would apply to all those theories of material objects which, while admitting their reality, doubt whether they have some or all of the properties they appear to have: colour, sound, taste, smell, etc. Now it is clear that, in the only sense ever given to these predicates, it is undoubtedly correct to apply them to material objects. We learn the use of such words as 'red', 'round', etc., by being shown material objects or processes in certain optimal conditions: other people, we note, have been taught to apply the same words in similar circumstances. Now in the only sense ever given to the words 'red', 'round', etc., it is plain that some material objects are red and round, for it is certain that we and others, who regard them in appropriate conditions, uniformly decide to call them so. If there is any *other* sense in which an object may be red (e.g. an incommunicable, private sense, if such were admissible), they may not be red in *that* sense, but they are red in the only sense in which we have been taught to use the word.

It is clear, none the less, that both scepticism and idealism hold considerable paradoxical illumination, if we do not treat them with the wrong seriousness. For it is worth while saying that there is

35

LANGUAGE, MIND AND VALUE

always a logical possibility of error in our material-object statements, and it is worth while stressing that the line between the real and the phantasmal is not an absolutely clear one, and might, in perfectly conceivable circumstances, become impossible to fix. If an object could be shown to *A, B* and *C,* but not to *D, E* and *F,* or if it vanished and recurred at intervals, we could not say, with our present rules of language, whether it was real or not. And it may be worth while, from an ethical point of view, to cultivate towards material objects, at least at times, that attitude of slight consideration which we normally adopt towards objects we regard as imaginary.

It would be interesting to pursue our linguistic analysis a little further, and show how philosophers have arrived at the view that we have an immediate, incorrigible awareness of our own mental acts of the moment, that these mental acts take place in our own bosoms and cannot be shown to anyone, that the behaviour in which they issue is merely an outward and visible sign of them, that we can never certainly *know* that such mental acts take place in others, and so on. All these 'views' have a foundation in our language, they spring from an exaggeration of certain significant ways of talking, but they all lead, as they stand, to 'posers' and mysteries which render them more confusing than helpful. If we considered carefully what we can and what we cannot say, by the very nature of our language as a language, we should be able to resolve the majority of these puzzles, retaining whatever modicum of picturesque illumination there is to be found in them. We might also with profit pursue our philosophy of language through other puzzles which arise in different fields: the problems of universals, of relations, of various logical and mathematical categories, of causation, of induction, of mechanical and biological categories, of space and of time, and so on. Until one sees the variety of its applications, one can form no notion of its fruitfulness. Enough has, however, been said to make plain what the essential principles of our philosophy are, and how they work out in practice.

Enough has also been said to make plain what we previously said of the view taken by our theory of the essential nature of philosophical activity, and of the proper task of the philosopher. If the philosophic impulse is, on the current confused view, merely a higher flight of the scientific impulse, it is, on the view we are expounding, an impulse different in kind from the scientific impulse, a fact genuine philosophers have always obscurely recognized. For it does not spring from any dissatisfaction with what we know, but, what is far more weighty

36

and deep-seated, with the way in which we say it. No philosophy augments our knowledge of reality by one iota, but it can alter our way of saying things in a highly misleading or a highly illuminating manner. Philosophy arises, in part, out of our confused wonder at the queer suggestions of linguistic expressions whose use has been forgotten. We wonder what adjectives 'stand for', or what numerical expressions refer to, and are led to affirm the existence of some very queer entities with extraordinary properties. We are baffled by the meaning of mental terms, and wonder how in the world a man can think or believe what is not the case at all, and construct some theory to meet it. We may fail to see how mental language is connected with physical language, and so be forced to invent the various 'theories' of the mind-body relation. In all these cases philosophical construction rests mainly on a confusion; the task of a genuine philosophy is to trace such confusions to their roots, to show why we are tempted to say what we say, and to indicate how little illumination or explanation we can derive from it.

But there are other cases where philosophical construction springs from the fact that our language recognizes only a few of the multitudinous analogies among the things of our experience, and that other analogies press in upon us at times, and create a stress which cannot be relieved till we have given them *some* recognition in our language. We are then tempted to abuse ordinary language, to utter paradoxes of various kinds, in short to create new usages which may ease or vary our handling of the world. To say we do not know whether our desk is real, or whether our wife suffers pain, is to abuse language, but also to stress an analogy, for there are deep resemblances between waking and dreaming, or between cunning automata and intelligent persons: there is also no clear dividing line between surmise and belief, or belief and knowledge. Again to say that value-statements are not really statements but interjections, is to abuse language, but it also brings out an unrecognized analogy, and stresses an unrecognized difference. And who can deny that the river of Heraclitus into which, very oddly, we cannot step twice, or the charmed arrow of Zeno, at rest throughout the course of its flight, has brought out features of change and process which our ordinary language fails to emphasize? The metaphysicians of the past often wrongly supposed that they were building up ontologies: they were in reality, in many cases, doing something far finer, creating new languages which bring out certain analogies more pointedly and more systematically than is possible in our current language. In any case there is nothing in the philosophy of language we are studying which renders it hostile to any form of philosophy, however great the element of confusion this may hold. It has little affinity with those trends of thought called 'positivistic' whose aim is to eliminate philosophical perplexity in order to 'get on with the work of science'. There may, from its point of view, be far more importance in the confusions of a Locke or a Kant, far more illumination in the exaggerations of a Berkeley or a Spinoza, than is to be found in the clearest papers of the best experimentalists. The effect of this philosophy is not to diminish our faith in the value of philosophy but rather to augment it: for it as for Plato καλὸν τὸ ἆθλον καὶ ἡ ἐλπὶς μεγάλη.

II

TIME:

A TREATMENT OF SOME PUZZLES[1]

(1941)

I

THE aim of this paper is to inquire into the causes of some of our persistent perplexities with regard to time and change. We do not propose to offer a solution for these difficulties, but rather to make clear how they have come to worry us. For we shall suggest that they have their origin, not in any genuine obscurity in our experience, but in our ways of thinking and talking, and we shall also suggest that the clear consciousness of this origin is the only way to cure them. It is plain that we do not, in any ordinary frame of mind, find time so hard to understand: we are in fact always competently dealing with what we may describe as 'temporal situations'. We are dealing with such situations whenever we say, without hesitation or confusion, that this lasted longer than that, that this took place at the same time as that, that this has just happened or that that will happen soon. We have no difficulty in showing other people what we mean by such forms of statement, nor in getting them to agree that we have used them truly and appropriately. Yet all these forms of statement, and the situations to which they refer, seem capable of creating the most intense perplexity in some people: people are led to say that time is 'paradoxical', 'contradictory', 'mysterious', and to ask how certain things are 'possible' whose actuality seems obvious. Thus it has been asked how it is 'possible' for anything to reach the end of a phase of continuous change, or how it is 'possible' for that which *is* the case ever to cease being the case, or how it is 'possible' for the duration of

[1] First published in the *Australasian Journal of Psychology and Philosophy*, December 1941.

39

LANGUAGE, MIND AND VALUE

any happening to have a length and a measure. In all such cases it seems reasonable to say that the burden of proof that there *is* a genuine problem or difficulty is on the person who feels it, and not on the person who refuses to depart from ordinary ways of speaking. And it certainly does seem odd that people who have always had to deal with changing objects and situations, and whose whole language is perfectly adapted to dealing with them, should suddenly profess to find time so very strange. If time is so odd, we may very well ask, in terms of what things more familiar and understandable shall we proceed to explain it, or to throw light on its possibility? We may indeed regard it as a strange disorder that people who have spent all their days 'in time', should suddenly elect to speak as if they were casual visitors from 'eternity'. And it must be our business to cure them of this disorder through a clear awareness of its causes. There is indeed 'a short way with puzzlers' who inquire into the 'possibility' of perfectly familiar and understandable situations: we may simply point to some instance of the kind that perplexes them and say: 'That's how it is possible for so-and-so to be the case'. Thus if a man were to ask me 'How is it possible that that which *is* the case should cease to be the case?', I might simply crook my finger and say 'Now my finger is crooked', then straighten it and say 'Now it has ceased to be crooked. And that's how it's possible for that which *is* the case to cease being the case'.[1] But such an expedient, though perfectly proper in itself, and more than a man has a right to ask for in most cases, would not suffice to allay our questioner's perplexity, since he, presumably, is quite as familiar with ordinary usage as we are.

A treatment of the puzzles of time will also serve to illustrate a treatment which might be applied to many other questions and difficulties. For some people quite readily fall into a mood in which they feel that there is something mysterious and doubtful about things that they would normally regard as elementary and obvious. They are then led to ask questions which seem queer, because it is not in the least plain how one should set about answering them. Thus a man may wonder how it is possible for a number of distinct things

[1] The example given and the general method indicated was suggested by Professor Moore's proof that external objects exist. He proves that there are such objects by proving that there are two human hands, the latter being proved 'by holding up his two hands, and saying as he makes a certain gesture with the right hand, "Here is one hand", and adding, as he makes a certain gesture with the left, "and here is another" ' (*Proof of an External World*, p. 25).

40

TIME: A TREATMENT OF SOME PUZZLES

to share in the same quality, or whether he really is the same person from year to year, or why *this* world exists rather than any other. Now in ordinary unreflective moods we should regard these questions as either unanswerable or not worth answering, but our questioner plainly wants an answer and he doesn't want an obvious answer. It is plain, in particular, that we couldn't remove our questioner's perplexity by 'appealing to experience', by pointing to anything that both he and we could observe. For he *has* all the kinds of experience that could throw light on his problem, and yet he is puzzled. It seems clear that, where the simplest and most familiar instances of something occasion profound perplexity, we cannot hope to remove such perplexity, or even to allay it, by indefinitely accumulating other instances of the same kind, some of which would be strange and others highly complex. We are accordingly brought back to our supposition that there are some questions which beset us, not because there is anything genuinely problematic in our experience, but because the ways in which we speak of that experience are lacking in harmony or are otherwise unsatisfactory. We are sometimes thrown into a mood of interrogation not because we are in quest of further facts, but because we are in quest of clearer, or less discordant, or merely different ways of verbally dealing with those facts. Such moods of questioning plainly have no answers, in any ordinary sense of 'answer'; we may nevertheless hope to relieve them by becoming clearly conscious of the underlying needs that prompt them, and by deliberately adopting ways of talking that provide appeasement for those needs.

There are other reasons why there is interest in our difficulties with regard to time. These difficulties form a relatively self-contained group of puzzles, which do not seem to share their entrails with too many other philosophical problems. We can find time difficult without finding anything else difficult, but we couldn't be puzzled by matter or mind or knowledge, without being puzzled by practically everything else. Hence we can deal more cleanly with these temporal puzzles than with other issues; they provide, accordingly, a simpler paradigm of method. These puzzles are also important in that philosophical difficulties seem to flourish more readily in the temporal field than in almost any other. It would be safe to say that rapid change and the 'nothingness of the past' are things which can always be relied on spontaneously to vex a large number of unsophisticated people, and so to constitute one of the standing mysteries of our universe.

We have reason, of course, to suspect such generalizations; for we know nowadays that there is no way of ascertaining the philosophical reactions of unphilosophical common sense, except by testing and questioning large numbers of people.[1] But in the absence of such testing, vague experience certainly bears witness to the generality of such puzzlement.

II

We may now point to a circumstance which is certainly responsible for *some* of our difficulties with regard to time. This is the fact that it is possible to persuade a man, by an almost insensible process, to use certain familiar locutions in ways which become, on the one hand, steadily wider and more general, or, on the other hand, steadily narrower and stricter. This persuasive process is only one of the many processes by which an able dialectician can twist or stretch or shift or tear apart the web of words with which we overlay our world. In doing so, he relies on the fact that the boundaries of linguistic usage are seldom clear, that there are always ranges of cases in which it is simply doubtful whether a given locution is or is not applicable, and that there are, in addition, a number of deep-seated tendencies in language which facilitate linguistic shifts in certain directions. In the particular case we are now considering there are, it is plain, words and phrases whose use very readily widens: it is easy to persuade a man that they really *ought* to be used in cases in which it has never before occurred to anyone to use them. And it is also plain that there are words and phrases whose use very readily narrows, so that we are easily persuaded to say that it was 'wrong' or 'improper' to use them in cases where we previously used them without hesitation. And it is possible for the adroit dialectician, by making repeated use of a big stick called 'consistency', on the one hand, and another big stick called 'strictness', on the other hand, to persuade us to use such forms of speech so widely that they apply to everything, or so narrowly that they apply to nothing: the result in either case is to turn a serviceable mode of speaking into one that is totally unserviceable.

Good examples of these dialectical processes would be arguments which led us to use the term 'know' so widely, on the one hand,

[1] See, e.g., Arne'Ness's *Truth as conceived by those who are not professional philosophers*, Oslo, 1938.

that we might be said, like the monads of Leibniz, always to know everything, or so narrowly, on the other hand, that we might never be said to know anything. There is, of course, nothing in such an exaggerated width or narrowness of reference which *necessarily* leads to paradoxes or problems. If we persuade a man to use words in new ways, we disorganize his linguistic habits for the time being, but there is no reason why he should not rapidly build up a new set of habits, which will enable him to talk of ordinary situations as plainly and as promptly as before. But the trouble is that such a sudden change of usage *may* produce a temporary disorientation, it is like a cerebral lesion from which an organism needs to recover, and in the interval before recovery sets in, and new connections take the place of the old, a man may readily become a prey to serious confusions. For even after a man has been persuaded to use certain phrases in totally new ways in certain contexts, he may still hark back to old uses in other contexts: he may even try to incorporate both uses in the same context, thus giving rise to statements and questions which cannot be interpreted in either way of speaking.

Now in regard to time it is plain that there is a strong tendency in language to use terms connected with the 'present' in an ever stricter manner, so that, if this tendency is carried to the limit, the terms in question cease to have *any* application, or, at best, a novel and artificial one. It is also plain that *some* of the problems of time are connected with this fact. We can readily be persuaded to use the present tense and the temporal adverb 'now' (as well as the imperfect past and imperfect future tenses and the words 'then', 'at that time', etc.), in stricter and stricter ways; and if we yield completely to such pressure, our normal habits of speech will be disorganized. Our use of the present tense and of the temporal adverb 'now' is not very strict in ordinary circumstances: we are prepared to say, even of happenings that last a considerable time, that they are happening *now*, e.g. we say 'The National Anthem is now being sung', 'The Derby is now being run', etc. Now the present tense and the temporal adverb 'now' *might* have been the sort of speech-form that we tended to use more and more widely, so that we might easily have been persuaded to say 'The history of England is now running its course', 'The heat death of the Universe is now taking place'. We might then have been persuaded to allow that, since a *whole* cannot be happening now, unless all its component *parts* are also happening now, John is now really signing Magna Charta, life on the earth is now really extinct,

LANGUAGE, MIND AND VALUE

and so on. The problems that this way of speaking might occasion, would certainly be serious.

The natural development of the speech-forms we are considering does not, however, lie in this direction. We tend rather, if pressed, to use the present tense and the temporal adverb 'now' more and more narrowly: thus if we had said that the National Anthem was being sung, and someone asked us 'But what are they singing *just now?*' we should not widen our reference to cover the whole evening's concert, but narrow it to apply to some line or phrase or word or note of the National Anthem. Now since our tendencies lie in *this* direction, we can readily be persuaded to give up saying that anything which takes an appreciable time is happening now. We can be bullied into admitting that this is a 'loose' and 'inaccurate' way of talking. And it is possible to force us to grant that the really strict speaker would not use these forms of speech in the case of anything but a happening which was so short that it took *no time at all.*

Thus we might force a man first to admit that nothing which was *past*, nothing which was *no longer there*, could possibly be said to be happening now. We might then press him to admit the additional principle that nothing of which a *part* lay in the past could properly be said to be happening now. We might then persuade him to grant, with regard to any happening that 'takes time', that it doesn't happen 'all at once', but that it has parts which happen one after the other, and that, when any *one* of these parts *is* happening, all the *other* parts either *have* happened or *will* happen. It then becomes easy to prove that no happening which takes time can properly be said to be taking place, and that the only parts of it of which such a thing could ever be rightly said, would be parts that took *no time at all*.[1]

[1] The typical historical case of this argument is Augustine, *Confessions* (Book XI: 19, 20): 'Are a hundred years, when present, a long time? See first, whether a hundred years can be present. For if the first of these be now current, it is present, but the other ninety and nine are to come, and therefore are not yet, but if the second year be current, one is now past, another present, the rest to come. And so, if we assume any middle year of this hundred to be present, all before it are past; all after it to come; wherefore a hundred years cannot be present. But see at least whether that one which is now current itself is present; for if the current month be its first, the rest are to come; if the second, the first is already past, and the rest are not yet. Therefore neither is the year now current present; and if not present as a whole, then is not the year present. For twelve months are a year; of which, whatever be the current month is present; the rest past, or to come. Although neither is that current month present; but one day only; the rest being to come, if it be the first; past, if the last; if any of the middle,

In all these arguments we are being persuaded to apply linguistic principles which are established in the case of happenings of *fairly long duration*, to happenings of very short duration; we are not obliged, but can be readily pressed, to be 'consistent' in this manner since there are no clear lines between the long and the short. But the result of yielding to this pressure is to turn a serviceable way of talking into one that has no use. For it is obvious that all the happenings that we can point to (in any ordinary sense of 'point to') take time, and that pointing itself takes time, so that if the only happenings of which we may say 'This is happening now' are happenings which take no time, there are no happenings which we can point to, of which we may say 'This is happening now'.

Now this does not, of course, imply that a clear and useful meaning cannot be given to phrases and sentences which mention happenings that take no time: it is plain, in fact, that very clear and useful meanings *have* been given to them by a long succession of mathematicians and philosophers. But it is also plain that these new forms of diction may, at first, merely serve to disorganize existing speech-habits, and that, while this lasts, we may fail to give any clear or serviceable meaning to 'happenings which take no time'; we may tend to talk of them as if they were happenings we could point to, in the same sense in which we can point to happenings which *do* take time, and we may further credit them unthinkably with many of the properties of happenings which *do* take time. Such ways of talking, it is plain, must lead to many quite unanswerable questions.

III

After this preliminary consideration of *one* source of our temporal difficulties, we may turn to Augustine's problem in the eleventh book

then amid past and to come. See how the present time which alone we found could be called long, is abridged to the length scarce of one day. But let us examine that also; because neither is one day present as a whole. For it is made up of four and twenty hours of night and day: of which the first hath the rest to come; the last hath them past; and any of the middle hath those before it past, those behind it to come. Yea, that one hour passeth away in flying particles. Whatsoever of it hath flown away is past; whatever remaineth is to come. If an instant of time be conceived which cannot be divided into the smallest particles of moments, that alone is it, which may be called present, which yet flies with such speed from future to past, as not to be lengthened out with the least stay. For if it be, it is divided into past and future. The present hath no space. Where, then, is the time which we may call long?'

45

LANGUAGE, MIND AND VALUE

of the *Confessions*. This we may phrase as follows: 'How can we say of anything that it lasts a long time or a short time? How can a time have length? And how can that length be measured?'[1] What was it, we may ask, that Augustine found so difficult in the length and measure of time? We may perhaps distinguish three aspects of his bewilderment, which might be grounds for anyone's bewilderment. He found it difficult, in the first place (we may suppose), to see how happenings which take *no* time could ever be 'added up' to make the happenings which *do* take time.[2] This difficulty is not peculiar to our thought of time, but applies to space as well. It seems absurd to say that an accumulation of events, the duration of each of which is zero, should have, together, a duration that is more than zero. The matter might be put more strongly. We are inclined to say that, if the duration of events were reduced to zero, 'there would be nothing left of them', they would 'just be nothing', and we obviously could not hope to make something out of an accumulation of nothings.[3] We may regard this as one side of the Augustinian problem. A second slightly different side consists in the fact that the stages of any happening that takes time are never there *together*. Now it seems absurd to say of a number of things which are never together, but always apart, that they can ever *amount* to anything, or form a *whole* of any kind: it would be as if one were to try to build a house with bricks that repelled each other, so that each one moved away when the next one was brought up to it. At such a rate, it would seem, one could build no house and no interval of time.[4] But Augustine's problem has a third side which seems to have worried him particularly: that if we measure an interval of time, we must be measuring something of which a vanishing section only has reality: all the other sections of it, which give breadth and bulk, are either *not yet there* or *not there any longer*. Now it is hard to grasp how we can measure something which is no longer there, which is 'past and gone', of which we are tempted to say that it is 'simply nothing'. And it is also hard to grasp how

[1] The interest in Augustine as a case of philosophical puzzlement is due to Wittgenstein.

[2] Augustine: 'The present hath no space. Where then is the time which we may call long?' See above.

[3] Augustine: 'If time present ... only cometh into existence because it passeth into time past, how can we say that either this is, whose cause of being is that it shall not be' (XI, 17).

[4] Augustine: 'Therefore neither is the year now current present; and if not present *as a whole* (our italics) then is not the year present.' See above.

46

TIME: A TREATMENT OF SOME PUZZLES

we can measure something which is not yet there, which is merely expected, which we are likewise tempted to describe as 'nothing'. It would be like trying to measure a building of which all but the tiniest fragment had been blasted by a bomb, or existed merely in a builder's blue-print. In such a situation we should have no building to measure, and it seems we should be in the same position with regard to lengths of time.[1]

We shall now briefly point to some ways—there are an indefinite number of such ways—in which we might avoid these Augustinian perplexities. We might, first of all, evade the whole argument by which we have been bludgeoned into saying that there are some events that take no time, and that only these are ever truly present. We might refuse to say, of certain happenings which are very short, that any of their parts lie in the past or future; we do not normally, in fact, make use of the past and future tenses in speaking of the parts of very short events contemporary with our utterance. Alternatively we might say that some sufficiently short events can be 'present as wholes', though most of their parts are past or future; this too agrees with ordinary usage, for we say that many fairly long events *are* happening, though we should talk in the past or future tense of some of their remoter parts. Or again we might deny—as Whitehead in his doctrine of epochal durations has denied—that certain very brief events come into being *part by part*.[2] There is, in fact, no plain empirical meaning to be given to the supposition that all events come into being part by part, since there must necessarily be a limit to the division of events by human judgements or instruments. Or again we might choose to follow certain other trends of language, and to say, of certain very brief events, that they 'took no time at all', thereby excluding from the start the whole issue of divisibility into successive parts.[3] It does not, in fact, matter, in all this choice of diction, *what* we say, provided only that we truly please ourselves: the facts are

[1] Augustine: 'In what space then do we measure time passing? In the future, whence it passeth through? But what is not yet we measure not. Or in the present by which it passes? But no space we do not measure. Or in the past to which it passes? But neither do we measure that, which now is not' (XI, 27).

[2] 'Accordingly we must not proceed to conceive time as another form of extensiveness. Time is sheer succession of epochal durations. . . . The epochal duration is not realized *via* its *successive* divisible parts, but is given *with* its parts' (*Science and the Modern World*, p. 158).

[3] *How* brief the happenings must be, of which we say any of these things, is of course, a matter for arbitrary decision.

47

LANGUAGE, MIND AND VALUE

there, we can see and show them, and it is for us to talk of them in ways which will neither perplex nor embarrass us.

It is desirable, in our choice of words, that we should be consistent, but it is not desirable that we should make a fetish of consistency. Consistency in language is most necessary if it means that we shall not, in a given context, fall victims to linguistic conflicts, that we shall not try to say something, while striving at the same time to unsay it.[1] Consistency is also very desirable if it means that we shall be guided by the analogies of things in what we say in *different* contexts; in the absence of *some* degree of such consistency, all language would be arbitrary and communication impossible. But consistency is wholly undesirable if it becomes a bogey, if it makes us say something in one context merely because we have said it in some other, more or less analogous context, and if it then leads us on to say further things which bewilder and confuse us. For the analogies of things are varied and conflicting, and it is impossible, without disrupting human language, to do justice to them all.

So far we have pursued a line which shakes the dialectic on which the Augustinian problem is founded. By so doing we avoid giving a sense to the phrase 'events which take no time', and are not obliged to say that these alone are truly present. Suppose, however, we are moved by this dialectic, or by some consideration of scientific convenience, to admit this talk of 'momentary presents', how then shall we proceed to deal with the various aspects of the Augustinian problem? As regards the first aspect, the building of a whole which has size out of parts which have *no* size, we may simply point out that it mixes up the familiar sense in which a pile of money is built up out of coins, with the new sense in which a happening which takes time may be built up out of happenings which take no time. Because one couldn't amass a fortune out of zero contributions, one tends to think one couldn't make a measurable duration out of parts with no duration. But the situations are quite different; no one has witnessed a lapse of time being built up out of instants, as he can witness a pile of money being built up out of coins, nor can the former be imagined as the latter is imagined.[2] Hence if we wish to speak of 'happenings which take no time', we are quite free to fix what may be said of

[1] Unless, indeed, a linguistic conflict is deliberately used to express some personal reaction to reality, as has been done by some philosophers.

[2] Though a sense might be invented in which we could be said to witness or imagine the former.

48

TIME: A TREATMENT OF SOME PUZZLES

them, and this means that we may simply rule that events which take time *are* made up of events which take no time. And once misleading pictures are avoided, we shall find no problem in this. We may in the same way dispose of the difficulties which spring from the tendency to say that an event which took no time would 'just be nothing'. Either we must restrain this inclination—to which we are not in duty bound to yield—or be prepared to say that certain parts of real temporal wholes are simply nothing, and that mere nothing can at times have definite properties. This way of talking would no doubt do violence to our habits, and abound in dangerous suggestions, but we should not, with a little practice, find it difficult.

The second aspect of the Augustinian problem involves a similar confusion. Because it would be absurd to say of certain wholes— houses, mountains or libraries, for instance—that they existed and were measurable, although their parts were never together, we think it would be absurd to say the same thing of happenings. But the fact that we shouldn't say that *some* of the things we call parts could constitute the things we call their wholes, unless they were present together, does not oblige us to say this in the case of *other* things we also call parts and wholes. For the sense in which the parts were parts, and the wholes wholes, and the former made up the latter, might be ruled to be different in the two sets of cases: we might say we were dealing with two totally different *sorts* of parts and wholes. And we do in fact rule so: for we regard it as nonsense to say of an event that takes time, that its parts are present together. And we recognize the difference between the two sets of cases by talking of *coexistent* parts in the one set of cases, and of successive parts in the other: the successive parts of a whole are, in fact, just those parts of it that *don't* need to be together. But if we feel ourselves unconquerably opposed to calling something a whole whose parts are not together, we may simply rule that some things may have magnitude although they are not wholes. And other similar expedients will meet other possible difficulties.

As regards the third difficulty of Augustine, how we manage to measure something which is in part past, we may again suggest a number of alternatives. We might, in the first place, reject the analogy between the measurement of a coexistent whole like a house, which isn't there to be measured if any parts of it lie in the past, and the measurement of a successive whole like a happening, which *must* have parts in the past. Or we might follow certain other trends of

D

49

LANGUAGE, MIND AND VALUE

language, and say that we have succession *in the present,* and that certain happenings which are not too long are able to be present as wholes and so to be measured directly. Other longer happenings might then be measured by means of the briefer and directly measurable happenings which entered into their remembered history. Or if it is the 'nothingness of the past' that troubles us, we must remember that we are not compelled to say that the past is nothing: we may, if we like, credit it with existence or subsistence or any other suitable status. For we are only worried by the 'nothingness of the past' because we think it will stop us from finding out any facts about the past, just as the nothingness of a bachelor's children stops us from asking for their ages or appearance. But there are so many clear and agreed ways of establishing what has happened in the immediate or remoter past, that it would be nonsense to put past events in the position of a bachelor's children. So that if we wish to say that they exist or subsist, there is no good reason why we should not do so. But if the 'existence' of the past is going to suggest to us that we could by some device revive or revisit the past, as we could revive a drowned man or revisit Palermo, then it is perhaps better to go on saying that the past is nothing, allowing meanwhile that there may be measurable wholes which have certain parts that are nothing.

IV

The puzzles of Augustine lead on very naturally to the problems of Zeno, or rather to a certain very general difficulty which seems to be involved in every one of Zeno's paradoxes. This is our difficulty in seeing how anything can happen, if *before* it happens something else must happen, and *before* that happens something else must happen, and so on indefinitely. If we make time continuous and infinitely divisible, we also feel obliged to say that before any happening is completed, an infinity of prior happenings must have been completed, and this seems to mean that *no* happening can ever be completed. We seem to be in the plight of a runner in a torch-race, who wants to hand on his torch to another runner *A,* but is told by *A* that he will only take it from *B,* who tells him he will only take it from *C,* who tells him he will only take it from *D,* and so on indefinitely. Or in the plight of a man who wants to interview a Cabinet Minister, and who is informed by the Minister that he must first discuss his business

50

TIME: A TREATMENT OF SOME PUZZLES

with the Under-Secretary, who informs him he must first discuss it with the Chief Clerk, etc. etc. Our runner obviously will never get rid of his torch, and our harassed petitioner will obviously never see his Minister, and it looks as if all happenings involve the same hopeless difficulty.

The difficulty we are presenting is, of course, not identical with any one of Zeno's historical puzzles: in all of these the difficulties of duration are complicated by the introduction of change and motion. But it is plain that all these puzzles could be so restated as to deal with happenings without regard to whether those happenings were changes or persistent states, and without regard to whether they involved motion or not. A plum continuing to hang on a tree for a certain period affords, less dramatically, the same species of philosophical perplexity as an arrow in its flight. Moreover, when we strip Zeno's problem of its spatial and other wrappings, its significance becomes clearer. For it is not, essentially, a problem of space or quantity, but solely one of time: it is only because all motion is *successive*, because an infinity of positions must be passed *before* any subsequent position, that the possibility of such motion seems so utterly ruled out. If the infinite stages of a motion could be there all at once, as the parts of a piece of space are, we should feel no problem in their infinite number. It is therefore foolish to imagine that we can meet Zeno's puzzles by the modern theory of the continuum or by the facts of infinite convergent numerical series.[1] And the problem assumes its most vexing form if we allow that ordinary happenings have ultimate parts that take no time. For of such parts it seems most natural to say that none can be next to any other,[2] and once this is said it is hard to understand how any ultimate part can ever pass away or be replaced by any other. For before such a part can be replaced by any other similar part, it must first have been replaced by an infinity of other similar parts. Our admission seems to leave us with a world immobilized and paralysed, in which every object and process, like the arrow of Zeno, stands still in the instant, for the simple reason that it has no way of passing on to other instants.

As before, we may deal with our difficulties in several different ways. We might, in the first place, deny that very short happenings

---

[1] This point is clearly brought out by Whitehead. See *Process and Reality*, p. 95.

[2] Unless we choose to say that there is a finite number of ultimate parts in any happening, or other queerer things.

LANGUAGE, MIND AND VALUE

are divisible as fairly long ones are divisible: the divisibility of *all* happenings is in any case without a definite meaning. This is the line followed by Professor Whitehead, who makes time flow in indivisible drops, and says that it is 'sheer succession of epochal durations'.[1] But, far less drastically, we might give to all this talk of instants and of infinite divisibility a sense consistent with the obvious facts of our experience, that things happen and that phases are outlived, that the world is not immobilized, and that we seldom have to cast about for ways of passing on to novel stages. For the infinite happenings that must first occur before a given thing can happen, are not like ordinary happenings we can see and show, of which it would be absurd to say that an infinite number ever were completed. They are happenings of a new sort to which a meaning must be arbitrarily given. And since *we* have to give a meaning to these happenings, it is for us to see that they mean nothing which conflicts with our established ways of saying things. And once we strip them of pictorial vividness, we also strip them of their puzzling character. Our problem also vanishes when we note that even to be 'desperately immobilized', to 'cast about in vain for means to pass to other stages', would both, if they were anything, be states that lasted and took time. Our problem therefore takes for granted the very thing it finds so difficult.

V

We turn, in conclusion, from these Augustinian and Zenonian difficulties, to a different set of temporal puzzles, quite unconnected with our tendency to use the present tense in more exact and narrow ways. We shall consider briefly the very general wonderment which professes to find something 'unintelligible' or 'contradictory' in time and change. 'How is it possible', we sometimes like to ask, 'for all the solid objects and people around us to melt away into the past, and for a new order of objects and persons to emerge mysteriously from the future?' This kind of wonderment is most strongly stirred by processes of *rapid* change: we wonder at things which have no constant quality for any length of time however short, at things which only reach a state to leave it, and so forth. A similar perplexity besets us in regard to 'truths' or 'facts': we wonder how what *is* the case can ever cease to be the case, or how what was false *then* can

[1] *Science and the Modern World*, quoted above.

TIME: A TREATMENT OF SOME PUZZLES

come to be true *now*, and so on. This week the peaches in our garden are not ripe; next week we find them ripe; the following week they are no longer ripe, but rotten: in certain frames of mind we find this difficult.

Our difficulty with regard to change may also be expressed in terms of 'happenings' and their 'properties' of 'pastness', 'presentness' and 'futurity', the form in which this problem was propounded by McTaggart. We wonder how it comes about that happenings which are at first remotely future, should steadily become more nearly future, how in the end they manage to be present, and how from being present they become past, and how they go on, ever afterwards, becoming more and more remotely past. McTaggart has shown plainly that we cannot solve this problem (if it is a problem) by bringing in the 'different times' at which events are present, past and future, since these themselves (whatever we may mean by them) have also to be present, past and future, and so involve the very difficulty they are called in to remove.

Now it is hard to see, if we remain in any ordinary, unreflective state of mind, what is the problem that is being raised by those who say they can't see how what *is* the case at one time, is not the case at other times, or that they can't see how a happening that is future can ever come to be a happening that is past. As we observed at the beginning of this paper, it should be possible to remove such difficulties by pointing to some ordinary happening around us, a man diving, for instance, and saying, as it happened, 'Now he's not yet diving', 'Now he's diving', 'Now he is no longer diving', or other similar phrases. And if a man were really puzzled by our usage in such situations, it would not take him very long to master it. We do not ordinarily have difficulty in knowing what to say of happenings as they pass, nor any tendency both to say and not to say the same thing in a given context, a kind of inconsistency that is seldom desirable. Occasionally, where change is rapid, we may find ourselves at a loss to say whether something is or is not yellow, or whether it is or was yellow: we may also have a tendency to say that it is both or neither. But all this only means we lack a settled and satisfactory way of talking about very swiftly changing things. But in the case of changes which are less rapid, we find ourselves quite free from conflict or confusion. *Before* an event occurs we say, if we have evidence, that it is not yet happening, that it hasn't yet happened, but that it will happen, while if it *is* happening we say that it is now happening,

53

LANGUAGE, MIND AND VALUE

that it hasn't ceased happening and that it isn't about to happen, and *after* it has happened we say that it has happened, that it is no longer happening and that it is not going to happen. Stated in words these semantic rules might seem circular, but taught in connection with a concrete situation they are wholly clear. And our conventions with regard to tenses are so well worked out that we have practically the materials in them for a formal calculus.[1] Where all is so desirably definite, what room is there for puzzles or perplexities?

To give an answer to this question, we must point to a certain aspiration which all our language to some extent fulfils, and which we are at times inclined to follow to unreasonable lengths. We desire to have in our language only those kinds of statement that are *not* dependent, as regards their truth or falsity, on any circumstance in which the statement happens to be made. We do not wish a statement which we call 'correct' and 'justified by fact' when made by one person, to be incorrect when made by another person, and to have to be superseded by some other statement. In the same way we do not wish a statement which we call 'correct' when made in one place, to be incorrect when made in another place, and to have to be superseded by some other statement. And there are occasions when we feel the same sort of thing about the *time* at which a statement is made: if we are right in saying something at a certain time, then, we sometimes feel, we must be right in saying the same thing at all other times. This means that we object, in certain frames of mind, even to the easy, systematic changes of tense which statements have to undergo when they are transmitted from period to period. We might express our general aspiration by saying that we wish our statements to be independent of 'extraneous circumstances' in regard to their truth or falsity: 'the facts' must settle whether what we say is true, and nothing else must come into consideration. But such a way of talking would be gravely question-begging, for it depends on the sort of language we are speaking whether a circumstance is or is not extraneous. If we spoke a language in which the statements permitted

---

[1] The calculus of tenses should have been included in the modern development of modal logics. It includes such obvious propositions as that

x present $\equiv$ (x present) present;

x future $\quad\equiv$ (x future) present $\equiv$ (x present) future;

also such comparatively recondite propositions as that

(x). (x past) future; i.e. all events, past, present and future, *will* be past. (Professor Prior's *Time and Modality* has now remedied the lack complained of in this note.)

54

TIME: A TREATMENT OF SOME PUZZLES

in one place differed systematically from the statements permitted in another place, then it wouldn't, in that language, be an extraneous circumstance, as regards the truth or falsity of a statement, whether that statement was made here or there. And those who used the language would protest quite legitimately that 'something was left out' by other languages which ignored all local circumstances of utterance. But the point is that we do *in part* say things which may be passed from man to man, or place to place, or time to time, without a change in their truth-value, and we look at things from *this* angle when we say that time, place and speaker are extraneous circumstances, and require our statements to ignore them.

Now the urge behind these austerities seems simply to be the urge towards more adequate communication, which is the fundamental impulse underlying language. We are prepared to sacrifice local and personal colour, or period flavour, in order that our statements may be handed on unaltered to other persons who are differently situated, or to ourselves in other situations. But it is not *this* sacrifice which gives rise to our perplexities: if we always spoke rigorously in the third person of everyone, ourselves included, if we avoided the adverbs 'here' and 'there', if we purged our language of tenses, and talked exclusively in terms of dates and tenseless participles, we should never be involved in difficulties. And for the purposes of science it is perhaps desirable that we should always talk in this manner. But our difficulty arises because we try to talk in this way but are also uneasy in doing so; we feel that something worth while has been omitted, and try to combine our old way of talking with our new one. Thus McTaggart first offers us an order of events in which there are no differences of past, present and future, but only differences of earlier and later, in which every happening always stays the sort of happening it is, and always occupies the same position in the time-series: he then slides back into another way of talking in which events are present, past and future, and always *change* in these modalities. And his attempt to combine these ways of talking results in the unanswerable question: how can a single happening have the incompatible properties of being past and present and future? Whereas if we talk in the ordinary way we never have to say these things at once, and if we talk in an artificial, tenseless manner the question can't arise, since the modalities in question can't be mentioned. It is as if a man tried to retain the use of personal pronouns, such as 'I', 'you', 'he', etc., in a language in which everything that could truly be said

55

LANGUAGE, MIND AND VALUE

by one man could be truly said by every other man, and were then led to ask: 'How can one and the same person be I and you and he?' And once we see the source of such perplexities, we should be easily rid of them.

III

GOEDELIAN SENTENCES:
A NON-NUMERICAL APPROACH[1]

(1942)

THE purpose of this note is to make clearer, for the benefit of those who have little taste for the intricacies of mathematical logic, the general significance of Goedel's important logical discoveries.[2] In Goedel's own exposition the relation between certain linguistic and certain arithmetical issues is extremely intimate: the reader is introduced, from the first, to a difficult and complex 'arithmetized syntax', in which all the symbols of a language are correlated with numbers, and all the logical relations among those symbols are mirrored in a set of corresponding numerical relations. It is not generally realized that this association of syntax with numbers, though interesting and important, is inessential, and that the basic import of Goedel's discoveries can be made intelligible without recourse to arithmetic. To free his discoveries from this association will clarify their meaning for all those persons who find mathematical methods a hindrance rather than a help in their thinking.

The discoveries of Goedel have their origin in the well-known puzzles connected with reflexive sentences, sentences that refer to themselves and predicate properties of themselves. Such sentences are at times wholly innocuous—as when a sentence says of itself that it is long, or written in red ink, or occurs on a certain page of a book—but lead us, at other times, into hopeless antinomies. The best-known example of this latter kind of sentence occurs in the ancient puzzle of

---

[1] Published in *Mind* (1942), pp. 259–65.
[2] These are to be found in an article in *Monatshefte für Mathematik und Physik*, Vol. 33, 1931. Philosophers will find all they want in Carnap's *Logical Syntax of Language*.

LANGUAGE, MIND AND VALUE

the Liar. A man says that the sentence he is now uttering is false, and immediately makes it impossible for us to determine the truth-value of his statement, for if what he says is true, it is false, and if it is false it is true. The antinomies connected with the notions of truth and falsehood are, however, quite peculiar, and will not concern us here. While it is possible that Goedel may have been inspired in his researches by the antinomy of the Liar, he chose to deal with the concept of *demonstrability* rather than with the notion of truth. The sentence constructed by Goedel, for examination of its curious consequences, was one that asserted of itself (by implication) that it could not be demonstrated, that is, that it could not be derived from the primitive propositions and definitions of the language of which it was a part, by applying the rules of inference of that language. The difficulties which confront us when we utter such a sentence are obvious at a glance. If such a sentence *can* be demonstrated, then it cannot be demonstrated, since this is what it says of itself. If, on the other hand, it can be refuted, then it can be demonstrated, since this is the contradictory of what it says of itself. The conclusion emerges that this sentence which proclaims its own indemonstrability, can neither be demonstrated nor refuted within the limits of the language to which it belongs, that it is, in technical parlance, 'undecidable' in that language. It can at best be decided in another higher language which has certain novel terms and notions at its disposal. The sentence considered by Goedel does not, however, directly say of itself that it is not demonstrable, but only that a certain *number*, which is uniquely correlated with the sentence in question, is characterized by a numerical property which corresponds to indemonstrability. It therefore raises the issue of undecidability in the arithmetical as well as in the linguistic realm. Into these intricacies of arithmetization we shall not, at the moment, enter: *instead of considering the arithmetical sentence propounded by Goedel, we shall first consider a purely linguistic sentence which corresponds to it*, and which possibly led Goedel on to his intricate arithmetical sentence.[1] Having developed the fundamentals of the problem at this level, we shall try to show, in a general way, how Goedel's arithmetical sentence can be built up, and how it entails the consequences it does entail.

A merit of the Goedelian sentence we are about to consider is that it describes itself in a *purely formal manner*, and does not merely

[1] I am quite ignorant of the precise psychological circumstances in which Goedel made his discoveries.

58

GOEDELIAN SENTENCES: A NON-NUMERICAL APPROACH

point to itself by means of a proper name or a demonstrative pronoun, nor describe itself by means of *contingent empirical features* which have nothing to do with its intrinsic structure. It describes a certain sentence as something to be arrived at by carrying out certain formal operations on certain purely logical materials, and, when we have carried out these operations, we find that the describing sentence is identical with the sentence it describes. Whereas if a sentence refers to itself as 'this sentence', or 'the fifth sentence in Euclid', or 'the sentence uttered by John between ten and five past ten', we can only discover that such a sentence is talking about itself by going beyond the bounds of logic, and acquainting ourselves with contingent matters of fact.

We turn from these general considerations to our actual Goedelian sentence. We shall proceed to build this up in a number of stages, so that its meaning may be perfectly plain.

I. We may, in the first place, direct attention to the general distinction between an expression in a language and the *name* of that expression. Logic is a science of second intentions, and is concerned with expressions rather than with the things those expressions mean: it therefore requires a sufficiency of names to refer to such expressions. Now the simplest way of constructing a name for an expression is simply to write *that expression itself* in quotation marks: we may then proceed to construct a name *for* that name by enclosing the same expression in two sets of quotation marks, and so on indefinitely. Thus if Charles is a man, 'Charles' will be his name, and ' "Charles" ' will be the name of his name, and so on.[1] It is not, however, necessary that we should use the quotation mark method in naming expressions: we might very well have given the independent name 'Henry' to the name of Charles, and the independent name 'William' to the name of this name. In this case Charles's name would be Henry, and the name of his name would be William. The use of quotation marks is in fact misleading, as people tend readily to omit them, and so to confuse expressions with their names. Thus while few people would

[1] If we *look back* on the sentence we have just written, then the symbol 'Charles' occurs in it first of all without quotation marks and is the *name of a man*, then with one set of quotation marks and is the *name of a name*, then with two sets of quotation marks and is the *name of a name of a name*. But when we *wrote* the sentence in question we were referring to a *man* on the first occasion, to a *name* on the second, and to a *name of a name* on the third. Names are obviously always one order higher than the things to which they are applied.

59

LANGUAGE, MIND AND VALUE

confuse Charles with 'Charles', many people would fail to draw a distinction between 'Charles' and ' "Charles" '. But for logical purposes it is all-important that this distinction should always be maintained; if not, absurdities will result, since the things that are true of an expression are not necessarily true of its name. Provided, however, that we *do* maintain the distinction, the quotation mark method is legitimate and less cumbrous than any other.

II. We may now briefly explain the distinction between a statement and a statement-form (or, to use an older terminology, between a proposition and a propositional function). A statement-form is an expression containing variables such as 'X', 'Y', etc., which gives rise to statements when expressions with a constant meaning are substituted for those variables. Thus 'X is long' is a statement-form: it will give rise to a statement if the constant symbol 'Art' is substituted for the variable 'X'.

III. Parallel to the distinction between a statement and a statement-form, we may lay down a distinction between a complete and an incomplete description. An incomplete description is a form of words involving variables which gives rise to a description if expressions with a constant meaning are substituted for those variables. Thus 'The man who married X' is an incomplete description of a certain person, which gives rise to a complete description if 'Xanthippe' is substituted for 'X'.

IV. We now construct the following incomplete description of a statement: it is '*the statement which is arrived at by substituting for the variable in the statement-form Y the name of the statement-form in question*'. This description is incomplete because it contains the variable 'Y': it would become a complete description if we replaced 'Y' by the name or description of some actual statement-form. Thus if we replaced 'Y' by ' "X is the first sentence in Euclid" ',[1] our description would run 'The statement which is arrived at by substituting for the variable in the statement-form "X is the first sentence in Euclid" the name of the statement-form in question', and this description would describe the statement ' "X is the first sentence in Euclid" is the first sentence in Euclid'.

[1] Since we are talking about the *name* of a statement-form we require the inner pair of quotation marks, and since, in order to talk about this name, we require a name *for* this name, we also require the outer pair of quotation marks.

60

GOEDELIAN SENTENCES: A NON-NUMERICAL APPROACH

V. We now construct a statement-form involving the incomplete description constructed in IV. This statement-form simply says of the statement incompletely described in IV that it is indemonstrable, that it cannot be proved. It runs as follows: '*We cannot prove the statement which is arrived at by substituting for the variable in the statement-form Y the name of the statement-form in question.*'

VI. We now construct the following description of a statement, that it is '*that statement which is arrived at by substituting for the variable in the statement-form formulated in V the name of the statement-form in question*'. If we substitute the actual name of the statement-form formulated in V, we get '*The statement which is arrived at by substituting for the variable in the statement-form "We cannot prove the statement which is arrived at by substituting for the variable in the statement-form Y the name of the statement-form in question" the name of the statement-form in question*'.

VII. We now say of the statement which we have described in VI that it cannot be demonstrated. We thereby arrive at our Goedelian sentence: '*We cannot prove the statement which is arrived by substituting for the variable in the statement-form "We cannot prove the statement which is arrived at by substituting for the variable in the statement-form Y the name of the statement-form in question" the name of the statement-form in question.*' To this statement we may give the name '*G*'.

Now *G* says that a certain statement cannot be proved, and it describes that statement by saying of it that it is the statement arrived at by replacing the variable in a certain statement-form, which is quoted in full, by the *name* of this statement-form. Now we can discover *what* statement is said by *G* to be indemonstrable, by replacing '*Y*', the variable in the statement-form quoted in *G*, by that same statement-form enclosed in quotation marks. When this operation is carried out we get '*We cannot prove the statement which is arrived at by substituting for the variable in the statement-form "We cannot prove the statement which is arrived at by substituting for the variable in the statement-form Y the name of the statement-form in question" the name of the statement-form in question*'. Now it is obvious, but also surprising, that the statement arrived at by carrying out the operation prescribed by *G* is simply *G* itself. *G* has therefore said of itself that it cannot be demonstrated. And from this situation flow all the curious consequences outlined in a previous paragraph.

We may clarify the situation by introducing a few abbreviations. Let 'dem' be an abbreviation for 'demonstrable', let 'subst (A, B, C)' stand for the result of replacing the expression B *in* the expression A *by* the expression C, let 'Qu A' mean the expression arrived at by writing A in quotation marks, and let 'Var A' mean the variable in the expression A.[1] G will now read

'not dem subst {"not dem subst $(Y, \text{Var } Y, \text{Qu } Y)$", Var "not dem subst $(Y, \text{Var } Y, \text{Qu } Y)$", Qu "not dem subst $(Y, \text{Var } Y, \text{Qu } Y)$"}'.

Now it is obvious that if we *do* substitute for the variable in 'not dem subst $(Y, \text{Var } Y, \text{Qu } Y)$' i.e. for '$Y$', the quotation-enclosed statement-form 'not dem subst $(Y, \text{Var } Y, \text{Qu } Y)$', we are back at G, our original statement.

We shall now proceed to show, in a general way, how Goedel's *arithmetical* sentence, which we may call 'G''', can be arrived at from the purely linguistic sentence G, which has just been given. This arithmetical sentence is arrived at by 'arithmetizing syntax', i.e. by constructing an exact numerical model of the linguistic situation sketched above. This arithmetizing of syntax involves, in the first place, that we assign *numbers* to all the symbols, primitive or defined, which occur in our language: the number of 'not' might, for instance, be 21, that of 'and', 24, and so on. This assignment of numbers may be done, in part, according to general rules, e.g. variables may have prime numbers assigned to them, predicates cubes of prime numbers, and so on. In this arithmetization it is important to note that there will also be *numbers assigned to numbers*, and these numbers will not, in general, be the same as those numbers, or else all the numbers would be used up in numbering numbers.

We then determine a method according to which whole expressions (including sentences), consisting of strings of symbols, can be arithmetized: the method chosen is to write down the prime numbers in ascending order for each successive symbol of the sentence, and then to attach the *numbers* of those symbols as exponents to these prime numbers, the number of the whole sentence being the *product* of all these primes raised to various powers.

Thus in arithmetizing the Law of Contradiction, 'Not (p and

[1] Note that 'A', 'B', and 'C' in the sentence just written are already names of expressions, and need not therefore be enclosed in quotation marks. In this note they are so enclosed since we are talking of the names and not of the expressions.

GOEDELIAN SENTENCES: A NON-NUMERICAL APPROACH

not p)' we have, say, 14 for 'not', 6 for the left-hand bracket, 7 for 'p', 24 for 'and', 14 for 'not', 7 for 'p' and 10 for the right-hand bracket.

The whole law arithmetized becomes

$$2^{14} \times 3^6 \times 5^7 \times 7^{24} \times 11^{14} \times 13^7 \times 7^{10}$$

if this product is multiplied out, it can always be uniquely factorized into its primes and their powers. We can in similar fashion assign numbers to *sequences* of sentences, e.g. to a sequence of sentences which constitutes a proof. Thus, if the first sentence in a proof had the number a (a very large number), the second b, the third c, the whole proof would have the number $2^a \times 3^b \times 5^c$.

When our whole language has been thus arithmetized, there will obviously be properties and relations of numbers corresponding to every syntactical property or relation of our statements or their component expressions. There will likewise be numerical operations corresponding to all the syntactical operations permitted in our language. Thus, if a sentence is demonstrable when it is of a certain form, or is related in certain ways to certain other sentences of certain forms, then the number corresponding to that sentence will have a parallel property, which we may call 'DEMONSTRABILITY', if it is built up in a certain way, or if it stands in certain relations to other numbers of certain kinds. And if a statement is formed from a statement-form by *substituting* a constant symbol for a variable, there will be a precisely analogous operation which can be performed on the corresponding numbers. We now add the finishing touch to our complicated picture by noting that we shall require special *names* and *symbolic devices* to refer to the various numerical properties, relations and operations which can be discovered in our arithmetized language, and that we shall further require special *numbers* which can be correlated with these names and symbolic devices, so that our whole account of our arithmetized language can *itself* be arithmetized. The adjective 'DEMONSTRABLE', for example, will not merely *mean* a numerical property: it will also *have* a special number which corresponds to it, and so will every sentence in which it occurs.

The stage is now set for the arithmetical sentence G' which corresponds to the purely linguistic sentence G given above. G, we may remember, ran: 'We cannot prove the statement which is arrived at by substituting for the variable in the statement-form "We cannot prove the statement which is arrived at by substituting for the

63

LANGUAGE, MIND AND VALUE

variable in the statement-form Y the name of the statement-form in question" the name of the statement-form in question'. To this will correspond on the arithmetical plane the statement '*The number is not DEMONSTRABLE which is obtained by substituting for the number of the variable in the number of the sentence-form "The number is not DEMONSTRABLE which is obtained by substituting for the number of the variable in the number of the sentence-form Y the number of the number of that sentence-form" the number of the number of that sentence-form*'. (In the actual statement the numbers will not be described as 'numbers of variables', 'numbers of sentence-forms', etc.: this will be evident from the numbers themselves.) Now this arithmetical sentence G' can be stated symbolically just as we stated the purely linguistic G given above, and then, since all its symbols have had numbers assigned to them, we can also assign a number to the whole sentence. Let us suppose that this number is n. Now we can also discover the number of the sentence-form quoted in G', i.e. the number of the sentence-form 'The number is not DEMONSTRABLE which is obtained by substituting for the number of the variable in the number of the sentence-form Y the number of the number of that sentence-form'. Let us suppose that this number is m. Now G' tells us that by carrying out a certain substitution in m we shall arrive at another number which is not DEMONSTRABLE. Here it is possible to prove, and Goedel has proved, that the number obtained by carrying out on m the substitution mentioned by G', is simply n, that is, G''s own number. So that we see that, just as G says of G that it is not demonstrable, so G' says of G''s number n that it is not DEMONSTRABLE. And the consequences which we have seen to follow in the case of G also follow in the case of G'. For it is easy to show that G', like G, can neither be demonstrated nor refuted in the language in which it occurs. For if G' could be demonstrated then its number could be shown to have the parallel property of DEMONSTRABILITY, which involves a contradiction, since G' says that its number is not DEMONSTRABLE. Similarly, if G' could be refuted, then its number could be shown to be non-DEMONSTRABLE, which involves a contradiction, since a refutation of G' is also a proof that G''s number *is* DEMONSTRABLE. And the whole argument has the very curious consequence that, even in the realm of numbers, where one would have imagined that every formulable question can be proved or disproved, there are some questions which cannot be decided within the limits of a given language. Such ques-

GOEDELIAN SENTENCES: A NON-NUMERICAL APPROACH

tions may, however, be decided in other, wider languages, which make use of new notions, and survey the whole situation from above, as it were: we have in fact just proved, in such a wider language, that G' is undecidable, and therefore indemonstrable in its own language, and this, in its turn, means that G's number is non-DEMONSTRABLE, which means that we have given, again in our wider language, a valid proof of G'.[1]

---

[1] It is perhaps worth suggesting that the whole logical situation here presented furnishes a very perfect example of Hegelian dialectic, of the 'swing over' of a notion or proposition into its contrary at a higher level, and one that Hegel himself would thoroughly have understood and enjoyed.

IV

MORALITY BY CONVENTION[1]

(1944)

I

FEW features in regard to our moral judgements have proved more distressing to philosophers, or have seemed more hopelessly to obstruct their efforts to build up a science of ethics, than our plain inability to reach agreement on many moral questions. There seem to be, by contrast, in other fields of discourse, methods of settling arguments which are both intelligible and final. We can, for instance, bring most mathematical arguments to an end by calculation, that is, by operating continuously on our symbols (according to a set of rules that follow from their meanings) until some satisfactory result emerges. And we can likewise settle most disputes concerning objects in the realm of nature, if we can only succeed in placing ourselves where we can use our senses or our instruments to make appropriate observations. But in the field of morals such methods do not seem to be available: there do not seem to be any acknowledged, easy ways of reaching answers that everyone will find acceptable. The situation seems, in fact, to be so desperate that some have had recourse, in dealing with their moral problems, to certain wholly private operations, described by them in terms of 'feeling' or 'immediate intuition'; these are, unfortunately, quite worthless from the point of view of settling arguments, since no one else can be quite sure what they involve, or whether, in a given instance, they have been properly performed. And there are others who have sought a remedy for their difficulties by assuming, rather uselessly, that while it may be impossible for *us* to know whether we have the right answers to our moral questions, yet there nevertheless *are* a comprehensive set of right answers, 'laid up' in some realm or mind or

[1] Published in *Mind*, April 1944, pp. 142–69.

MORALITY BY CONVENTION

medium to which we have no means of access. And there are yet others who have simply ceased to worry about the hopeless character of disputes in ethics, and have even found a reason for this hopelessness: our ethical utterances have their origin in private feelings, which vary without principle from one man to another; it is not meaningful to say that any of these feelings are true or valid, or that others are the opposite.

Against the boundless nihilism of these doctrines, we shall attempt to argue that there is not, in fact, and cannot be, that wide variety of ethical feeling and opinion, that some have imagined possible, and that men only have assumed such variability because they simply have not understood, or have not analysed, what we really *mean* by saying that a feeling or opinion is an ethical one. And we shall also try to argue that we have, in morals, many quite definite methods by which our questions may be approached and dealt with, that a substantial range of questions can be satisfactorily disposed of by these methods, and that certain residual questions, which remain unanswered in this manner, are quite incapable of receiving any answer. We may, in fact, attribute the despair of many moral philosophers to their forgetfulness of the Aristotelian warning: that we should never seek for a higher degree of exactness in a science than is appropriate to its subject-matter and the type of its inquiry. It seems therefore plainly to be incumbent on the moral philosopher, before he poses a problem or considers an answer, to probe into the ways by which we settle ethical arguments, as well as the ways by which we test our moral judgements.

Before we pass on to these questions, we may align ourselves, quite definitely, with a theory of the moral judgement which has been put forward recently by the so-called positivists, but which was also stated, in a less clear manner, by writers of the sentimental school in the eighteenth century. This is the view which holds it to be the function of an ethical statement, particularly in regard to certain crucial words occurring in it—words such as 'good', 'bad', 'right', 'wrong', 'ought', 'duty', and so on—to *evince* or *express* the sentiments of the speaker. A man who makes an ethical statement, and uses some of these peculiar words, is not, while he uses them, trying to 'discover objects as they stand in nature, without addition or diminution':[1] he is rather trying to give voice to the demands and feelings which the notion of such objects arouses in him.

[1] Hume, *An Inquiry Concerning the Principles of Morals*, Appendix I.

LANGUAGE, MIND AND VALUE

He is not, in any ordinary sense of 'description', trying to describe objects,[1] or say what they are like, but may be said, rather, to be allowing himself to be moved or stirred by them. It does not seem, at the present stage of the argument, which has prolonged itself for centuries, that any other way of talking is clearer or more profitable. We might say, as some have said, that ethical terms had as their meanings certain peculiar ethical properties and relations, that these were not to be identified with anyone's feelings and demands, that these were not located on the natural level, but in some sphere or territory of their own, that they were not accessible to sense-perception but revealed themselves to some non-sensuous scrutiny: all these would constitute a body of utterances to which (although they cannot be readily interpreted as they stand) it might nevertheless be possible to give some perfectly good meaning.

But even if we managed to give them such a meaning, the picture that they yielded would still remain extraordinarily misleading. For it assimilates our situation in the moral judgement to the situation we are up against in judgements of perception. It definitely suggests that it is possible, in either case, to observe dispassionately and report accurately, that others will be able to understand and to verify our statements, and that any emotions and wishes which accompany our reports, are purely incidental and 'our own affair', and are not in any way important in interpreting our utterances. Whereas we find, in fact, that we are quite unable either to say or hear of anything that it is good or bad, or right or wrong, or that it should be done, or that it ought to be the case, without either actually experiencing feelings and demands in connection with these words, or, at least, coming rather close to having such experiences. We are disposed to say that we can 'only really understand' these words, when we are actually experiencing such demands and feelings. We are also disposed to say that, if there were some property or relation, however singular and unique in status, which we could contemplate without the faintest stirring of desire or feeling, then such a property or relation would have no special relevance to ethics, nor be of any particular interest to the moralist. And even if there were moral philosophers who dignified it with the name of 'good', or gave it any other axiological title, this would not in the least be sufficient to give it the slightest connection with that familiar goodness which, in

[1] Of course, we might so use the word 'describe', that someone who said that something was good or bad might be said to be describing it.

68

Aristotelian phrase, is 'capable of being practised or possessed by men'.

It seems clear, further, that we have absolutely no way of teaching someone how we use an ethical word or phrase, unless we can express or evince before him (by manner, tone, gesture or some other feature of behaviour), and so successfully communicate to him, some ethical demand or feeling. If the analogy with perceptual judgements were at all close, these facts would constitute a most mysterious and anomalous situation. We simply could not say why we could never think or talk of ethical properties or relations, without experiencing or showing feelings and demands, while, in the case of other properties and relations, there was no such close and necessary association.

II

That moral judgements are emotional, is the truth which really underlies Moore's well-known doctrine of the 'naturalistic fallacy'. For what this doctrine really succeeds in bringing out, is the profound disparity between our ethical judgements, which evince attitudes, and all those other judgements which describe objects in the world around us, which tell us where they are, when they happen, how big or small they are, how long they last, how they are shaped and coloured, and even what they think or feel. These questions differ totally from ethical questions: it is only when we know (or have imagined) answers to them, that we are in a position to raise the genuinely ethical questions: 'Is it a good thing for this to be like this?', or 'Would it be a good thing if this were the case?', and so forth. Even questions of the type called 'metaphysical', which try to penetrate beyond experience and the world of nature, but which nevertheless resemble empirical questions, and which leave experience at quite definite points: these questions, too, are plainly quite different from ethical questions.

But though Moore made it very clear, in his early expositions, that there *was* a difference between such ethical and such non-ethical questions, he never in the least succeeded in saying what that difference really was. For though he held that the predicate 'good' could neither be reduced nor analysed, he did not tell us how this made it so fundamentally different from all those very numerous non-ethical predicates which are equally irreducible and equally incapable of analysis. And though he also maintained that ethical predicates accrued

LANGUAGE, MIND AND VALUE

to objects as secondary consequences of their 'nature' (in a somewhat narrow sense of 'nature'), he again failed to show how this rendered them fundamentally different from many non-ethical predicates, 'simplicity' for instance, which are, to an equal extent, secondary and consequential. But if we make it the essential function of our ethical words and phrases to evince or voice the feelings and demands which the thought of certain objects arouses in us, we shall have no difficulty in understanding why ethical and non-ethical utterances are so widely different, and why no combination of the latter could ever conceivably yield us an exact equivalent of the former.

We may, in passing, emphasize a merit of the modern sentimental doctrine, which differentiates it markedly from the much less clearly stated doctrines of the early sentimentalists. The modern sentimentalist is quite clear that, if we say: 'This thing is good', 'This should be done' and so forth, we are not talking *of* our own demands and feelings, but rather *giving voice* to them. Whereas the doctrines of the earlier sentimentalists leave it vague whether they think the moral judgement *voices* sentiment, or that it merely *talks about* it. And, if they mean the latter, there is, of course, no fundamental difference between a moral judgement and any other sort of judgement. It is also clear that, if they mean the latter, we should be able to settle all disputes in ethics by simply finding out what certain people actually wish and feel. But this is obviously not the case.

If, further, the feelings talked of in a moral judgement were the speaker's own, then obviously the moral judgements of different speakers could not really be in conflict, since they would be talking about entirely different things, and there would be no reason why anyone should seek to influence anyone else to accept *his* moral judgements, or to give up his own. Yet all agree that it is perfectly sensible to attempt to do this, and that it very often is our duty to do so. But if an ethical judgement serves, among other things, to voice an attitude, then it may very well be 'part and parcel' of that attitude to insist, and rigorously demand, that others should agree with us in experiencing certain feelings and desires. We see in Hume, the best and clearest of the older sentimentalists, a constant vacillation between the true and the mistaken doctrine. He utters the true doctrine when he tells us that 'from circumstances known and supposed the former (reason) leads us to the discovery of the concealed and unknown', and that 'after all circumstances and relations are laid before us the latter (taste) makes us feel from the whole a new

70

MORALITY BY CONVENTION

sentiment of blame and approbation'. But he gives us the mistaken doctrine when he says: 'The hypothesis which we embrace is plain. . . . It maintains that morality is determined by sentiment. It defines virtue to be whatsoever mental action or quality gives to a spectator the pleasing sentiment of approbation'.[1]

There is, however, one respect in which the older sentimentalism was wholly superior to the newer theories. It never allowed itself, like the modern doctrines, to say a number of very bizarre and curious things: that moral judgements are not really judgements, that they do not express propositions capable of truth or falsehood, and that they are wholly lacking in 'factual content'. Nor did it hold that ethical predicates have no meaning, that they express no genuine properties of objects, and that they may properly be likened to ejaculations which accompany our references to objects and objective situations. These statements are, no doubt, valuable in bringing out the difference between a moral judgement, which gives voice to an attitude, and other judgements which we should describe as 'factual' in a narrow sense. And it was also valuable to stress the previously unnoticed likeness between an ethical predicate and an exclamation. But it is altogether arbitrary, and also contrary to accepted usage, to say that what we usually *call* moral judgements, have not, in strictness, any right to be classed as judgements. It is also wholly arbitrary to deny the right of certain of these judgements to be denominated 'true' or 'valid'. For, as we shall make it our business to show, there is a whole gamut of tests to which a moral judgement, just *because* it is a moral judgement, must necessarily submit itself: it is customary and proper to say of judgements that survive these tests that they are true or valid. The tests required to validate a judgement differ, in any case, according to the character of the judgement; we should not say that mathematical judgements were not really judgements merely because we do not test them as we test our judgements about natural objects. So that it would be quite unreasonable to refuse to speak of 'moral judgements' merely because the testing procedures applicable in their case have many singularities. And while we should not lose sight of the resemblances between an ethical predicate and an exclamation, this will not in the least justify us in ignoring their many important differences. Nor should we say that ethical predicates have no meaning, merely because the way in which we learnt to use them differed in many respects from the way in which we learnt to use such

[1] *An Inquiry Concerning the Principles of Morals*, Appendix I.

71

predicates as 'round' or 'sweet'. For ethical predicates occur integrally in statements that are capable of truth, and so it is both permissible and correct to say that they have meaning, and that they stand for properties of objects.

We may, however, point to one respect in which all the sentimental schools have gone seriously astray; that is, in thinking that, because our ethical judgements had their origin in feeling, there could be no limit to their possible objects. They often speak as if it would be possible to have ethical emotions in regard to absolutely *anything*, and to voice one's sentiment in the corresponding judgement. Or if they have conceded any limit to the objects of our ethical emotions, they have tended to ascribe this to some merely constitutional bias, to some accident of our human make-up, or to some mere contingency of circumstance or of 'social conditioning'. They have never for a moment imagined that there might be definite *claims* involved in moral attitudes, claims capable of being tested, and capable, through the outcome of such testing, of rendering the attitudes in question either justifiable or unjustifiable.

It seems quite obvious, however, that, even in the case of the most familiar and elementary emotions, we find some definite limitation to their possible range of objects, and also certain definite claims involved in them, whose validation would serve to *justify* a man in feeling them. Thus in the emotion that we call 'fear' we see some object 'in a menacing light': it must seem dangerous, a source of possible harm; we couldn't be afraid of something that was *obviously* harmless. And it is plain that, if an object was not really harmful, our fears of it would forthwith *lose their justification*. It is also plain that, if we *knew* an object wasn't really harmful, and nevertheless continued to fear it, our fear would rightly be denominated 'neurotic'[1] or 'abnormal'. To be afraid of objects therefore means, in part, to treat them as having certain properties, to make a claim with regard to them, a claim which may be true or false, whose verification will serve to justify our frightened state, and whose refutation will altogether remove this justification. And while, in normal mental life, the refutation of the claim involved in fear will suffice to dissipate the emotion, there are, of course, a large number of abnormal states in which things continue to *look* sinister and menacing although we know that they are really harmless. This case resembles the case of scenes in mirrors, which

---

[1] The normative meaning of 'neurotic' has seldom been realized by abnormal psychologists.

72

MORALITY BY CONVENTION

still seem situated at a place beyond the mirror, although we know that they are not really there. All these are things which are implied in, which follow from, the nature of the emotion known as 'fear'; we should not *call* a feeling 'fear' if any of them were not present: they enter, if one likes the phrase, into the 'constitution of the affect'.

It would be possible, in a similar fashion, to show that jealousy and anger have a constitution, that they make various complicated claims regarding actual situations, and that they immediately lose their justification if any of these claims should prove unfounded. What is true of all these elementary affects will obviously be true of ethical demands and feelings, which are, much more plainly, complex and derivative: there will be definite limits to their possible range of objects, and they will make a number of claims by testing which we may pronounce them either justifiable or unjustifiable. These obvious truths have hitherto escaped notice only because men have tended to operate with a picture of emotional life which has been, to an impossible degree, reduced and simplified. They have tended to picture emotions as 'simple stirrings in men's bosoms', only accessible to an inward eye, and quite without any necessary relation to the objects in the environing world, or to the ways in which such objects lead us to behave. They have also tended to talk as if there were obvious surface marks by means of which the inward eye could recognize and classify these 'stirrings'. Whereas we plainly cannot hope to talk of our emotions to other people, in terms of wholly inward happenings which nobody can set side by side nor compare in any way. We can only bring such feelings into the range of public discourse through traits which are themselves public and revealed, or which are capable, in favourable circumstances, of becoming such. We can only pin them down, for other people, by referring to the objective situations which such feelings presuppose, or to the ever varied yet quite characteristic ways in which they might lead someone to 'take' such situations.

It is also abundantly clear that the stirrings in men's bosoms are seldom simple in their quality, and they do not readily assort themselves into a small number of obvious types. Rather, if we may follow the lead of the few psychologists who have genuinely striven to build up a satisfactory introspective language—we shall leave aside the problems involved in such an enterprise—we have to speak of our inward states as highly complex, varied and obscure, as altogether

LANGUAGE, MIND AND VALUE

shifting and elusive. Nor can we class them as instances of this or that emotion by virtue of some simple surface quality, but by the type of situation which we face in them, and by the general *policy of action* which we follow in facing such a situation. If we can state completely the sort of situation that confronts us in a given attitude, and how we are preparing and nerving ourselves to cope with it, then we shall not require to appeal to subjective shades in order to construct an exhaustive picture of the 'constitution' or 'anatomy' of that attitude. And it is precisely such a 'constitution' or 'anatomy', developed in terms of objective situations and of objective ways of responding to them, that it is now our business to furnish in the case of *ethical* demands and feelings.

III

Before we embark on this dissection of morality, we must, however, pause to think what really may be involved in such anatomizing. We might here follow Husserl, or others who have yielded to the dangerous charm of Plato, and say that we were embarking on 'a pure phenomenology of the moral attitudes', on some intuitive study of the essences involved in moral attitudes, and of their *a priori*, necessary relationships. To speak in this manner might prove harmless: it nevertheless involves suggestions which might, in the end, plunge us into senselessness or misconstruction. But we might also say, with much less chance of being misled, that we were trying to discover what *conventions* governed us in using words like 'ethical' and 'moral' in connection with demands and feelings. We might say we were endeavouring to determine what conditions must be present before we were prepared to *call* some attitude an ethical one.[1] This would be a better way of speaking than the last, since it would not lead us to imagine that there necessarily was one single, standard meaning of such terms as 'ethical' and 'moral', and that this simply lay before us for analysis, like some quiescent patient under anaesthetics. We should expect that 'ethical feelings', like many other phenomena to which a common name is given, would constitute a varied family of

[1] The words 'ethical' and 'moral' are, of course, sophisticated words, more used by philosophers than by ordinary people. But they have been so tightly anchored by definitions to such ordinary words as 'right' and 'wrong', that they are, to all intents and purposes, a part of ordinary language.

74

MORALITY BY CONVENTION

cases, linked to each other by many, very different likenesses, and not inevitably displaying *one* generic trait.[1]

But this linguistic mode of treatment has other, even greater, advantages. Philosophers of essence have not generally adhered closely to the current meanings of familiar words and phrases; they have, only too frequently, played fast and loose with these. They have given such words and phrases more polished and precise meanings than are customary, they have ironed out anomalies in our usage, or have extended it in new directions. But they have tended to do these things unconsciously, saying that they were discovering what those words and phrases 'really meant', or how they should, 'in strict propriety', be used, or how the essences they stood for really were related to each other. A philosopher of language may, however, do intentionally and consciously what the philosophers of essence have done unconsciously and unintentionally. He may deliberately lay down new conventions, and give familiar terms preciser and more serviceable meanings. He may endeavour to remove anomalies and vaguenesses, or to throw light upon unnoticed likenesses and differences. If these innovations are to be justifiable, however, they must not break abruptly with prevailing usage, nor must they readily be capable of leading, by covert slips and shifts of meaning, to statements that are merely queer or merely paradoxical. They must develop tendencies present in ordinary diction in ways that lead to more light or greater uniformity. We shall, accordingly, deliberately present a somewhat stylized, much more simple picture of 'the ethical reaction', than really corresponds to any common feature of those very varied attitudes that we know as 'ethical' or 'moral'. But we shall try to do this in a profitable way, so that the concept which results, while it promotes more smoothness and more light, may also be acceptable to a fair sprinkling of reflective speakers.[2]

We shall also find it profitable, in laying down the constitution of our ethical responses, to draw a distinction between 'developed' ethical responses, and those that we shall characterize as 'undeveloped' or 'distorted'. Such a distinction is valuable because there has, in fact, been a definite line along which all the attitudes that we call

[1] There are, for instance, more differences than resemblances between an ethical attitude based on fellow-feeling and compassion, and one based on blind obedience to some authoritative code.

[2] The ideas in this paragraph obviously owe a great deal to Wittgenstein, Wisdom and others.

75

LANGUAGE, MIND AND VALUE

'ethical' have developed, as life has grown progressively more secure and easy, and as men have had more time to ponder over moral questions. That ethical feelings have, with many sideways shifts and setbacks, moved steadily in this direction, may be regarded as a mere fact of history, but it is also possible to show that such a movement represents a natural extension of certain traits present from the outset in all the attitudes that we call 'ethical' or 'moral', as well as a gradual dropping out of other factors that are highly variable. We may sufficiently suggest the kind of movement we are thinking of if we say, somewhat banally, that it leads from arbitrary taboo and tribalism to the reasoned pursuit of what is genuinely best for everyone. It is, in fact, the kind of movement that occurs in every field, as soon as men become conscious of the strangeness of including certain objects or phenomena in a class, although they differ widely from the majority of its members, and of excluding other objects or phenomena from the same class, although they very much resemble the majority of its members. In all such cases, reflective thought tends readily to *drop* the former from the class in question, and to *extend* the boundaries of that class till it includes the latter.

We may therefore quite legitimately frame the notion of 'developed' ethical feelings' and 'developed ethical judgements' to represent the limit towards which our reflective ethical responses seem to be tending. To fix the content of this notion is, to a very large extent, an arbitrary proceeding: we could determine this content in a merely tiresome way by laying down that only those responses were 'developed ethical responses' which happened to accord with some peculiar, private set of preferences of our own. But, if we wish to use the notion profitably, we must be at some pains to cover in it most of the features that reasonably reflective people would incorporate in it, and we must not determine it in so narrow and so precise a manner that every moral problem would be thereby straightway decided. For, while our ethical responses have their limits, they also leave, within those limits, much that remains unsettled and debatable. And we should not be characterizing them truly, nor in a manner that accords with accepted ways of speaking, if our description of them were to take away entirely, or reduce very seriously, their quite fundamental vagueness and debatability. It is for us to fix the meaning of 'developed moral feelings and demands', but we must also try to do so in a manner that has some chance of winning a fair measure of acceptance.

MORALITY BY CONVENTION

IV

We may begin our sketch of 'the developed ethical reaction' (and of the less developed forms which lead up to it) by trying, first of all, to determine the appropriate *object* of an ethical reaction. Just as the appropriate object of fear is something dangerous and menacing, of anger something hostile and obstructive, so there is obviously something which may be said to be the proper object of an ethical reaction. It must be a proper object, in that we simply should not *call* an attitude an ethical one, *unless* it had an object of this sort. We may start our sketch with some textbook commonplaces, for even the textbooks, with their quite naïve views of language, and their quite naïve picture of our mental workings, have not suggested that it is possible to have ethical emotions in regard to absolutely everything. While they have fearfully envisaged the possibility that certain people might approve ethically of manslaughter or adultery, they have at least avoided the absurdity of supposing that someone might approve ethically of his own boots and shoes, and of thinking it strange that none of us actually does so.

Quite plainly the appropriate object of an ethical emotion or demand is, in the first place, *something done* or *something to be done*, and, in the second place, *the man who did it* or *who might do it*. We could scarcely be said to be diverging from current usage if we held that *acts* and *agents* are the appropriate objects of an ethical reaction. For while one may have feelings in regard to objects that are not acts and agents—feelings not necessarily very different qualitatively from ethical feelings—and while one may in certain circumstances feel an urge to call such feelings 'ethical'—as when a man censures some art-form as 'debased' and 'mean'—we recognize that it is only on account of some *analogy* that such a way of talking can be tolerated. Our object only is *as if* it were an action or an agent, and so our feeling only is *as if* it were an ethical one.

We may lay down, in the next place, that the proper object of our ethical reactions must be a *conscious* action or a *conscious* agent. We may respond emotionally to hurricanes or pestilences or our own digestive tracts, but we could only call such emotions 'ethical' by a momentary abuse of language, since these are very plainly agents who 'know not what they do'. And it is only, further, *to the extent* that agents know what they are doing, that we should say that we were *ethically* affected by them: whatever they may do unwittingly,

LANGUAGE, MIND AND VALUE

even if it happens to be a part or a consequence of some conscious action, can never be a source of *ethical* emotion. There are, of course, a large number of primitive reactions to conduct which we should still call 'ethical', although the acts which prompt them are not conscious, and may even be known to be unwitting. But we should only call them 'ethical' on account of their close association, and their affinity with innumerable other attitudes, quite richly represented even in animals and savages, which *do* take cognizance of the distinction between conscious and unwitting actions. We should further qualify our references to them, by saying that they were 'undeveloped' or 'perverted' ethical reactions, thus bringing out a difference, at the same time that we emphasized a likeness.

We may lay down, thirdly, that the kind of act to which an ethical emotion is appropriate, is an act which is not merely conscious but also *voluntary*. An agent, in order to be morally commended or condemned, must not merely *know* what he is doing, but what he does must also be in harmony with his cooler and more reflective preferences, with his premeditated purposes in unimpassioned moments, and with the whole policy and tenour which are characteristic of his reasoning self. A given action need not actually be considered and deliberate, in order to be ethically relevant, but it must nevertheless be the *sort* of action that the agent *would* have chosen if he had been able to consider and deliberate sufficiently. Acts of this kind we say are 'voluntary', and they are the only acts that we regard as suitable objects of an ethical reaction. Further, we should not call some feeling 'ethical', if it could not be shown to be very finely sensitive to the distinction between the involuntary and the voluntary, if it were not immediately *inhibited* by the knowledge that a certain act could not be helped, or greatly *strengthened* by the knowledge that an action *was* deliberate and considered. Even animals and savages are frequently responsive to such differences—a dog discriminates between intentional and unintentional injuries—and if we sometimes call an attitude 'ethical' although it is *not* sensitive in this manner, this again can only be on account of some connection or affinity with other attitudes which are so sensitive. We should qualify our use of 'ethical' in such cases by adding some such adjective as 'undeveloped' or 'distorted': we say, for instance, that it shows an undeveloped moral sense to blame a man for some involuntary but abnormal sexual preference, or for some genuine but utterly fantastic conscientious scruple. We therefore call responses 'ethical' *without reserve* if they have voluntary acts and agents as their objects, but we may also find it profitable to regard certain other attitudes, which are directed to non-voluntary acts and qualities, as instances of distorted or aberrant ethical feeling.

We may lay down, finally, that the voluntary acts which are appropriate objects of our moral attitudes need not be overt, visible acts; they may be inward ponderings in which such overt acts are hatched or planned, or are even merely played with in imagination. In legislating in this manner, we are only carrying one stage further the tendency, profoundly rooted in our ethical responses, to stress the inward, conscious side of action, and to discount all the mere details of outward execution. Not what we actually do, but what we really *mean* to do is ethically important, and it remains important even if we get no farther than sincerely meaning to do it. This ruling is, of course, in harmony with the usage of many quite early moral 'sages' and illuminati.

V

Having determined that the objects of ethical reactions are voluntary acts and agents, we may now proceed to fix more narrowly the *character* of such reactions. Here we shall draw a distinction, from the outset, between *two* kinds of ethical reaction, one that *demands* that something should be done or that it should be omitted, and one that merely sits back and *appraises* actions, and finds them (or the men who did them) either *satisfactory* or *unsatisfactory*. The former type of attitude is more obviously 'conative', the latter mainly contemplative and 'affective'. We should not be untrue to our prevailing usage if we were to say that words like 'ought', 'should', 'right' and 'wrong', were mainly used to express the former sort of attitude, while words like 'good' and 'bad', 'virtuous' and 'wicked', served mainly to express the latter. In saying that an action *should* be done, that it is *right* to do it, we are not merely, in the vast majority of cases, giving vent to feelings roused by conduct: we are also uttering an *imperative* by which we hope to influence conduct. Even when we sit in judgement on some act done in a far-off place or period, we still preserve in our voices a somewhat magisterial tone: we talk as if we were present on the spot, and able by our utterances to modify the deeds that men are doing.

LANGUAGE, MIND AND VALUE

We may lay down, further, that our ethical imperatives have a number of distinct degrees of urgency or insistence. Some acts or abstinences are demanded unconditionally—they are absolutely or perfectly obligatory—while other acts and abstinences are demanded much less stringently: it would be exceedingly proper if we did them, but no one has nevertheless a right to expect them from us. There are, of course, some speakers who would exclude all non-stringent obligations and all 'works of supererogation' from the ethical field; our ruling accords, however, with the majority usage in this matter.

Quite different from the attitude just dealt with, which urgently demands some action or omission, is the attitude which sits back quietly and appraises action. In this we do not regard an act as something to be done (or left undone), we do not insist on its performance or omission: we rather look upon it as something altogether over and done with, and then proceed to find it either satisfying or dissatisfying. We dwell upon its various inner aspects, we try to understand the 'character' and 'style of life' of which it is an instance, endeavouring by these means to form some estimate of his 'moral value'. If the action satisfies us when we regard it thus, we evince our satisfaction in the words 'virtuous' and 'morally good', whereas we use the contrary adjectives if it pains us or dissatisfies us.[1] Such responses order themselves quite differently from the ethical imperatives just considered; we do not find them tending towards some upper limit of rigorous insistence, but rather stretching out in two unending series from a single centre of indifference. Above each satisfactory act or style of living there are others which are more intensely satisfactory; below each painful act or unsatisfactory style of living, there are others which are more keenly painful and unsatisfactory. (If we were endeavouring to describe completely the complicated 'phenomenology' of this region, we should have to point out, further, that there are obviously 'depths' and 'breadths' in moral satisfaction as well as differences of intensity. Some acts seem fine, but in a thin and narrow way, while others yield a broader sort of satisfaction. And there are obviously many other complicating and enriching overtones in our moral satisfactions: there are, quite plainly, virtues that we love, and virtues that we admire, virtues which charm, and virtues which inspire awe. There are also, in the same way, vices that mildly vex us, vices

[1] We are not suggesting that this is a complete account of how we use these terms: that will only be provided in the whole article.

80

MORALITY BY CONVENTION

that shame us, vices that provoke wrath, and vices that make us shudder and be sick. Nothing could be more misleadingly simplified than to speak as if we always felt, in regard to every piece of conduct, some single, stereotyped experience of 'moral valuation'.)

VI

We may now pass on to sketch another trait of our ethical responses which some might think unduly narrowing in its effect. We shall deliberately restrict the object of our ethical reactions to those voluntary acts *that have some bearing on the welfare of sentient beings*. Either these acts may actually be productive (or destructive) of welfare, or they may aim at ends which would, if realized, have some influence on welfare, or they merely *mean* to achieve welfare (or the opposite) in ways that may be quite misguided. These differences are interesting, and would occupy separate compartments in a systematic ethical treatise, but this is obviously not the place to dwell upon them. We shall only rule that actions, in order to be morally commendable or censurable, must have some tendency to help or injure somebody, even if only in the imagination of the agent.

In laying down this ruling we are not coming out baldly in favour of some form of utilitarianism. For we have laid down no principles with regard to the distribution of welfare: we have not decided whether anyone's welfare is to be preferred to anyone else's in given circumstances, or whether every man's welfare is to be equally regarded. Nor have we made one of those depressing, blanket statements to the effect that welfare must be heaped up into as large a pile as possible, regardless of the precise persons who are to experience this welfare. Nor are we questioning in any way that some personal claims may be too sacred to be set aside on any ground of *general* welfare: we are only saying that even such personal claims are *claims to welfare*. Even when someone feels bound to carry out some promise to a dead friend, this can, we rule, only be an ethical experience in so far as he regards the dead as being capable of a sort of posthumous welfare. To do so is not absurd, for, whether one has experiences after death or not, to be a person whose wishes will be posthumously disregarded and overridden, is not, to that extent, to be 'well off'.

We rule, accordingly, that moral feelings are, in their developed form, invariably bound up with the notion of actual or intended

F 81

LANGUAGE, MIND AND VALUE

benefit or harm to someone. In legislating in this manner, we are deliberately not taking account of, and failing to cover many attitudes of savages and civilized people which would, in common parlance, be denominated 'ethical'. The life of savages is full of very bizarre, unmotived prohibitions and imperatives, whether of marrying, eating or performing certain ceremonies, in which some act seems ultimately and mysteriously right or wrong, without being apparently connected with anyone's welfare. And there are doubtless many members of more civilized communities who venerate similar taboos in certain regions of behaviour. But we should not be saying anything very questionable if we were to hold that all such attitudes tended to lose their grip on reflective minds once it became quite clear that certain acts, previously censured or commended, had absolutely *no* effects on welfare. The welfare involved might be gross and material, or spiritual and impalpable, but if an action had no bearing on any sort of well-being, we should certainly feel inclined to cease praising or condemning it. Or, if we went on doing so, we should feel disposed to say that our feelings were no longer ethical. Or, alternatively, we might continue to react ethically to some action which seemed, at first, to have no bearing on welfare, because we discovered it to have some subtle, long-term influence on welfare which was not obvious at the first glance. It is clear that, even in savages, the majority of the feelings that we call 'ethical' are concerned with acts that *have* an influence on welfare; e.g. where one man steals his neighbour's landmark or has intercourse with his wife or robs him or breaks faith with him. So that we find it profitable to rule that only those acts are proper objects of an ethical reaction which have some bearing on welfare, allowing meanwhile that there may be many 'undeveloped' and 'distorted' ethical reactions in which this relevance to welfare is slurred over or ignored. When we call the latter 'ethical reactions', we are stressing their manifold affinities with what we should unhesitatingly call 'ethical reactions', but we add the qualifications 'undeveloped' or 'distorted' to show that they have some features which make us hesitate to call them 'ethical reactions'.

VII

We may now proceed to fix a number of traits of ethical reactions which will give rise to much less question than the relation to welfare

82

we have just considered. We may lay down, first of all, that there is involved in every ethical reaction a *demand* that a certain primary response to conduct should be *tested* by a process of reflection, as well as a *claim* that this primary response will be able to survive this process. Both this primary response to conduct, and this secondary demand and claim with regard to this primary response, may be ruled to be essential elements of an ethical reaction.

The reflection which our ethical reaction demands in this manner is an exhaustive and intense examination of what we commonly call 'the facts and values of the case'. We test some response to conduct by probing into or reviewing *all* the circumstances of some action, the persons who are involved in it, the means employed to compass it, as well as all its probable or certain consequences. Only if our response survives such testing, and is not liquidated in the process, do we denominate it 'true' and 'valid'. And only if our reaction includes, in addition to a certain primary response to conduct, the *claim* that this response can be validated in this manner, can we denominate the whole reaction 'ethical' at all.

We also test our responses to conduct by trying either to *perceive palpably*, or to *imagine very vividly*, all the circumstances thus reviewed in thought: our response must not only survive the most lucid knowledge, but also the most vivid imagination. Above all, we try to enter sympathetically, with as much vividness as possible, into the feelings of all the persons involved in the action, and to conceive the situation as it must appear to them. We also test a response to conduct by trying to review, and feel keenly, all increments of spiritual or material benefit or injury (assessed according to some standard, and in some manner, which we need not consider here) of every circumstance and consequence of the action. Only if our response withstands such tests can we call it a justifiable response. We should not be experiencing an ethical reaction unless, in addition to experiencing such a response, we also claimed that this response was justifiable in this manner.

We may lay down, as a consequence, that every ethical reaction claims *stability* for a certain attitude to conduct; it claims that this attitude will not be modified or superseded when the action it concerns is viewed in different moods and circumstances. If we find a certain response tending to waver when we reconsider an act, the ethical reaction of which it is a part will tend to become proportionately less assured, whereas, if a given response does not fluctuate when we reconsider an act, the ethical reaction of which it is a part will tend, in

LANGUAGE, MIND AND VALUE

consequence, to become more confident and unwavering. So that all responses which we are wholly unable to stabilize will tend to be abandoned, while those which are stable will tend to become, for that very reason, more and more firmly stabilized. So that any person's ethical reactions must inevitably tend to an ever higher level of consistency and fixity. However disparate and variable they may be at first, they must necessarily end by achieving considerable uniformity and agreement.

VIII

We may now lay down that every ethical reaction involves the further demand that our primary response to conduct (which is also a part of it) *should be acceptable to other people*. When we speak ethically, we are not merely voicing some private upset of our own, as some have rather simple-mindedly imagined; we are addressing our utterance to the world at large, we are endeavouring to legislate for men in general, we are, to some extent, displaying an authoritarian and intolerant spirit. Often, indeed, we show ourselves as crudely masterful: we use the somewhat clumsy violence of praise and blame, or of reward and punishment, or the milder violence of ethical persuasion and exhortation, in order to impose our attitude on others. But even where our proselytism is not overt, or has been curbed for reasons of politeness or of policy, we should not be responding ethically at all, if there were not some modicum of this deep intolerance in our attitude. Even a moral attitude which is tentative, which readily yields to other men's persuasion, pretends faintly, while it lasts, that it is final and authoritative. The same holds good, of course, for certain other types of attitude, our attitude to the beautiful, for example, or to 'the really worth-while things of life'. In these fields, too, we cannot rest content while others fail to share our feelings: we experience a powerful *nisus* to convert dissenters. But few would question that this essentially intolerant and authoritarian pose was far more characteristic of our moral attitudes than of our axiological or aesthetic ones.

We may lay down, further, in close connection with this trait, that every ethical reaction submits itself to a process of *testing by the attitudes and sentiments of other persons*. Not only do we *demand* that others should accept our attitudes, we also positively *expect* that they will do so. And if, at first, they do not seem to share our feelings,

84

we think that this is so, only because they have, as yet, been insufficiently reflective. We think that they have not yet dwelt upon the matter long enough, that they have not yet pictured all its aspects with sufficient vividness, or that they have not adequately taken account of the various values, the items of material or spiritual benefit or injury, that are involved in it. We tend to think that, if they would only carry out the searching scrutiny that we press for, they can hardly fail to reach complete agreement with us. In all such cases, we make our appeal above the unreflective heads of 'present company', to the 'great company of reflective persons', wherever they may be situated in space or time; we do this all the more emphatically that present company proves unsympathetic. But we should not be speaking ethically at all, if we were not making our appeal to some such company, if we were not submitting our immediate, primary attitude to some form of social testing.

Since we thus look for agreement on the part of all reflective persons, it follows that our moral attitudes and judgements will become more confident whenever we find such persons in agreement with us, and that they will, in a similar manner, be weakened and discredited whenever such persons cast their vote against us. Such a strengthening or weakening is not accidental nor unjustifiable, but follows from the nature of the moral attitudes. For the moral sphere is really one of those spheres in which the *orbis terrarum* may be said to judge securely. And since our ethical attitudes are strengthened by agreement, and weakened by disagreement, we may reasonably expect that all those attitudes which altogether fail to secure agreement will gradually be abandoned, while all those attitudes which *do* secure it will become, in consequence, much more firmly fixed. So that we find again that men's moral attitudes must, in consequence of their nature and their mode of testing, tend steadily towards an ever higher level of agreement. However varied they may be at first, the process of social attrition to which they are continuously subjected must necessarily leave them highly uniform.

We may rule further, just as we have ruled in other contexts, that there are certain 'undeveloped' or 'distorted' ethical reactions, in which a man appeals, not to the verdict of *all* reflective persons, but to the verdict of some narrower, and not necessarily reflective set of persons, to all the members of some nation, or some race or sect, or clique, or other social group. We call these attitudes 'ethical' since they resemble ethical responses in many ways, and since we seldom

85

LANGUAGE, MIND AND VALUE

find them wholly proof against reflection, or wholly unaffected by the judgements of persons who are not members of the chosen group. But we prefix the qualifying adjectives 'undeveloped' or 'distorted', to show that we are also somewhat hesitant to admit these attitudes to the class of ethical responses, on account of these arbitrary limitations and restrictions.

IX

We may now lay down a feature of the ethical reaction which, more than any other, determines its content and its flavour, the feature, namely, that an ethical reaction claims *impartiality*, that it aspires to be *unbiassed*, to *take no sides* among the persons who may be involved in some action. This is the feature brought out in so masterly a manner by Adam Smith, who has located an 'impartial spectator' as the moral subject in our bosoms, a spectator who has sympathy with *all* the parties to an action, and yet divests himself of fear or favour in regard to *any*. It also comes out in the Kantian principle that we can only will something *morally*, if we are also prepared to will it *universally*. And it comes out in the three Sidgwickian maxims of equity and benevolence: that one man's well-being deserves as much consideration as another's, that what is right for one man cannot be wrong for others, if their circumstances are identical, and that it cannot be right for one man to treat another in a way in which it would be wrong for that other man, whose circumstances are similar, to treat the first man. These rules and axioms were not made known to us by any supernormal intuition, nor is it in any way queer that every ethical consciousness should acknowledge them; we simply should not *call* a set of feelings 'ethical' in which they were not followed or approved. A man might find it personally amusing to see one person riding roughshod over others, he might even demand and love brutality and ruthlessness, but it would be quite impossible to keep to our accepted use of terms, and still maintain that these were *ethical* reactions. It is plainly only by a very liberal stretch of usage that the codes sponsored by Thrasymachus or Nietzsche, or those upheld by various lesser, later persons, could be described as ethical codes.

It is further plain that, if on our examination of some moral attitude, we were to come upon a hidden source of prejudice or bias in it, in favour of certain persons, we should immediately discard this attitude

86

MORALITY BY CONVENTION

as unjustified, whereas, the more we were assured of its freedom from such bias, the more we should feel justified in holding to it. We might, however, choose to speak of 'undeveloped' or 'distorted' ethical reactions, in all those cases where the persons, whose interests we impartially consider, are members of a limited social group, and there are many outside persons whose interests we ignore entirely. Such feelings, highly sensitive to the claims within a chosen circle, and quite insensitive to other claims beyond it, may be called 'moral' (with some qualifying tag), because they are free from partisanship within their chosen limits, and also because the gentle force of analogy will always lead them on to take account of other outside claims, and to extend the same impartiality to them. Even the most hardened member of the Teutonic master-race could scarcely imagine with vividness the feelings of some hounded Jew, without being momentarily tempted to extend to him the sympathy and mercy that he showers so freely on himself and his compatriots. We may also speak of 'undeveloped reactions' in cases where we simply take for granted inequalities of status which are neither natural nor irremovable, nor a necessary condition of anything extraordinarily valuable. For if we project ourselves impartially into the skins of all the parties to such arbitrary distributions, we can see no reason why welfare should be so richly concentrated in some of them, while it remains so very thinly spread in others.

All moral attitudes are, by their nature, levelling and egalitarian: they tolerate no differences and no degrees for which no very cogent reasons can be given. All these facts simply render silly those arguments which suggest that there might very well be people who approved morally of torturing innocent persons, or of committing other similar enormities, and that no one could do more than harry or abuse them for their very singular moral taste. Whereas, if anyone approved of such acts, he could not, on our ruling, be responding ethically at all, since no one could maintain that he was even attempting to achieve impartiality. Or, if we said he was attempting to achieve impartiality, he would be failing so grossly, that no one could regard his feelings or his judgements as anything but totally unjustifiable.

X

So far we have been showing that the moral responses of different people, must, since they are *moral* responses, agree in very many

LANGUAGE, MIND AND VALUE

ways, and that the testing processes to which they are subjected must bring them into ever closer harmony. But we have still left open a somewhat dangerous avenue of variability: different people may not take the same view of human welfare, or of the factors which compose it. For we have said that acts, in order to be ethically relevant, must have some bearing upon welfare, and, if men differed widely in their view of welfare, their moral attitudes might also differ very widely. Two sets of moral attitudes that were both well-considered, stable, unbiassed, and acceptable in a given social setting, might yet be utterly at variance if they built on notions of welfare that were widely different. If some people could be of the opinion that welfare consisted entirely in editing Greek authors and visiting fashionable watering-places, while others found it wholly comprehended in trout-fishing and lion-taming, we could scarcely hope for much agreement in their ethical responses. And some have seriously argued as if such differences were thinkable. Whereas we shall attempt to show that there are processes of appraisal, very similar in many ways to the moral tests we have just dealt with, by which we can determine whether anything is 'genuinely worth while', and how high we may rank it among human goods. And we shall also try to make plain that certain views of well-being can be shown by these tests to be utterly invalid, and that we have, in fact, a very narrow range of liberty in determining the content of well-being.

What is, in fact, the attitude behind the statement that some experience or way of living is 'really worth having', or the contrary? Plainly it involves a state of satisfaction or dissatisfaction, which will be actual if the experience or way of life is actual, and hypothetical if it is imaginary. But it is not, as an attitude, exhausted by such feelings, nor does it merely seem to hold for one occasion, or for one person only. Quite obviously it also includes claims and expectations, which may be tested, and by which it may be validated or invalidated. A man who thinks some way of life to be authentically worth while, thinks, in the first place, that it will not cease to satisfy him, however long he ponders on it, and however long he continues to see it in relation to the whole of life, or to other ways of living. It must not merely be a satisfactory form of living: it must also be a source of *stable and enduring satisfaction*. And if, after a due course of reflection and comparison, it shows itself as paltry and meretricious, or if we find it varying inconsequently in our estimation, then our original appraisal must be withdrawn.

88

MORALITY BY CONVENTION

To hold a way of life to be genuinely worth while means, further, that we think it will be able to establish itself in the regard of *all* who have sufficiently experienced it, or who have thought about it long enough; we also think that it will be able to *maintain* itself in the regard of all such persons. Our estimate accordingly subjects itself, by virtue of its nature as an estimate of well-being, to a form of social testing. Not only do we *wish* to communicate our attitude to others, to lead them to set store by whatever we cherish ourselves: we also positively *expect* that they will do so, if they will only try our cherished ways of living long enough, so that they 'really know what they are like'. It is in such a spirit that we recommend to others the satisfactions of the adventurous life, or of the life of intellectual effort, or of self-sacrificing love. And, if our estimate finds no echo in the bosoms of our contemporaries or our neighbours, then we appeal to the judgement of *all* reflective persons, wherever they may be situated in space or time, and firmly trust that *they* will corroborate us.

That this communicability to others is a touchstone of authentic value, shows itself also in the fact that, in endeavouring to assess such value, we try, as far as possible, to divest ourselves of any merely personal preferences that we could never hope to render catholic. No one would hold, for instance, that beagling, playing cards and having wilful love-affairs were in themselves intrinsically valuable, since there must necessarily be many who have absolutely no taste for these amusements. Only what *everyone* must inevitably cherish, or come to cherish, can be genuinely worth while. The importance of communicability also shows itself in the great seriousness with which we trouble to *discuss* our way of life with others; we take the mere fact that someone says or feels that something is worth while, as evidence that it really *is* worth while. There is, in the unemotional sciences, no such value attaching to the mere multiplication of heads and voices. We are now in a position to see that, by virtue of the testing they receive, our estimates of the genuinely worth while must always tend to greater uniformity. For every estimate that is neither stable nor communicable will tend to be discredited and abandoned, while those that fluctuate only slightly, and are readily shared by others, will thereby come to be more firmly fixed and justified.

We should not, however, be giving a complete account of welfare, unless we touched upon the difference, so puzzling to philosophers, between the *higher* and the *lower* forms of welfare. Some ways of living do not merely seem satisfactory, they also seem *to have dignity*;

89

LANGUAGE, MIND AND VALUE

we should sometimes choose them even if they were not so intensely satisfactory as other, less distinguished forms of living. Mill's talk about the quality of pleasures, his well-known dictum about Socrates dissatisfied and a pig satisfied, are sufficient to describe the situation. But, from our point of view, we cannot merely take this difference for granted; we must discover the *attitude* that underlies it. For to say that something has dignity, that it represents a higher way of living, is to evince or express a certain emotional attitude in regard to it, and we cannot interpret the utterances in question without understanding the nature of this attitude. What is, in fact, our attitude when we say that something has dignity?

Once we raise this question, the answer leaps to view: the 'higher things' are things that we do not merely prize, but that we are also *able to admire*. There are, in welfare, elements so needful that they form its indispensable core, but there are other things that we only begin to demand when these primary goods are present, things which seem in some way to be rare or fine or difficult, and which accordingly attract our admiration. The higher ways of living are *admired* ways of living, not merely satisfactory ones. Accordingly, when we attempt to grade the various forms of life and experience, we have to remember that there are at least two ways of grading them, according as we find them merely satisfactory, and according as we find them admirable. We have, in short, *mere* well-being and the *higher* well-being. (And there may very well, in addition, be other forms of well-being, which correspond to such attitudes as awe or passionate love, and which we might qualify by such adjectives as 'sublime', 'glorious' and so forth: we could scarcely hope to cover, in one comprehensive scale of values, the very numerous, mutually incomparable forms of human bliss and blessedness.)

We shall now proceed to point to certain necessary and inevitable agreements in our preferences both in the sphere of mere welfare and in the sphere of the higher well-being. It is not hard to see, first of all, that if we eliminate all questions of higher and lower, and look on ways of living as merely satisfactory, and if we are careful to discard all merely personal preferences and idiosyncrasies, there is nothing left to make a way of living satisfactory to *us* but the fact that it is actually satisfactory to someone. The *content* of a way of life thereupon becomes irrelevant: the *fact* that it is satisfactory alone remains significant. We are, in short, brought back to common hedonism, which seems, in consequence, to be the one unquestionably

90

correct account of what we have described as 'mere welfare'. For one could not make stamp-collecting or horse-breeding integral parts of welfare, since many find them utterly boring, and since no one who took the trouble to divest himself of any personal likings could discover the ghost of a reason why anyone who *didn't* care for them *should* care for them. But even those who have divested themselves of personal likings in the matter, still find it satisfactory that those who actually care for horse-breeding or stamp-collecting should devote themselves to these activities, merely *because* they find them agreeable or satisfactory. The activities themselves therefore lack what we may call 'interpersonal value', but the fact that something is personally valuable and agreeable to someone, *has* interpersonal value. The source of pleasure doesn't count for impartial judges, but the pleasure itself does.

Even if we turn to certain standard acts, which all or most men find highly agreeable, the acts of eating or having sexual intercourse, for instance, we are still unable to regard these as integral parts of welfare since we can so readily *imagine* beings who would not find them pleasant. And no one could find a reason why anyone who *didn't* find them pleasant *should* find them so. But even those who didn't find them pleasant, would necessarily, in so far as they were impartially sympathetic, be agreeably affected by the pleasure of those who found them pleasant. There is also another good reason for excluding these generally pleasurable acts from welfare: our liking for them is utterly unstable. They may, at a given moment, seem all-important and supremely sweet, but in a flash they are capable of becoming distasteful or indifferent. It is only the pleasurableness of the activities that does not pall, not the activities themselves. It seems therefore that only pleasantness, and freedom from unpleasantness, will qualify as marks of our lower form of well-being, when this is assessed by judges who have divested themselves of all tastes and preferences that are not necessarily shared by everybody.

Turning, however, to our higher form of well-being, we shall try to show that here, too, there must be *much* inevitable agreement. For it is not possible to admire everything: some ways of living are simply not a possible object of this attitude. One could not, for example, think that enormous dignity attached to a life of brainless tea-drinking punctuated with mild gambling. To awaken admiration a way of life must, at the least, be *extraordinary* in some manner: it must be rare in its strength, in its purity, in its thoroughness, or unusual in its harmony or range. It must achieve or perform *more*

LANGUAGE, MIND AND VALUE

in a certain direction than is normally achieved or performed: it cannot represent a merely humdrum or average level of accomplishment.

If some way of living is then to be rated as a higher form of well-being, it must, further, be able to *keep* our admiration, however long we think about it, and however clearly we see it in relation to other ways of living. Activities whose rarity soon wears off, or which only arouse wonder when our experience is limited, would certainly not deserve incorporation in a list of higher goods. It is further plain that nothing could be regarded as a higher form of welfare which we could not *unreservedly* admire, or which was essentially mixed up with other things that we could not help shunning or despising. Thus military glory could obviously never be reckoned among the higher forms of welfare, though equally obviously there is an immense amount of higher welfare involved in it.

We may lay down further, just as we did in other cases, that justifiable admiration is always capable of communication: things *truly* admirable are things that *all* reflective persons will ultimately come to admire. Is it unreasonable to suggest that the higher goods whose listing has been so prominent a feature of recent ethical discussion, really represent a well-attested summing-up of the ways of living that are enduringly, unmixedly and necessarily admirable to everyone? For practically everyone would agree that knowledge, contemplation of beauty, personal affection and moral virtue are to be included among the higher goods. Profound and penetrating intellectual vision, enjoyment of rare harmonies of form or rare felicities of expression, passionate and profound personal love and understanding, and determined choice of what is right and proper: these, and a few other similar things, are undoubtedly to be included among the higher forms of well-being. Nor need we fear that any of them could ever lose our admiration: for, by the use of such adjectives as 'passionate', 'profound' and 'rare', we have ensured that they must always lie on the upper borderline of our experience (wherever that may be); they never could, accordingly, become commonplace or facile.

XI

We may now claim to have established that the ethical judgements of different people, although they express emotions, must necessarily

MORALITY BY CONVENTION

agree in many ways, and that they must also necessarily tend towards greater and greater agreement. We have tried to show that they cannot have that boundless variability which some have thought inevitable in emotional expressions. We have thereby taken away the main grounds for so-called 'intellectualist' and 'realist' theories of the ethical judgement, i.e. theories that assimilate ethical judgements to judgements of perception. A moral attitude, we have tried to show, is not one capable of being directed at *any* object, nor one to which *no* object is more peculiarly suited than any other. It is, by virtue of its nature, oriented towards a certain sort of object, and subject to a definite type of testing. Its proper object is a voluntary act which has some relevance to welfare. It is, moreover, tested by a careful weighing of all the facts and values of the case, by a careful purge of prejudice and partisanship, and by a submission to the judgement of all conscientious and reflective persons. It is further limited in its scope by the processes by which we test the genuineness of some apparent form of welfare: only a few forms of living will approve themselves as genuinely good, whether in the higher or the lower manner, to the unanimous and considered verdict of mankind. In fine, we see no vestige of that random subjectivity, that indefinite variability, that moralists have expected and feared to find in different people's ethical responses.

It is now, however, time to stress another aspect of the matter. We must emphasize that there are many differences in morals that we simply cannot compose or settle, and that there are also many moral questions which will never have one satisfactory answer. And it is just because a realist ethics might lead us to suppose that every ethical question has some definite answer (although we may not know it), that such a theory becomes so definitely misleading. For the techniques by which we test our moral judgements are plainly quite incapable of leading to precise results in countless cases of doubt and conflict. And it is altogether unhelpful to suppose that there are objective differences where we are quite unable to draw distinctions.

We may, in fact, point to *two* major zones of indeterminacy in the moral field: the zone of *justice*, where we balance and compare the claims of different persons, and the zone of *welfare*, where we balance and compare the claims of different sorts of well-being. Must I keep faith with *A*, though *B* and *C* will suffer in consequence? How great a possible benefit to *B* and *C* would justify a breach of faith with *A*? These, and countless other similar questions may be regarded as 'posers' of justice, and it is only too plain that we shall *never* be able to answer them. Again we may ask: Is virtuous ignorance preferable to unvirtuous (not necessarily vicious) knowledge? And how much virtue is equivalent to a certain depth and range of knowledge? These, and innumerable other similar questions may be regarded as 'posers' of welfare, and it is again plain that they are *wholly* unanswerable. Indeed a mere perusal of the ethical literature of the present century would show the utter hopelessness of these inquiries: whatever the ethical questions on which we may at length achieve agreement, we shall *never* agree on these. There is, of course, a 'sound man's judgement' in these dubious territories, to which many thinkers, following Aristotle, have appealed, but this is surely nothing but the very sensible proceeding of making up one's mind, and shaping one's conduct, quite arbitrarily in circumstances where self-torturing conscientiousness would be utterly profitless. There may, of course, be a heuristic value in postulating that there *are* answers to every ethical question, but we must remember that the heuristic value of false assumptions can be much exaggerated, both in this and in other fields of investigation.

We may conclude our very sketchy 'anatomy' of the moral attitudes, by dwelling for a while on the task of moral philosophy. To regard this as an analytical study, which finds out how we actually *do* use ethical words and phrases, to what objects we apply them, and under what conditions: all this would be in harmony with the view of most contemporary moralists. But, in reality, as we have shown, moralists have never merely been analysts: they have always sought to better and to simplify the language that we use in morals. While such changes may be dangerous if carried out unconsciously, there is no reason why the conscious emendation of our ethical diction should not be regarded as a very valuable function of the moral philosopher. To iron out anomalies in usage, to stretch it where restrictions seem unnecessary, to coin new uses that bring out new likenesses: all these are tasks that may be profitably performed by moralists. But there has also been a third, time-honoured task of moralists, at present very largely neglected: to preach and edify, to inculcate new duties and devotions, or to make men more profoundly conscious of the old ones. Only our more than eighteenth-century horror of enthusiasm, as well as our quite fantastic reverence for the unemotional sciences, have led philosophers to hand over this function to the unreflective, or to fulfil it only in some furtive, shamefaced manner. There is nothing proper in a situation where only dolts, bigots and sentimentalists are responsible for the upkeep and development of our ethical systems: there seems no reason why philosophers, who have at least some clearness in regard to what they are doing, should not participate in this task of sustaining morals, or of edifying individuals.

V

CAN GOD'S EXISTENCE BE DISPROVED?[1]

(1948)

I

THE course of philosophical development has been full of attempted proofs of the existence of God. Some of these have sought a basis in the bare necessities of thought, while others have tried to found themselves on the facts of experience. And, of these latter, some have founded themselves on *very general facts*, as that something exists, or that something is in motion, while others have tried to build on *highly special facts*, as that living beings are put together in a purposive manner, or that human beings are subject to certain improbable urges and passions, such as the zeal for righteousness, the love for useless truths and unprofitable beauties, as well as the many specifically religious needs and feelings. The general philosophical verdict is that none of these 'proofs' is truly compelling. The proofs based on the necessities of thought are universally regarded as fallacious: it is not thought possible to build bridges between mere abstractions and concrete existence. The proofs based on the general facts of existence and motion are only felt to be valid by a minority of thinkers, who seem quite powerless to communicate this sense of validity to others. And while most thinkers would accord weight to arguments resting on the special facts we have mentioned, they wouldn't think such arguments successful in ruling out a vast range of counter-possibilities. Religious people have, in fact, come to acquiesce in the total absence of any cogent proofs of the Being they believe in: they even find it positively satisfying that something

[1] First published in *Mind*, April 1948. I have added a few words at one or two places to indicate that I think my argument holds for all who accept all that Kant says in criticism of the Ontological Proof, and not only for linguistic philosophers.

CAN GOD'S EXISTENCE BE DISPROVED?

so far surpassing clear conception should also surpass the possibility of demonstration. And non-religious people willingly mitigate their rejection with a tinge of agnosticism: they don't so much deny the existence of God, as the existence of good reasons for believing in Him. We shall, however, maintain in this essay that there isn't room, in the case we are examining, for all these attitudes of tentative surmise and doubt. For we shall try to show that the Divine Existence can only be conceived, in a religiously satisfactory manner, if we also conceive it as something inescapable and necessary, whether for thought or reality. From which it follows that our modern denial of necessity or rational evidence for such an existence amounts to a demonstration that there cannot be a God.

Before we develop this argument, we must, however, give greater precision to our use of the term 'God'. For it is possible to say that there are nearly as many 'Gods' as there are speakers and worshippers, and while existence may be confidently asserted or denied of *some* of them, we should feel more hesitant in the case of others. It is one thing, plainly, to pronounce on God's existence, if He be taken to be some ancient, shapeless stone, or if we identify Him with the bearded Father of the Sistine ceiling, and quite another matter, if we make of Him an 'all-pervasive, immaterial intelligence', or characterize Him in some yet more negative and analogical manner. We shall, however, choose an indirect approach, and pin God down for our purposes as the 'adequate object of religious attitudes'.

Plainly we find it possible to gather together, under the blanket term 'religious', a large range of cases of possible action, linked together by so many overlapping[1] affinities that we are ready to treat them as the varying 'expressions' of a single 'attitude' or 'policy'. And plainly we find it possible to indicate the character of that attitude by a number of descriptive phrases which, though they may err individually by savouring too strongly of particular cases, nevertheless permit us, in their totality, to draw a rough boundary round the attitude in question. Thus we might say, for instance, that a religious attitude was one in which we tended to abase ourselves before some object, to defer to it wholly, to devote ourselves to it with unquestioning enthusiasm, to bend the knee before it, whether literally or metaphorically. These phrases, and a large number of similar ones, would make perfectly plain the sort of attitude we were speaking of,

---

[1] This word is added to avoid the suggestion that there must be *one* pervasive affinity linking together all the actions commonly called 'religious'.

G

LANGUAGE, MIND AND VALUE

and would suffice to mark it off from cognate attitudes which are much less unconditional and extreme in their tone. Clearly similar phrases would suffice to fix the boundaries of religious *feeling*. We might describe religious frames of mind as ones in which we felt ready to abase ourselves before some object, to bend the knee before it, and so forth. Here, as elsewhere, we find ourselves indicating the *felt* character of our attitudes, by treating their inward character as, in some sense, a concentrated and condensed substitute for appropriate lines of action, a way of speaking that accords curiously with the functional significance of the inward.[1]

But not only do we thus incorporate, in the meanings of our various names for attitudes, a reference to this readiness for appropriate lines of action: we also incorporate in these meanings a reference to *the sorts of things or situations to which these attitudes are the normal or appropriate responses*. For, as a matter of fact, our attitudes are not indifferently evoked in *any* setting: there is a range of situations in which they normally and most readily occur. And though they may at times arise in circumstances which are not in this range, they are also readily dissipated by the consciousness that such circumstances *are* unsuitable or unusual. Thus fear is an attitude very readily evoked in situations with a character of menace or potential injury, and it is also an attitude very readily allayed by the clear perception that a given situation isn't really dangerous. And anger, likewise, in an attitude provoked very readily by perverse resistance and obstructive difficulty in some object, and is also very readily dissipated, even in animals, by the consciousness that a given object is innocent of offence. All attitudes, we may say, *presume* characters in their objects, and are, in consequence, strengthened by the discovery that their objects *have* these characters, as they are weakened by the discovery that they really haven't got them.

Not only do we find this out empirically: we also incorporate it in the *meanings* of our names for attitudes. Thus attitudes are said to be 'normal', 'fully justified' and so forth, if we find them altered in a certain manner (called 'appropriate') by our knowledge of the actual state of things, whereas we speak of them as 'queer' or 'senseless' or 'neurotic', if they aren't at all modified by this knowledge of reality. We call it abnormal, from this point of view, to feel a deep-seated fear of mice, to rage maniacally at strangers, to greet disasters with a

---

[1] Whatever the philosophical 'ground' for it may be, this plainly is the way in which we *do* describe the 'inner quality' of our felt attitudes.

CAN GOD'S EXISTENCE BE DISPROVED?

hebephrenic giggle, whereas we think it altogether normal to deplore deep losses deeply, or to fear grave dangers gravely. And so an implicit reference to some standard object—which makes an attitude either normal or abnormal—is part of what we ordinarily mean by all our names for attitudes, and can be rendered explicit by a simple study of usage. We can consider the circumstances in which ordinary speakers would call an attitude 'appropriate' or 'justified'.

All that philosophy achieves in this regard is merely to push further, and develop into more considered and consistent forms, the implications of such ordinary ways of speaking. It can inquire whether an attitude would still seem justified, and its object appropriate, after we had reflected long and carefully on a certain matter, and looked at it from every wonted and unwonted angle. Such consideration may lead philosophers to a different and more reasoned notion of the appropriate objects of a given attitude, than could be garnered from our unreflective ways of speaking. And these developments of ordinary usage will only seem unfeasible to victims of that strange modern confusion which thinks of attitudes exclusively as hidden processes 'in our bosoms', with nothing but an adventitious relation to appropriate outward acts and objects.

II

How then may we apply these notions to the case of our religious attitudes? Plainly we shall be following the natural trends of unreflective speech if we say that religious attitudes presume *superiority* in their objects, and such superiority, moreover, as reduces us, who feel the attitudes, to comparative nothingness. For having described a worshipful attitude as one in which we feel disposed to bend the knee before some object, to defer to it wholly, and the like, we find it natural to say that such an attitude can only be fitting where the object reverenced *exceeds* us very vastly, whether in power or wisdom or in other valued qualities. While it is certainly possible to worship stocks and stones and articles of common use, one does so usually on the assumption that they aren't merely stocks and stones and ordinary articles, but the temporary seats of 'indwelling presences' or centres of extraordinary powers and virtues. If one realizes clearly that such things *are* merely stocks and stones or articles of common

LANGUAGE, MIND AND VALUE

use, one can't help suffering a total vanishing or grave abatement of religious ardour.

To feel religiously is therefore to presume surpassing greatness in some object: so much characterizes the attitudes in which we bow and bend the knee, and enters into the ordinary meaning of the word 'religious'. But now we advance further—in company with a large number of theologians and philosophers, who have added new touches to the portrait of deity, pleading various theoretical necessities, but really concerned to make their object worthier of our worship—and ask whether it isn't wholly anomalous to worship anything *limited* in any thinkable manner. For all limited superiorities are tainted with an obvious relativity, and can be dwarfed in thought by still mightier superiorities, in which process of being dwarfed they lose their claim upon our worshipful attitudes. And hence we are led on irresistibly to demand that our religious object should have an *unsurpassable* supremacy along all avenues, that it should tower *infinitely* above all other objects. Not only are we led to demand for it such merely quantitative superiority: we also ask that it shouldn't stand surrounded by a world of *alien* objects, which owe it no allegiance, or set limits to its influence. The proper object of religious reverence must in some manner be *all-comprehensive*: there mustn't be anything capable of existing, or of displaying any virtue, without owing all of these absolutely to this single source.

All these, certainly, are difficult requirements, involving not only the obscurities and doubtful significance of the infinite, but also all the well-worn antagonism of the immanent and transcendent, of finite sinfulness and divine perfection and preordination, which centuries of theological brooding have failed to dissipate. But we are also led on irresistibly to a yet more stringent demand, which raises difficulties which make the difficulties we have mentioned seem wholly inconsiderable: we can't help feeling that the worthy object of our worship can never be a thing that merely *happens* to exist, nor one on which all other objects merely *happen* to depend. The true object of religious reverence must not be one, merely, to which no *actual* independent realities stand opposed: it must be one to which such opposition is totally *inconceivable*. God mustn't merely cover the territory of the actual, but also, with equal comprehensiveness, the territory of the possible. And not only must the existence of *other* things be unthinkable without Him, but His own non-existence must be wholly unthinkable in any circumstances. There must, in short, be no conceivable

CAN GOD'S EXISTENCE BE DISPROVED?

alternative to an existence properly termed 'divine': God must be wholly inescapable, as we remarked previously, whether for thought or reality. So we are led on insensibly to the barely intelligible notion of a Being in whom Essence and Existence lose their separateness. And all that the great medieval thinkers really did was to carry such a development to its logical limit.

We may, however, approach the matter from a slightly different angle. Not only is it contrary to the demands and claims inherent in religious attitudes that their object should *exist* 'accidentally': it is also contrary to those demands that it should *possess its various excellences* in some merely adventitious or contingent manner. It would be quite unsatisfactory from the religious standpoint, if an object merely *happened* to be wise, good, powerful and so forth, even to a superlative degree, and if other beings had, *as a mere matter of fact*, derived their excellences from this single source. An object of this sort would doubtless deserve respect and admiration, and other quasi-religious attitudes, but it would not deserve the utter self-abandonment peculiar to the religious frame of mind. It would deserve the δουλεία canonically accorded to the saints, but not the λατρεία that we properly owe to God. We might respect this object as the crowning instance of most excellent qualities, but we should incline our head before the qualities and not before the person. Wherever such qualities were manifested, though perhaps less eminently, we should always be ready to perform an essentially similar obeisance. For though such qualities might be intimately characteristic of the Supreme Being, they still wouldn't be in any sense inalienably His own. And even if other beings had, in fact, derived such qualities from this sovereign source, they still would be *their own* qualities, possessed by them in their own right. We should have no better reason to *adore* the author of such virtues, than sons have reason to adore superior parents, or pupils to adore superior teachers. For while these latter may deserve deep deference, the fact that we are coming to *participate* in their excellences renders them unworthy of our *worship*. Plainly a being that possesses and imparts desirable qualities—which other things might nevertheless have manifested though this source were totally absent—has all the utter inadequacy as a religious object which is expressed by saying that it would be *idolatrous* to worship it. Wisdom, kindness and other excellences deserve respect wherever they are manifested, but no being can appropriate them as its personal perquisites, even if it does possess them in a superlative degree. And

LANGUAGE, MIND AND VALUE

so we are led on irresistibly, by the demands inherent in religious reverence, to hold that an adequate object of our worship must possess its various qualities *in some necessary manner.* These qualities must be intrinsically incapable of belonging to anything except in so far as they belong primarily to the object of our worship. Again we are led on to a queer and barely intelligible Scholastic doctrine, that God isn't merely good, but is in some manner indistinguishable from His own (and anything else's) goodness.

III

What, however, are the consequences of these requirements for the possibility of God's existence? Plainly (for all who share a contemporary outlook) they entail not only that there isn't a God, but that the Divine Existence is either senseless[1] or impossible. The modern mind feels not the faintest axiomatic force in principles which trace contingent things back to some necessarily existent source, nor does it find it hard to conceive that things should display various excellent qualities without deriving them from a source which manifests them supremely. Those who believe in necessary truths which aren't merely tautological, think that such truths merely connect the *possible* instances of various characteristics with each other: they don't expect such truths to tell them whether there *will* be instances of any characteristics. This is the outcome of the whole medieval and Kantian criticism of the Ontological Proof. And, on a yet more modern view of the matter, necessity in propositions merely reflects our use of words, the arbitrary conventions of our language. On such a view the Divine Existence could only be a necessary matter if we had made up our minds to speak theistically *whatever the empirical circumstances might turn out to be.* This, doubtless, would suffice for some, who speak theistically, much as Spinoza spoke monistically, merely to give expression to a particular way of looking at things, or of feeling about them. It would also suffice for those who make use of the term 'God' to cover whatever tendencies towards righteousness and beauty are actually included in the make-up of our world. But it wouldn't suffice for the full-blooded worshipper, who can't help finding our actual world anything but edifying, and its half-

[1] I have included this alternative, of which I am not fond, merely because so many modern thinkers make use of it in this sort of connection.

102

CAN GOD'S EXISTENCE BE DISPROVED?

formed tendencies towards righteousness and beauty very far from adorable.

The religious frame of mind seems, in fact, to be in a quandary; it seems invincibly determined both to eat its cake and have it. It desires the Divine Existence both to have that inescapable character which can, on Kantian or modern views, only be found where truth reflects a connection of characteristics or an arbitrary convention, and also the character of 'making a real difference' which is only possible where truth doesn't have this merely hypothetical or linguistic basis. We may accordingly deny that these approaches allow us to remain agnostically poised in regard to God: they force us to come down on the atheistic side. For if God is to satisfy religious claims and needs, He must be a being in every way inescapable, One whose existence and whose possession of certain excellences we cannot possibly conceive away. And the views in question really make it self-evidently absurd (if they don't make it ungrammatical) to speak of such a Being and attribute existence to Him. It was indeed an ill day for Anselm when he hit upon his famous proof. For on that day he not only laid bare something that is of the essence of an adequate religious object, but also something that entails its necessary non-existence.[1]

The force of our argument must not, however, be exaggerated. We haven't proved that there aren't beings of all degrees of excellence and greatness, who may deserve attitudes approximating indefinitely to religious reverence. But such beings will at best be instances of valued qualities which we too may come to exemplify, though in lesser degree. Not only would it be idolatrous for us to worship them, but it would also be monstrous for them to exact worship, or to care for it. The attitude of such beings to our reverence would necessarily be deprecating: they would prefer co-operative atheists to adoring zealots. And they would probably hide themselves like royal personages from the anthems of their worshippers, and perhaps the fact that there are so few positive signs of their presence is itself a feeble evidence of their real existence. But whether such beings exist or not, they are not divine, and can never satisfy the demands inherent in religious reverence. The effect of our argument will further be to discredit generally such forms of religion as attach a uniquely sacred meaning to existent things, whether these things be men or acts or institutions or writings.

[1] Or 'non-significance', if this alternative is preferred.

103

LANGUAGE, MIND AND VALUE

But there are other frames of mind, to which we shouldn't deny the name 'religious', which acquiesce quite readily in the non-existence of their objects. (This non-existence might, in fact, be taken to be the 'real meaning' of saying that religious objects and realities are 'not of this world'.) In such frames of mind we give ourselves over unconditionally and gladly to the task of indefinite approach toward a certain imaginary focus[1] where nothing actually is, and we find this task sufficiently inspiring and satisfying without demanding (absurdly) that there should be something actual at that limit. And the atheistic religious attitude we have mentioned has also undergone reflective elaboration by such philosophers as Fichte and Erigena and Alexander. There is, then, a religious atheism which takes full stock of our arguments, and we may be glad that this is so. For since the religious spirit is one of reverence before things greater than ourselves, we should be gravely impoverished and arrested if this spirit ceased to be operative in our personal and social life. It would certainly be better that this spirit should survive, with all its fallacious existential trimmings, than that we should cast it forth merely in order to be rid of such irrelevances.

[1] To use a Kantian comparison.

VI

VALUES IN SPEAKING[1]

(1950)

I

I AM addressing you this evening on a somewhat unfamiliar theme: that of 'logical values' or 'values in speaking'. I do so since the points I want to raise come up very constantly in contemporary discussion, and yet are seldom made the object of explicit reflection. There are, it is plain, a large number of qualities which appeal to us in our utterances, whether in the setting forth of our notions in words, or in the weaving of such words into sentences. And they may be said to appeal to us in a peculiar manner, and to satisfy a special set of interests in us, which we may group together as the 'logical side' of our nature. Thus most people would say that clarity, relevance, coherence, solid significance and simplicity were merits in speaking, and that so also was truthful conformity to the facts of experience, whether in their general outline or their concrete detail. And everyone would admit readily that such excellences 'belonged together', that they were somehow akin, and that they differed profoundly from such virtues in speaking as poetic felicity, practical helpfulness, or moral and religious inspiration.

Most people would also be willing to say, with a great deal of obscurity and most puzzling conviction, that the appeal of such qualities wasn't 'merely momentary and personal', but had something 'solid' and 'universal' about it, that a man would be *foolish* not to value such qualities, and that he couldn't *help* valuing them if he only thought of them sufficiently. And we should recommend such qualities to the approval of others with an air of earnestness and authority, setting them on a level, in this respect, with those other excellences

[1] An Inaugural Lecture delivered at King's College, Newcastle upon Tyne, on February 10, 1949. Published in *Philosophy*, January 1950.

that are called 'ethical' and 'aesthetic'. But while we could back our recommendation in the last two types of case with a great deal of systematic doctrine, built up in centuries of reflection, we should have little to bring forward in the former case, since the excellences that I want to call 'logical', though often acknowledged, have seldom been made the objects of systematic reflection.

This last is perhaps due to the fact that the 'true' has generally been ranged alongside of the 'good' and the 'beautiful' as a species of 'ultimate value'. Now 'truth' is a word which readily carries with it a connotation of mere agreement with something, of passive registering of whatever comes before us, of situations where our use of terms is fixed, and we wait upon experience to determine us what to say. Truth, so spoken of, becomes a thing beyond the range of human preferences and valuations, and therein quite unlike our moral and aesthetic values, which have the closest connection with our likes and preferences. And by this stress on truth, as *all* that is logically admirable and desirable, we may be brought to forget entirely that we adopt statements confidently (and call them 'true') for a large number of *other* reasons than that they agree with experience, or agree with anything. We adopt statements for their perspicuity and definiteness, we adopt them for their economy and simplicity, we adopt them because they gather facts together in a unified manner. Though we may say, of *any* statement we accept and adopt, that it 'agrees with reality', it isn't *on account of* any such agreement that we accept it or value it.

We want therefore to sort out all those qualities in our diction which could be said to yield us 'logical satisfaction', and we want also to characterize, as simply and as generally as we can, the precise *sort* of satisfaction that they yield us. We are, in short, trying to build up a conceptual model in terms of which a large number of important human attitudes can be classified and graded. We shall regard such a characterization as successful to the extent that it enables us to make plain just *why* a given quality in our speech *is* logically satisfactory. We are, in short, embarking on the same sort of simplifying work in logic, that has been carried on for centuries in ethics and aesthetics.

II

Before we go further, we must, however, make plain just what we mean by speaking of the *values* of diction. Now recent thought has

106

VALUES IN SPEAKING

emphasized strongly, in my opinion rightly, that all statements of value should be regarded as expressing emotion in ourselves, and also as expressing the endeavour to evoke similar emotion in others. We can't genuinely understand what is meant by saying such things as 'That is a right way of acting', 'That is an admirable picture', 'That is a well-conceived and well-developed theory' without either feeling (or feigning) satisfaction with the objects in question. And we also shouldn't normally utter such statements, without wishing to communicate our attitudes to others, so as to influence them in their feelings and their practical life. Quite plainly, too, we *learnt* the meanings of the value-words in such statements, when those around us evinced emotional attitudes in our presence, and managed to evoke the same attitudes in ourselves. Remove the emotional background to our value-terminology, remove all wish to communicate our attitudes to others, and I should say that all such terms lose their function entirely, and become idle impediments in the stream of language.

It is true, of course, that we may acknowledge things to be worth while or the contrary in some wholly cool and detached mood, much as we might acknowledge the dodecahedron to be the one regular solid with pentagonal sides. But the proof of the pudding is in the eating, and while this eating, in the case of geometrical objects, consists in processes of construction, comparison, superposition, reasoning from axioms and the like, which can be carried out in the same detached manner as our final judgement, the proof of a value-statement inevitably involves a stirring-up of some satisfaction or dissatisfaction in ourselves, without which we should be quite unable to give it either meaning or validity. We may, if we like, say that men come to *see* or *apprehend* or to *intuit* certain values—there is nothing reprehensible in such phrases—but we should only say so if we are willing to make the readiness to experience certain emotions 'of the essence' of such processes. Without this willingness, we can only use such terms in a wholly empty and misleading manner.

But the modern conception of value-statements as expressive of emotion, has generally gone together with the view that *no* value-statement can be either justified or unjustified, that all are on a level, like the emotions behind them, and that we can only hope to alter other people's judgements of value by working *irrationally* on their sentiments and feelings. In such irrational evocation, it may indeed be possible at times to waken some desired attitude by calling attention

LANGUAGE, MIND AND VALUE

to unnoticed aspects of fact. But all appeals to fact may prove utterly unavailing, and, in the last resort, emotional attitudes and their corresponding judgements, whether weakened or strengthened by suasion, 'fight it out' blindly in the soul of the individual.

There can, however, be nothing farther from the psychological realities and linguistic proprieties than the notion we have just out-lined. For human emotions are nothing if they aren't states in which we are *ready*, and *feel* ourselves ready, to respond in some more or less definite way, to some more or less definite sort of situation. They may involve bodily disturbances of different sorts, and their accom-panying sensations, they may involve various barely describable trends of feeling, but we certainly shouldn't regard them as instances of this or that emotion, if they didn't seem to point to a certain style of action, in the face of a certain sort of presumed situation. As Titchener said, very paradoxically, in criticizing the Lange–James theory, the essence of an emotion lies in a *logical meaning*[1] which is put upon or carried by a certain bodily condition: the state or pose of our body signifies (for us and others) a certain policy of action or inaction, in the face of certain presumed circumstances. That Titchener thought such a meaning quite beyond the province of psychology, is nothing to the point. He showed that, without such a signified policy, or such presumed circumstances, there would be nothing to distinguish any given emotional disturbance from count-less other disturbed states of mind and body. In anger we are plainly out to destroy some object that offends us and obstructs us, in fear we are plainly in retreat from something menacing and dangerous, in surprise we feel ourselves at a loss before something wholly unexpected, and so on in every other case one might care to analyse. Quite plainly we have only 'picked out' certain emotional attitudes, and distinguished them in our language, on account of certain com-munities of policy in the face of certain presumed similarities of situation. Both policies and presumptions are part of what we nor-mally *mean* in speaking of the emotions in question. Empirically, too, it is obvious that our various types of response are adjusted to the

---

[1] Many will doubtless be shocked by the 'intellectualistic' suggestions of this phrase, but it is my view, which I cannot here defend, that however much 'dynamism' we may admit in our actions, or in the *objects* of our experiences, we must still give a purely *cognitive* analysis of those experiences themselves. To *feel* an emotion is, in short, to *perceive* (whether clearly or marginally) that we are ready to behave in certain ways.

108

VALUES IN SPEAKING

properties of objects, that they are strengthened by the discovery that an object really *has* some property, or weakened by the discovery that it really hasn't got it. And not only high-grade ethical and aesthetic emotions are subject to such 'norms', but even the commonest stirring of envy, or the most disreputable attack of malice or disgust or sexual lust. Thus envy tends to vanish if we find that our envied person is really an inferior, malice if we find that one we hate is only a fellow-sufferer devoid of ill-will to ourselves, disgust if a seeming drop of spittle proves to be a rare jewel, and sexual interest if some seemingly artless, lovely young woman proves, on a closer scrutiny, to be a scheming, ageing and bedizened harlot.

There are, of course, occasions where we go on responding in a certain manner regardless of the ascertained or ascertainable circumstances, but we mark our sense of the unusual character of these cases by speaking of them as 'abnormal', 'pathological' or 'neurotic'. Now it is doubtless thinkable that our impulsive responses might *all* have been of this unbiassed type, in which case what is now a pathological phenomenon would have been the human norm. Men might have been so made that they shrank from *anything* whether helpful or offensive, or were sexually moved by *any* object regardless of its shape or species or dimensions. In such a case we should have built up our language quite differently: names for impulsive responses would have signified only certain policies of action, and not a presumed set of properties in the objects of such policies. Philosophers with their talk of a boundless variability in the objects of our ethical and other emotions, have in fact adjusted their language to this wholly imaginary situation, instead of to the real emotions of actual human beings. We, however, prefer to adjust our language to phenomena that actually exist, and so to include an orientation to a given type of object in the very meaning of our names for emotional attitudes. We shall, accordingly, speak in the manner of Brentano, who founded his 'phenomena of love and hate' upon the more basic phenomena of judgement and idea. All this implies that an emotional attitude can be justified or the reverse according as the assumptions it is built on prove true or otherwise.

We suggest, therefore, that, even if our statements of value are only expressions of emotions in ourselves, they may none the less express emotions which are justifiable or unjustifiable, and so themselves be fitly spoken of as (in a sense) justifiable or unjustifiable statements. They will be justified whenever the properties whose

LANGUAGE, MIND AND VALUE

presence they presume are actually there, unjustifiable when this is not the case. And so when we sketch the character of a given emotional attitude, we must not be content to say what sort of *response* it inwardly represents, but also what sort of *object* it outwardly requires, whose presence would *justify* the emotion in question. We must now try to do this in the difficult case of 'logical demands' and 'logical satisfactions'.

Now some would object, from the outset, to our whole enterprise, on the ground that there isn't necessarily any single standard reaction covered by each name for an emotional attitude, but that each stands for a vast 'family' of quite different reactions, linked together by a large number of distinct affinities, and not truly exemplifying any single 'common nature'. And they would regard it as the typical philosophic, or Platonic error to imagine otherwise. They would doubtless think such an error particularly heinous in the case of so vague and artificial an assemblage as the 'logical emotions'. We, however, see no way of dealing profitably with a vast host of disparate cases, except by ranging them under certain conceptual models,[1] rather more simple and 'typical' than the majority of cases that we meet with, and then treating all such cases either as 'normal' or as 'undeveloped' or as 'deviating' instances of this model. If this is Platonism, then such Platonism should be consciously cultivated. And if ordinary language is as deeply unplatonic as some modern thinkers suppose, then ordinary language stands in grave and constant need of philosophic correction.

III

What then shall we say is the policy pursued in our logical emotions, and what are the characteristics required in their objects? They are, very plainly, forms of 'cherishing' or 'valuing', of states where our policy is to keep objects in existence or to keep them in view, or, contrariwise, to banish them from existence, or from the range of our vision. This much may be simply taken over from the very competent accounts of valuation put out by certain modern analysts. But we may say, further, that they are all forms of *impersonal valuation* of states where we recommend objects both to ourselves at future times

[1] In this idea I have been influenced (not perhaps in a way he would approve) by Stevenson's use of 'working models' in *Ethics and Language*.

VALUES IN SPEAKING

and to the world at large, and where we *claim* tacitly that the things valued by us will also attract us reliably in the future, and will prove attractive to all genuinely reflective and unbiased persons. Plainly the valuations in question are the fine fruits of that sympathetic interaction of persons in a civilized society, which leads them to look on their own individuality as a trammel, and to desire nothing more passionately than to think and feel after a universal pattern.[1]

Lest this whole desire should seem vain and chimerical, I shall emphasize at this point that there are laws governing human desires and satisfactions which ensure that there *must* be certain very general, higher-order objects which will appeal reliably to all reflective persons. For men are creatures whose desires can lose their cruder urgency, and yet, mysteriously, retain an influence over action: we can plan meals when we aren't hungry, and marriages when we aren't sexually inflamed. And human passions, unlike metals, are extremely *malleable* in their cooler state: they can be bent and twisted in most various directions by whatever seems practicable or likely, and they can be welded and alloyed into most complex schemes and policies which yield us great and many-sided satisfaction. Men are also creatures who can throw themselves imaginatively into the situations of others, and who can then weld the interests of a group of persons into comprehensive plans and policies. All this is part of what one ought to mean by calling men 'rational', and would scarcely be worth mentioning were it not now so constantly forgotten. And, for beings constituted as we are, there must *of necessity* be certain very general, formal objectives, which will appeal reliably and upon unbiassed reflection. We may not agree in our basic, first-order interests—though God knows we are similar enough in respect of these—but it is sheer tautology to maintain that we *must* agree in our unbiassed and reflective admiration of such higher-order abstractions as 'integrated and successful living' (whether personal or social), or of 'rare and difficult achievement' whether in art, knowledge, skill or practical life. The concrete content of the 'good life' may be personal and private, but its form is necessary and universal: here as elsewhere it is merely nonsense to think men can vary in a limitless manner.

We shan't, however, spend more time upon this difficult theme of our impersonal valuations: we must say how the valuations called 'logical' differ from *other* impersonal valuations. Here we have hardly any traditions to go on, since our field hasn't been worked over

[1] I am influenced here by the great, strangely neglected work of Adam Smith.

LANGUAGE, MIND AND VALUE

through the centuries like the fields of ethics and aesthetics. If we were trying to characterize our ethical emotions we might follow reputable traditions, and say they were feelings of approval or disapproval concerned with voluntary conduct, and with such conduct in so far as it bore upon the interests of persons, and might secure some adjustment or impartial equalization of such interests. We might then go on to show how such an account made it understandable that we should react ethically to this or that line of conduct, or experience this or that obligation. We might then also show how certain reactions, commonly called 'ethical', which couldn't readily be squared with our account, could be treated either as undeveloped or distorted forms of ethical feeling. By so doing we might not only achieve a better *understanding* of our ethical reactions, but might also succeed in changing them into simpler and more rational forms.

We could likewise carry out the same sort of clarifying work in the case of our aesthetic feelings. For these might be fitly characterized, on lines following tradition, as states where we approve or disapprove the 'sensuous look' of objects, and this to the extent that such a look 'brings out', as tellingly and unconfusedly as possible, some surface form or character of objects, or some deeper notional meaning. And we might then show how our account covered the wide ranges of aesthetic appreciation, and how cases that it didn't readily cover could be classed either as rudimentary or perverted variants. But in the logical field we have nothing to go on, and must start our clarifying work from the beginning.

We may therefore say, at a venture, that the emotions covered by the word 'logical' are concerned with symbols and *symbolic structures*, and this to the extent that such symbols yield us *mastery* over the detail offered by the senses, and reconstituted in thought. And we may say, further, that they concern such symbols as yielding us another sort of mastery: that over all those minds who have access to the same empirical material, and can thereby share the same references. Plainly we have certain satisfactions *not* concerned with states of things, but with the *way* in which such states are spoken of or formulated. And there are some such satisfactions not concerned with any effect our words may have on people's conduct, nor with their telling expression of some single form or meaning, but solely with the *hold* they give us over all the dark masses of particularity, as well as over all those fellow minds who fish conceptually in the same dark waters. In calling such satisfactions 'logical', we aren't

112

VALUES IN SPEAKING

deviating far from established usage, and we are gathering together, under one conceptual model, feelings connected with such diverse qualities as clearness, truth, coherence, adequacy, lack of empty verbiage, plausibility, simplicity and the like. The success of our characterization will then lie in our ability to show that just these qualities (or some supplemented and amended list of them) must necessarily attract seekers after that linguistic mastery which is (for us) the essence of the 'logical'. To such a demonstration we address ourselves.

Our task will, however, be simplified, if we distinguish from the outset between *two* kinds of symbolic excellence, corresponding to the traditional distinction of the 'form' and 'matter' of our discourse. There are things which satisfy us in our formulations, which are, as it were, features of their manner alone, in the sense that it isn't important on *what* content that manner has been used. There are other features in our ways of speaking which satisfy us on account of the content (whether directly or derivatively empirical) to which those ways of speaking are applied. Our speech may be said to have formal excellences, treated as a well-made instrument applicable to anything, but it also has material excellences, as an instrument adapted to the actual course and content of experience. To these formal and material excellences we now turn ourselves.

IV

What then shall we pick out as the first and most important formal merit of speaking? We shall be recognizing a virtue much sought after in the traditional logic, as well as in its modern mathematical successors, if we make our first virtue 'definiteness'. A good form of speech must be one that never lands us in situations where we become lost in linguistic hesitation, or are torn between the impulses both to say and not to say something. For situations of hesitation and conflict are situations of linguistic impotence, and of inability to communicate our meaning to others. And if our attitude is approvingly oriented to linguistic mastery, we must necessarily dislike such situations.

This need for definiteness underlies the traditional demand that we should try to offer *definitions* of all but the simplest terms in our language, an obligation that we can't always readily fulfil, since ordinary speech pursues only that degree of definiteness and mastery which is necessary for practical purposes. This requirement also underlies that standard use of the term 'not' which is embodied in

H   113

LANGUAGE, MIND AND VALUE

our laws of Contradiction and Excluded Middle. We so contrive our speech that we shall always have *something* definite to say, either that such and such is the case, or that it is *not* the case. And we so lay down the meaning of 'not-such-and-such' that it precisely covers *every* possibility but the one covered by its positive counterpart, so that the same conflict felt between saying and not saying something, is now felt between saying something *together with* its negative. Obviously the ideal here indicated is one to which ordinary language only very distantly approximates. For there are countless situations where our ordinary speech leaves us hesitant and torn between conflicting impulses, and must be helped out by arbitrary rulings. At what precise point in some fatal illness shall we say of a man that he is dying? Shall we say that dragons are or are not fire-breathing reptiles, in view of the fact that there aren't really any dragons?

We may note at this point that our requirement of definiteness isn't bound up with that scheme of *bifurcated* possibility associated with our standard use of 'not'. We could speak with perfect definiteness, even if we used 'p' and 'not-p' of two non-exhaustive fields of possibility, and kept a third phrase for an intermediate set of cases, *provided* only that we were never in doubt as to *when* we should apply each of these ways of speaking. There is nothing logically sinful in that use of 'not' which leads us to say, in a Scotch mist, that it is both raining and not raining, or even that it is neither raining nor not raining: sin only enters when the Scotch mist confuses us, and ties us up linguistically, so that we don't know clearly *what* we ought to say. And this, be it noted, is the genuine logical fault in the Hegelian dialectic, as well as in its Marxist derivatives. For there is no harm at all in saying of this conflict-ridden, often nebulous and changeable world, that it abounds in contradictions: this is, in fact, a very common sense of 'contradiction'. But the true evil enters when we abrogate the plain rules of speaking, without setting up new principles which will tell us what to say in given circumstances. Despite talk about the 'cold march of necessity', or the rigorously 'scientific' character of certain deductions and predictions, everyone knows that it is often nothing but the most arbitrary inspiration which decides the dialectical speaker what to say next. No game so played can yield us that linguistic mastery which we require both in theory and practice: hence the tragedy of a situation when populations are reared, and communities run on a logic so distorted.

All this doesn't mean that definiteness is the only logical virtue,

VALUES IN SPEAKING

and that there aren't times when its unmeasured pursuit may not lead us into antinomies or profound falsifications. We shouldn't, for instance, try to speak too definitely of the shape, size or position of a stomach-ache, and *perhaps* similar reservations should be made in regard to the doings of electrons or the future actions of men. Nor should we question the aesthetic expressiveness of certain stammering and contradictious forms of speech: they may bring out the packed richness of certain experiences which defy precise formulation. And there is a long and legitimate tradition, from Heraclitus through Hegel to the modern existentialists, of men who have given us their 'sense of life' in a poetic, rather than a logically proper manner. But, if we are to set store by such works, we should do so from a consciously non-logical point of view.

V

If definiteness is the primary formal virtue in our speaking, there are other virtues, none the less fundamental, connected with the simplification and the unification of our diction. The first has traditionally been called *economy*: the second may be spoken of as *harmony* or *coherence*. The first may be said to secure unity in speaking by eliminating the superfluous, the second by ironing out the anomalous, and by filling in connecting or explanatory links. Both virtues are seen at their best in artificial symbolic languages. Plainly we shouldn't get the best use from our linguistic devices, if they offered us a large number of needless, unequated alternatives, and so were full of unconfessed redundancies. We should be led by such forms of speech into drawing distinctions between more sorts of situations, and more sorts of entities, than it is profitable to postulate, and hence also into many puzzling and unnecessary questions. And it is this requirement of economy which leads us to build up language-systems with the smallest number of 'basic notions', or of basic axioms and rules of inference. It underlies also the whole movement to replace 'inferred entities' by 'logical constructions', which was started by Russell in the early years of this century. It culminated in the *Tractatus* of Wittgenstein who wanted us to build up a language so free from deceptive alternatives that it would be physically impossible for us to express anything in it that was logically absurd.[1]

[1] Such at least is my interpretation of some of the proposals of this treatise, which have not been sufficiently examined by philosophers.

LANGUAGE, MIND AND VALUE

Beside this virtue of economy, we may range the sister virtues of coherent unity and harmony in speaking. Plainly we shall be working in the interests of communicability and increased linguistic mastery, if we bridge the gap between distinct ways of speaking by continuous transitions, or look on them as limiting cases of each other, or as special cases of more general forms of speaking. Plainly it will also serve the interests of linguistic mastery and communicability, if the necessary principles postulated in our language are, as far as possible, inferrible from each other. This virtue of formal unity in speaking coincides largely with the virtue of economy, for we generally increase unity by eliminating the superfluous. But there are times when we increase unity by adding new and unfamiliar notions to our speech, or by complicating it with axioms and rules of inference which don't, at first, seem evident or natural. The obvious case of such complicating unification is the introduction of the 'stroke' or 'not-both' notion into modern mathematical logic, and the consequent condensation of several logical axioms into one axiomatic principle. And Popper's rules,[1] which do away with any need for axioms, are a more modern instance.

VI

Having thus set apart the formal virtues of definiteness, economy and unity, we now turn to those excellences of speech which lie in its relation to the empirical material that it describes and anticipates, and without which it would be wholly vain and empty. We have said that the proper objects of our logical approval were ways of speaking that afforded us mastery over empirical material; it is therefore truistic if *one* of the basic virtues of symbolic combinations is said to lie in their *conformity* to the combinations actually met with in experience. And this conformity may assume several forms, according as we consider different types of symbolic combinations, and different aspects of experience.

From one point of view this demand for conformity is a demand for an adequate *richness* in our various linguistic tools and devices: we must have enough names, predicates, relational terms and so forth, so as never to feel that we are 'leaving out something' in our dis-

[1] See 'New Foundations for Logic', *Mind*, 1947.

116

VALUES IN SPEAKING

course, simply passing over some discriminable feature or factor in experience. This demand inspires our various philosophical and non-philosophical attempts at 'analysis': we don't want any aspects of the real to slip unregistered through our linguistic nets. But there are times when our ideal of conformity to experience doesn't seem to call for such enrichment of diction, but rather for an impoverishment, and for the deliberate refusal to say something we might otherwise be tempted to say. Thus in trying to do justice to the nebulous contours, qualities and dimensions of our sense-data, or the shadowy contents of our thoughts, we must refrain, purposely, from saying all those definite things that would be quite appropriate in other contexts.

This demand for conformity to experience appears also in the special store we set on statements that have actually been *verified* by empirical data, or, if not verified, then continuously *confirmed*, and never refuted by such data. If the goal of our speaking be linguistic mastery over the detail of experience, we shall be obviously drawing nearer to that goal, in proportion as our statements square with all that has, or will come before us in experience. It isn't possible, at this point, to consider the many interesting questions connected with what are called by the modern logician 'degrees of confirmation', a topic very much to the fore in recent discussion.[1] But it is obvious that a statement will have greater conformity to empirical data (and hence afford us greater linguistic mastery) the *more* empirical data it conforms to, and the *more exactly* it anticipates their character. And it is also obvious that the logical value due to such conformity with experience, will be greater as confirming data come from widely separated fields, since mastery of any sort would be said to increase with the *range* of material mastered. We master experience in our speaking, in proportion as we wipe out wider and wider ranges of the merely possible, and replace them with the actual and the definite. The more widespread our data, the wider are the ranges that are thus wiped out. And positive data have a much higher confirmatory value than negative, since the ranges of possibility wiped out by the former indefinitely exceed the ranges ruled out by the latter. More possibilities of natural law are, for instance, ruled out by a single hoopoe with a crest, than by innumerable cases where there aren't any hoopoes and also no crests.

[1] See particularly the articles of C. G. Hempel in *Mind*, January and April 1945.

117

LANGUAGE, MIND AND VALUE

VII

The logical value of conformity to experience may, however, be blended with the two previously mentioned virtues of economy and unity, which then become, not purely formal excellences of our speaking, but of that speaking as applied to empirical material. And here economy takes the special form of demanding that the modes of speech in our language (with the exception of such as have a purely formal function) should be anchored to the firm ground of experience, and should have no meaning but in terms of what we *have* experienced, or what we *might* experience in conceivable circumstances. It may be an innocent pastime to weave symbols together without troubling to attach them to empirical points of reference: quite possibly such uninterpreted combinations may one day find most fruitful applications and interpretations. But, as Kant pointed out, notions without intuitive filling are empty: they yield us no mastery over anything we are capable of dealing with. While their logical value isn't simply *nil*, since they may still exhibit economy, unity and other logical virtues, they are none the less lacking in a most essential respect. We may say of them what Augustine said of the virtues of the pagans, that they were only examples of splendid vice. Even wholly untutored speakers and listeners crave for 'solid significance', and detest nothing more strongly than a diet of 'hot air'.

If we now turn from concepts to statements, we shall find the demand for economy developing into a recommendation to exclude from our talk, as empty and unprofitable, all statements (not purely formal and linguistic) which aren't either empirically verifiable or falsifiable, or which aren't even empirically confirmable or disconfirmable. When we affirm something, we must make its truth entail differences somewhere in the course and content of experience. Otherwise it is an empty utterance, yielding no intellectual mastery over anything. Now in the last decades this ideal of economy has led men to say that the meaning of a statement is its manner of verification, that it means no more than the sum of those tests that would prove it true, or render it probable. It is well that the vogue of this confusing formula is passing. For not only is it contrary to established usage to identify the circumscribed *meaning* of a sentence, with the countless circumstances that bear upon its truth, but it also sins

VALUES IN SPEAKING

against a fundamental logical requirement, which we may, by anticipation, call the demand for explanatory simplicity.

It is our constant practice, in dealing with the bewildering multiplicity of what we do or may experience, to import into our talk certain simplified objects, clothed only in the barest selection of the properties of things around us, or conceived only on some dim analogy with them, and to say of such simplified objects that they *underlie* the data of experience, and that they form the *ground* of their variety. Thus the ordinary speaker always puts a 'real table', much more simple and constant than its varied appearances, 'beneath' such appearances, and also makes the former *responsible* for the latter. And men of science are but carrying this process several stages farther, when they place their much more rarefied electric particles beneath the same appearances. In the same way ordinary speakers and the older unsophisticated psychologists always put simple flashes of insight, throbs of feeling, strains and stresses of the will, described in all the natural metaphors of our introspective diction, beneath that bewildering array of grimaces, gestures, words and deeds through which such experiences *might* evince their presence. To see the simple outlines of the 'real' under its complex manifestations, to make everything merely possible an adjunct of the actual, all that is, for our natural understanding, to explain, elucidate and render intelligible.

There is nothing contrary to a true empiricism in the introduction of such entities, which aren't identified with anything to which we have direct access, provided that we conceive them on a clear analogy with experienced things, and, more importantly, *that we establish two-way bridges of deducibility between them and experienced data.* Thus we can raise no valid objection to the underlying entities of physics, since they are characterized on a definite (if remote and hesitant) analogy with experienced objects, and since we can always make inferences as to their state or character *from* the data of experience, and, *vice versa*, from their state or character *to* the data of experience. Because we have built such two-way bridges of deducibility, we can connect the complex detail of experience by such simplifying entities. The same applies, despite sophistical objections, to the explanation of our outward actions by the thoughts, feelings and decisions of the introspective psychologist. In fact, if we weren't intimately acquainted with such inner states, we should have had to invent them, and should probably have spoken of them in much the same metaphorical,

LANGUAGE, MIND AND VALUE

analogical manner that we now actually employ.[1] If there were reliable, two-way bridges of deducibility between either the monads of Leibniz, or the entelechies of Driesch, and actual data in experience, then it would be as unobjectionable and as unmetaphysical to introduce them into our talk as to make use of mental states or atoms. For it isn't the unobservability of such entities which renders them suspect, but only their uselessness from an explanatory point of view.[2]

It is, however, nothing but a very short-sighted passion for economy which has led to the modern *identification* of an underlying, explanatory entity with the outward signs of its presence. This is an act which brings the whole edifice of reason down in ruins. For it bids us build up a new way of speaking of a ramifying complexity[3] that would tax the capacities of a demigod, and which could never be more than a hollow programme for men. It also leaves the vast array of our possible experience hanging loose and unsupported in the air, with no simplifying tie to bind them, and no actual basis to explain their possibility. To turn talk about Cleopatra's nose into an infinite set of unintelligibly complex statements about what *might* have been observed, in circumstances requiring a formulation quite as complex, and as little intelligible, might be a diverting exercise for an unemployed archangel, but even he could derive from it none of that linguistic mastery which underlies our logical values. But though one may deplore these economical excesses, one must respect the ideal that they stand for, and recognize the abiding value of economy. We should practise a most rigorous austerity in regard to all those underlying entities which can't be given a definite character, and are not linked by two-way bridges of deducibility with the data of experience. *Some* of the references called 'metaphysical' need ruthless pruning, even if others are legitimate and indispensable.

[1] That introspective talk *is* analogical is argued in my article 'Recommendations regarding the Language of Introspection', in *Philosophy and Phenomenological Research*, December 1948, reprinted in the collection of articles *Clarity is not Enough*.

[2] To take an illustration from chess, we might successfully turn what seemed a very anomalous game of chess into one that was perfectly orthodox, by postulating the presence of several invisible pawns, bishops, etc., which the players were moving 'in their heads' (since the actual pieces had been lost).

[3] For this see Price: *Hume's Theory of the External World*, Chapter V.

VALUES IN SPEAKING

VIII

We now turn from economy in relation to empirical material, to the cognate virtue of harmony and unity in relation to the same material. And here we are faced by so many logical duties and values, that we shall have to content ourselves with a very brief enumeration. Most of them are beautifully set out in Kant's appendix to the Transcendental Dialectic. Plainly we want, in speaking, to subsume as many empirical predicates as possible under more general predicates, for clearly our linguistic mastery will be augmented thereby. And we proceed regularly *as if* such general predicates were there to find, for only by proceeding in this manner should we discover them if they were actually there. And we desire also, in our speaking, to connect the things spoken of by as many relationships as possible, and by such relationships, in particular, as *arrange* those things in orderly dimensions. We want everything to be 'placed' in regard to everything else, and to be *reachable* from other things along continuous routes or transitions. The perfect instance of this sort of arrangement is the little appreciated order of time and space, as well as the order of transmitted causal influence which depends on this. It is only since we speak in terms of such an order, that we can put the things we speak of in a single world or cosmos.

We must emphasize strongly at this point that our only justification for speaking in terms of such an order is the logical value that it embodies. Time and space are doubtless realities, but as such they are not fully present in our fragmentary experiences: they are in fact 'nothing to us', and can never yield a reason for our saying anything whatever. But we must try to place the things we speak of in a single time and space order because, only if this is possible, can we achieve the needed measure of symbolic, cognitive mastery over experience and its detail. We speak of unbroken spatio-temporal transitions between the disjointed shows of our actual experience, and of continuous influences bridging such transitions, because, only if our data fit this verbal framework, can they be dealt with in a logically tolerable manner.

This quest for unity and connection is exemplified, also, in the way in which we *interpolate* and *extrapolate*, processes seen at their highest level of abstraction in the formal arguments of analogy and induction. We fill in gaps in experience, as well as all the unknown territories beyond experience, with whatever fits most smoothly on to data

LANGUAGE, MIND AND VALUE

previously experienced, so as to yield the largest possible measure of linguistic mastery and of logical value. And here we may glance briefly at the historical puzzle of induction, which arises obstinately when men crave that assurance which they can only have from actually *seeing* things, in situations where their best available assurance is one resting on a logical value. For we can have no other reason for saying that what we *don't* see, will none the less follow on the lines of what we *do* see, than that it is logically proper to do so. Clearly we shall never achieve any verbal mastery over experience, if we prepare ourselves carefully for a situation in which such mastery will be totally impossible.

Our obligation, in this regard, can probably be treated as a simple case of courage: here, as elsewhere, we should never enfeeble ourselves (except in spells of philosophic play) with desperate, paralysing and defeatist talk. No doubt nature will reward this 'faith', if 'faith' it is proper to call it: we may even say we *know* that she will do so. But here as elsewhere we can give no other reason for our confidence but its logical propriety. There is, of course, no novelty in these contentions. We are merely saying rather frankly and proudly what is often said ashamedly, and as some desperate last resort. We may add further that it is high time that the whole foundations of the theory of probability, whether in its abstract mathematical or more concrete branches, were removed from the incompetent hands of exaggeratedly empiricist philosophers, and given a firm basis in our logical values. There is much in the theory of J. M. Keynes, with its stress on 'rational belief', that would fit in well with such an enterprise: not so all the writings of his critics and successors.

IX

We have, for our purpose, picked out enough of the formal and material excellences in our speaking, and have linked them with that goal of linguistic mastery which is (for us) the end of speaking. We must, however, utter a warning at this point against one general misinterpretation of all that we have said. It might be imagined that our approach was, in some manner, covertly subjective or idealistic, that we were doing no more than recommend certain convenient postulates or *façons de parler*, without seriously claiming that 'the Real' will conform to them. Against such an interpretation we must

122

VALUES IN SPEAKING

set our face. For to speak in a certain manner, and at the same time call it nothing but a mere postulate, or à mere *façon de parler*, is to take away with one hand what one grants with another.

We haven't made the slightest suggestion that there may not be the most complete conformity between the 'real nature of things' and our logical values: we have only said that our reason for speaking in a certain manner must necessarily be a logical value. We say what we say because it is clear, definite, economical, harmonious, and conformable to experience, and not because it corresponds with reality, which isn't, in any case, known to us completely, and isn't, thus far, anything to us at all. But when we speak carefully, and with due regard to our logical obligations, we may *also* say that we are approaching steadily to conformity with reality, if for no other reason than that it would be extremely silly to call anything 'reality', and make it our ideal to conform to it, if we didn't (in addition to making it independent, 'mind-transcendent' and what not) also make it *approachable* in our speaking.

Reality *must*, in fact, fall in with our formal logical requirements, since they, being formal, impose no limitations on its content, and it also *will*, in fact, fulfil our various more material requirements. Nor do we need a better 'justification' of this latter statement beyond the humble tautology that a world of which we can intelligibly speak, must necessarily fulfil the conditions of intelligible speaking. There is therefore no discrepancy between the most sincere realism and an approach through logical values.

X

It might now be profitable, if we had the time, to pass on to applications of our logical values, whether in the formal fields of mathematics or logistics, or in the various empirical sciences. This has, however, been, for years, the best cultivated portion of the logical field, and so we shall devote what time remains to us to the more neglected case of metaphysical speaking. Here is a field subject, in recent times, to much wilful misunderstanding, and it is also one that offers very great difficulties for a general characterization. We can't, unfortunately, work up to an argued characterization through accounts and instances, and so must say, at a hazard, that metaphysical speaking is a kind of talk where we endeavour to adjust our language to our

LANGUAGE, MIND AND VALUE

logical values with a degree of thoroughness and passion which is never met with at the ordinary level, or even at the scientific level of speaking. The metaphysician is a man pursuing economy, systematic simplicity, conformity to experience and the other logical values, with far more devotion and consistency than an ordinary speaker thinks necessary or possible. We must now try to show *how* he pursues these values in a few special cases.

We may say, in the first place, that metaphysics strives after conformity to experience in a much more sweeping, penetrating manner than is ever attempted in the market-place or in the laboratory. This is often denied, but is none the less the case. For the metaphysician doesn't merely apply established ways of speaking to new ranges of material: he will never merely tell us that a fountain-pen needs filling, that the barometer is rising, or that someone looks disgruntled. He attempts rather to *modify* our diction in various queer and searching ways, so as to bring out new aspects in familiar material, or to emphasize alignments and affinities that have so far passed unnoticed. No more than a great creative artist can represent nature in some merely hidebound and conventional manner, but must of necessity import his own style and emphasis into everything he depicts, so little can the metaphysician achieve conformity to experience in the blunted phrases that we ordinarily use. He will say of science that it is nothing but a series of plausible guesses, or that it rests on nothing but faith, thereby bringing out the analogy between a procedure which rests solely on a logical value, and one that has no foundation whatever. He will say, with Heraclitus, that one can't step twice into the same river, thereby bringing out the close analogy between states of change where identity is said to be preserved, and states where we deny that there is any enduring identity. Or he will say, with Whitehead, that Cleopatra's needle is nothing but a stream of happenings, in which certain patterns are maintained, thereby bringing out the almost negligible difference between being and becoming. In such cases, he is altering language in what seems an arbitrary and paradoxical manner, but he is really *adjusting* it to the richness of experience, so as to throw light on sides that have previously lain in shadow. Such procedures are as sober and empirical, in their own peculiar way, as any of the bald reports we ordinarily reckon as informative.

We may note further, that, although the metaphysical glove may often fit the empirical hand somewhat loosely, yet it nearly always

124

VALUES IN SPEAKING

does try to fit it: it isn't ever without some vague prospective reference to the detail of experience. For this reason, every metaphysical account is always undergoing slight confirmations or disconfirmations by everything that happens. Thus when Hegel said that everything in our world was but a stage in the development of 'Spirit', or when Bosanquet called our world the 'vale of soul-making', they were both certainly implying some general trend or drift in things towards wiser, kindlier arrangements: their views will accordingly be faintly confirmed by a meeting of friends, or weakened by a bicycle accident. We are certainly more willing to accept their theories in the former kind of situation than in the latter. Though Bosanquet went a little far in saying that it should be impossible, on his system, for a town with the spiritual significance of London to be ruined by an earthquake, it is none the less clear that there is always some *general* relevance of a philosophical theory to the course and content of experience. The *long-run* expectations of monists, pluralists, atheists, theists, spiritualists, materialists, determinists, indeterminists, and so forth, are certainly different, and it is wilful myopia to ignore this fact.

If conformity to experience is among the goals of metaphysical speaking, it is even more obvious that this form of speaking will pursue such goals as definiteness, economy and unity. We may illustrate the metaphysical pursuit of definiteness by the philosophic treatment of that vague, disturbing phrase 'in the mind'. For we are quite notoriously unsure, in many cases, whether to say or not to say of something—whether imaginary, abstract, dispositional or the like— that it is present 'in our minds', and we experience very powerful impulses both to say and not to say such things. This is a situation that the ordinary speaker finds tolerable, while it is wholly intolerable to the philosophic lover of the definite. Our philosophic pursuit of unity may, at the same time, be illustrated by that idealistic form of speech in which *everything*, whether real or imaginary, concrete or abstract, is located 'in the mind', or that equally extreme realism in which all these entities are given the most utter independence of our minds and their states. A similar example, both of the pursuit of definiteness and unity, would be our philosophic unease with all the vague, anomalous talk about the *present*—for we say indifferently that this hour, this minute or this century are present—together with the attempts to remedy this anomaly by saying, with one long tradition, that the 'true present' is without length, or, following a less popular and more mystical route, and saying it embraces *all* the past

LANGUAGE, MIND AND VALUE

and *all* the future. And if one wants instances of *economy* in philosophic speaking one has only to think of how Aristotle criticized the forms of Plato, or how the Renaissance criticized 'occult qualities', or how some modern philosophers have criticized cruder formulations of the Freudian psychology. Metaphysicians have, in fact, throughout their history always been doing that simplifying work which is now thought to be the peculiar prerogative of the anti-metaphysician.

In all this philosophic pursuit of the best way of speaking, it may at time happen that *some* logical values are sacrificed to others, and this so completely as to lead to very warped and strange accounts of things. It may happen, in particular, that no place is left in some system for conformity to experience, as in that long, weird, interesting tradition which began with the Eleatics and ended with McTaggart and Bradley. Very often the one-sided pursuit of certain logical values and neglect of others, has led philosophers into much greater nonsense and confusion than are ever found in ordinary language. Only too often has the last state of a philosopher been worse than his first. Hence has arisen, both in ancient and modern times, that deep *misology*, spoken of by Plato in the *Phaedo*, which makes men turn disgustedly from all philosophic inquiries. This misology has, in recent years, taken the special form of looking on philosophy as a sort of a pathology of diction, which arises out of the misunderstanding or abuse of ordinary language. And it has been held that the only cure for our philosophic *aporia* lies in seeing all the deepseated and unconscious confusions from which it arises, after which we can return tranquilly to our ordinary forms of speech.

There can be little doubt that this modern misology has had a regrettable influence, even though its author was responsible, also, for some of the most profound and positive appraisals of the task of philosophy. There is, of course, much that is rotten in philosophy, as in all human products and achievements. But it is not the case that the difficulties of philosophy cannot be philosophically removed, nor is it the case that we cannot build up systems of philosophy which at once conform penetratingly to experience, as well as satisfying other logical demands. There is undoubtedly much soundness in some traditional systems, and there is no reason why we, with our modest and more conscious ideals, should not even be sounder.

We may note, at this point, that it would in no sense be a genuine reproach to philosophy if there weren't any single, absolutely *right* account of things, but rather a large number of alternative accounts,

126

VALUES IN SPEAKING

of varying excellence, which illuminate the 'facts' from different angles. For where usage is settled, and we have only to apply it to empirical material, it is impossible to talk very *differently* without also talking contradictorily. But where usage is unsettled and creative, as it always is and must be in philosophy, there are far fewer cases of such gross incompatibility. We should, perhaps, no more regret that things can be spoken of metaphysically in a large number of distinct manners, than that things can be painted in a large number of distinct styles, or life lived in a large number of distinct and different ways.

All this does not mean, however, that all metaphysical schemes of speaking are on a level, and that there aren't some most decisively superior to others, as well as some of such tried soundness that it would be folly to reject them entirely. I myself would place a certain moderate realism, which does full justice both to ponderables and imponderables, in the latter category. However that may be, a wildly metaphysical way of speaking may still be preferable, logically, to our ordinary accounts of things. For ordinary language is the breeding-ground of every metaphysical system: it is only innocuous because it holds them *all* in germ, in which state they may cancel out each other's defects, but do not develop any of their compensating excellences. It is clear, finally, that to live and talk without philosophic examination is a mode of life not 'liveable by a human being'; it is much better, plainly, to be Socrates dissatisfied and confused than the ordinary speaker competent and satisfied.

We have now finished our survey of the field of logical values. We have tried to show that, although valuations in the logical sphere are emotional preferences, they are none the less not at all lacking in objectivity or validity. For all human emotions are essentially oriented to definite states of things, and will be justified or the reverse according as those states are actual or otherwise. All our rational and social emotions, moreover, which arise out of the reflective integration of our own and other people's interests, must, of necessity, have certain long-term, higher-order objectives, which all men must seek, and which philosophers must try to illuminate and develop. However little they may care to be either censors or mentors, philosophers are under a plain obligation to teach themselves and others how to act and feel and speak.

VII

LINGUISTIC APPROACH TO PSYCHO-PHYSICS[1]

(1950)

I

I WANT this evening to discuss the time-honoured question as to whether or not we should credit ourselves (and our human and animal associates) with two distinct 'lives', one consisting in the gross movements of the parts and particles of our bodies, and the other consisting of much more impalpable, ghostly and secret changes, which not only elude outside observers, but also prove somewhat elusive even to those to whom they actually happen, and are with some difficulty circumscribed in language. I also want to consider how, if we admit two such lives, we should conceive them as related to each other, whether as the histories of distinct agents, or of the same agent differently regarded, and whether we should separate them rigorously or credit them with overlapping phases, and to what extent, finally, we should conceive of them as impinging on each other and modifying each other's course of development. It is this second set of questions rather than the first in which I am principally interested.

My questions are, as I said, time-honoured, but it is not easy to discuss them at the present moment, nor to count on a tolerant hearing. For the whole subject has become hedged about with a large number of prohibitions and warning pronouncements, and ghosts have been laid with such ceremonious finality that one dreads to raise them even for the most wholesome reasons. There used to be a *Verbot*, now happily breaking down, against talking about anything that one couldn't hope to show to other people, in the same sense in

---

[1] Read at a meeting of the Aristotelian Society, on January 9, 1950. Published in the *Proceedings*, 1949–50.

LINGUISTIC APPROACH TO PSYCHO-PHYSICS

which one could show them a pen-wiper or an inkwell, and there also has been a *Verbot* against mixing up different kinds of talk, so that one shouldn't refer to a sensation in the same breath in which one talked about a physical object, there has been a general discouragement, practically amounting to a *Verbot*, against any deviation from the plainest, first-order speech, and latterly there has been a threat, not wholly intelligible to me, that if we say there is anything ghostly under the smooth surface of our outward saying and doing, we shall be then forced to locate a second ghostly process under the first, and so on indefinitely. Now I react very unkindly to any *Verbot* unless it is backed up by reasons that I find conclusively persuasive, and I shall therefore not scruple to consider whether or not we should be said to have a ghostly side to our nature, and how it should be said to be related to our grosser manifestations.

I shall, however, try to say at the outset what sort of inquiry I believe myself to be embarking on, and how I think it ought to be conducted. I should call our inquiry predominantly 'metaphysical', in that its main purport wasn't to discover new facts, but to decide upon a satisfactory way of speaking about the familiar or recondite facts which are laid before us in our common experience or by science. But I should also say that our inquiry was, to a subsidiary extent, empirical, in that our final choice to speak in one manner rather than another, would depend upon the character of the facts to be spoken of (many of them as yet undiscovered) as well as upon pure considerations of linguistic fitness.

In saying all this, I am of course giving an unconventional account of what is involved in metaphysical inquiry, and one that would require more expansion and more justification than I can give it this evening. I am suggesting, first of all, that we can be said to have a certain number of common, impersonal aims in speaking, and that speech can be evaluated as good or bad, as it fulfils or falls short of such aims. And I am also suggesting that, by describing metaphysics in this manner, one isn't giving too warped or too misleading an account of the activities of actual philosophers, who could be classed as metaphysicians, but that one covers those activities fairly and squarely, and throws light upon their detailed procedure.

Now I think good arguments could be advanced for both of these contentions: I could point out that, as beings concerned to communicate and remember, we can't help demanding clarity and definiteness at all points in our discourse, and that, as beings concerned to make

LANGUAGE, MIND AND VALUE

penetrating references to vast masses of detail we must necessarily seek for simple formulations from which such detail follows smoothly, and with a minimum of clumsiness. And while our ordinary interest in clarity and smoothness may be limited by the occasion or by the subject-matter on hand, yet we can't help experiencing an unpractical, almost aesthetic prolongation of this interest, which leads us to pursue smoothness and clarity to the limit, and to tolerate no mode of speech in which anything is left indefinite, or apparently conflicting, or merely juxtaposed.

That these linguistic aims operate in the work of actual meta-physicians might be shown by examining their books, in which connection one could find no better illustration than the careful masterpieces of C. D. Broad. For though these books are written, for the most part, in what has been called the 'material mode of speech', yet they suffer remarkably little if translated into the formal mode, and most of the arguments which are put up in justification of a 'theory' will provide good reasons for preferring some way of speaking. Thus Broad's long weighing of the merits and demerits of the 'sensum' and the 'multiple-relations' theory of the relation of percipients to perceived objects, gain greatly in clearness, and can be freed from many senseless complications, if we regard them not as theories, but as essays in improved speech about familiar facts in ordinary experience.

In regarding our inquiry as one concerned mainly with ways of speaking I am not, of course, regarding it as trivial: it remains exactly what it always was, and to me, at least, the question 'What shall I say to speak well?' is as solemn and important as the old question: 'What shall I do to be saved?' While I disapprove of philosophy by pronouncement or philosophy by prohibition (as also of philosophy by ignoring or not understanding) I am as unfriendly to that facile tolerance which readily agrees to differ. To me philosophical preferences should be based upon good reasons and good reasons are by definition those which can't help wringing some measure of recognition from others, even if those others aren't ultimately moved by them.

II

I turn now to consider, first of all, whether we ought or ought not to split up a person's history into two separate 'stories', that we

LINGUISTIC APPROACH TO PSYCHO-PHYSICS

may roughly distinguish as gross, outward and material, and inward, subtle and spiritual. Now this question I propose to consider with some brevity, both because I have written and spoken on it several times recently, and am rather tired of it, and also because I want to pass on to other questions that I find more interesting. Now it seems to me, that there nearly always are, in a very plain sense, two separate stories about a man involved in certain situations, and engaged in certain activities, and those are, on the one hand, the story which tells us what the man did or underwent, or what he was about to do or undergo, or what he would have done or undergone (in the ordinary sense in which we don't do or undergo anything when we merely 'sit and think'), and the quite different story which tells us how things *felt* or *seemed* to the man in question, when he was involved in this situation or engaged in these activities.

These are distinct stories in the quite obvious sense of being made up of quite different sets of words, quite differently arranged, and they are also distinct in requiring quite a different background and preparation in an understanding auditor. For the experience, the sympathy and the interpretative capacity that are necessary for the understanding of the one story, are quite superfluous in the understanding of the other. And while the one story can be set down in words that bear a plain meaning and can be readily connected with features of our common environment, the other story abounds in phrases involving a 'sort of', a 'rather as if', a 'rather like', a 'just as if' and so forth, which require quite a different training and effort if we are to interpret them properly. Even if there *is* a strained, sophisticated sense in which the one story can be regarded as a 'translation' of the other, it is only when we have understood both stories in the ordinary manner, that we can come to say that this is possible.

I shall now illustrate my meaning by considering a case very carefully dealt with by Professor Ryle, that of a man doing something with a great deal of attention or conscious 'heed'. Now I think that Professor Ryle has told us *one* of the stories concerning this man, the one, namely, that would ordinarily be called 'outward', with very great accuracy and beauty: he has told us how a man doing something in a heedful manner is always able and ready to tell us what he has been doing, and what he is about to do, that he can report on it accurately afterwards, that he becomes tired by his activity in a way in which heedless actions do not tire him, that his activity can be touched off or finely regulated by general orders issued by himself or

LANGUAGE, MIND AND VALUE

other persons, that it may be based on past learning, but adjusts itself neatly to the novel features of the situation, and so on and so forth.[1]

This is, as I say, an admirable account of the heedful activity, and one that discriminates many features not previously noted. But it none the less altogether fails to tell us how this heedful activity *feels* to the heeder, except to the extent of telling us that it *doesn't* consist of murmuring to oneself, uttering comments, strictures, encouragements or diagnoses to oneself, which are obviously not at all of the essence of heeding. But how heeding feels to the heedful person is surely something of immense interest and importance, and it isn't something that presents insuperable obstacles to description.

For quite obviously, when we heed something carefully, an extraordinary phenomenon occurs—it is only extraordinary since we so seldom heed our heeding—which we are wont to describe by a number of more or less suitable metaphors: it is as if all we were not heeding faded away into the background, or vanished altogether, however powerfully it might be assaulting our physical sense-organs, or impressing their more sensitive portions. And it is as if certain objects, or, strange to say, even abstract phases of objects, were set in brilliant light, while everything else passed into penumbra or was totally obscured. The phenomenon in fact appears more saliently and impressively, whenever one keeps one's fleshly eyes and ears fixed and immobile, and lets what I may call one's ghostly eyes and ears rove over their deliverances, dwelling as heedfully on the dim and marginal as upon the vivid and central, and *then* notes retrospectively —as one can do without difficulty—how various features in the picture appeared and disappeared, and were at times, in a curious manner, half-apparent. To note all this is certainly to become aware of a 'light' and a 'clarity' that are in many ways deeply different from anything else that goes by these names.

We are, of course, bound to describe our phenomenon metaphorically, since the whole process of looking back with descriptive intent on one's just past experience is a trifle unusual. Yet it isn't by any means a difficult proceeding, nor need it be described in terms of that contemporary 'phosphorescence' which some have found so dubious and objectionable. For while the more absorbed passages in our inner life take place, as it were, *in camera*, yet we have but to interrupt their session to receive at once a full, circumstantial, wholly confident report, embracing much queerly worded detail that would

[1] *Concept of Mind*, pp. 135–49.

LINGUISTIC APPROACH TO PSYCHO-PHYSICS

never otherwise have been released. While we may quarrel about metaphors, and particularly so when they have been frozen into technicalities, yet the very fact that we *do* quarrel about them, could be said to indicate that we understand them.

Not only does the heedful experience show the quasi-luminous effects I have mentioned, but it also frequently involves what one can only call an accumulated sense of what one has accomplished, as well as a concentrated sense of what one is about to do, both of which 'senses' disappear entirely whenever we can carry out activities in a less heedful and more routine manner. And one could, in the same manner, furnish two distinct stories for any of the other activities that one wouldn't call entirely 'unconscious', though some, doubtless, would present more difficulties than others. But we find, curiously enough, that those stories which are most exciting on the level of saying and doing, often correspond to the poorest stories on the level of seeming and feeling, while those which involve the most vivid appearances and feelings, correspond to the dullest tales upon the level of action.

All this being as tritely obvious as it is, what possible ground could anyone have for saying that there is only *one* story covering every type of human activity, and that proposals to bifurcate it are due to the confusions of philosophers? One might, I think, say so because one thought no clear line could, or should be drawn between the two stories: certainly the same things and persons may occur in both of them, and certainly there is a sense in which the one may be said frequently to carry on what has been started in the other. There are, plainly, quite as many likenesses as differences between solving some problem on paper, and turning it over in one's head.

If one wants to consider what is logically possible, though with small empirical warrant, one can certainly conceive of situations and senses, in which the one story could be said to have become *as* public as the other. If experiences of a foreign flavour, yet manifesting a characteristic, independent pattern, and seeming to refer back and forth to other experiences similar to themselves, haunted us on occasion or beset us recurrently, we should doubtless feel a strong temptation to say that they were experiences of some other person, that had temporarily strayed among our own. This inclination would be strengthened if we could find affinities and affiliations between such experiences and those that we attributed to the fleshly persons about us, whom we could meet and talk to in the ordinary manner.

LANGUAGE, MIND AND VALUE

Wittgenstein, too, has taken great trouble to imagine what it *might* mean to feel another's pain.

Those who would adhere, even in such cases, to that strict convention which makes it nonsense to say that anyone could enjoy the experiences of another, seem to me to be shaping their language too much to suit the circumstances and the communications of this transitory life. They remind me, also, of those determined Euclideans, who, on being transported from London to London by way of the whole circuit of spherical space, still said that this couldn't possibly be London, but was only a town exactly like it, since one couldn't return to one's point of origin by going away from it in a straight line.

But though I have the greatest sympathy with the line of objection I am considering, and though I certainly don't want to set up any rigid barriers between an inner and outer, or between the 'public' and the 'private', still the two tales in question do seem to me to mention *some* rather different matters, e.g. the 'light' of attention that we just considered, and they also seem to me (in this life at least) to require to be understood in a somewhat different manner, so that we still have the best of reasons for keeping them separate.

Some might object to speaking about the two stories for a different reason: because they thought the one story, the supposedly 'inner' one, wasn't really a story, because they held it 'hadn't any separate sense', that it told us nothing that couldn't have been better put in the other story, that it merely expressed certain passages in that story in a set of startling 'pictures', which might have an illustrative or a regulative value, but whose usefulness was outweighed by their quite misleading suggestion that they were conveying important and peculiar information. Now this line of objection seems to me to be very strange, and it also seems to me to make use of words in a manner that would need much justification.

For it is surely odd to say that one isn't communicating anything different when one says how things look or feel to a person, and when one says how that person would behave in certain circumstances? The strangeness wouldn't vanish even if one limited this behaviour to such as would provide evidence for the fact that things actually did feel or look in this manner to the person in question. It also seems strange to say that our whole difficult activity of putting ourselves into someone else's position, whether in fancy or fact, subjecting oneself to similar influences and provocations, trying to feel oneself into someone's actions and descriptions, and then testing and retesting one's readings by a further study of those actions and descriptions—all of which things would be said to be helpful in the understanding of another person's experiences—it would be strange to say that all this activity could result in nothing but the construction of an irrelevant 'picture', which couldn't by itself convey the slightest degree of information or knowledge.

Now all this may be said—one can certainly use the words 'information', 'knowledge', 'communication', 'picture', 'sense' 'different' and so forth in this manner—and to speak in this way may have the merit of stressing that the techniques we use to obtain insight into other people's experiences do not, in this life at least, operate independently of their utterances and actions, but are always prompted and tested by the latter. But it seems, at the same time, gravely misleading to speak in such a way, since it suggests that the 'picture' we are forming is idle and superfluous, that we might readily dispense with it, that we could easily replace it by some wholly lucid, 'outward' story. Whereas it is only by keeping such a 'picture' before us, that we can work out all the innumerable, highly indirect, surprising ways in which some of a man's more retiring attitudes *might* manifest themselves. We can also obviously never give a final outward rendering of this 'picture', but can at best come indefinitely nearer to doing so. For all these reasons I can see no good ground for departing from that ordinary mode of speech which talks in terms *both* of an inward and an outward story.

III

Having decided to say, therefore, that there nearly always are two stories about a man's activity at a given moment, we must now decide how we shall say that these two stories are related to each other. And here we must decide, at the outset, whether to attribute them both to a single agent or person, or whether to consider them as tales about distinct agents, a man's mind or spirit, on the one hand, and his body on the other. Now the mere fact that our common speech follows the former pattern more frequently than the latter, as well as the fact that some philosophers have spoken in the latter manner, would suffice for some to settle the whole issue: we, however, must give better reasons for our preferences.

What then are the circumstances in which it would be reasonable to say that our inward story was descriptive of *one* agent, and our

LANGUAGE, MIND AND VALUE

outward story of another? I shall answer this question on principles that I think we actually *do* follow in such matters, and which require only a little further elaboration and development to be the principles we ought to follow. It would, I think, be reasonable to speak of two agents in a situation like this, if we could work out, on the basis of our actual data, two hypothetical courses of development, each following its own independent and unbroken line, the one representing how our inner story *would* develop (from a given point onwards) if it were unaccompanied by an outward story, and the other representing how our outward story would develop if it were unaccompanied by an inward story. Both these lines of hypothetical development should have their own characteristic pattern, their own natural *nisus*, they should proceed without gaps, and they should *not* follow each other slavishly in their curves and windings.

Not only should it be then possible for us to work out two such lines, but we should also be able to light upon principles which connected deviations in the one pattern of development with certain features in the other, so that the one line could be looked upon as *interfering* with, modifying the direction of, the other. And if the deviations that we had to account for were extremely *sharp* and *notable*, we should have *stronger* reason for speaking in terms of a plurality of agents than if they were trivial and gradual. For, in the latter case, we could perhaps more reasonably say that our single agent had altered, or that it was really different from what we had originally supposed, whereas it wouldn't be so reasonable to say this in the case of marked and sharp changes. Quite plainly we regard a magnet as one agent, and a piece of iron as another, because we think we know how each would behave in the absence of the other, and also because we can see how the behaviour of the one alters in spectacular fashion when the two are brought together.

We may even say that talk in terms of two distinct agents would be reasonable, if we knew *no* way of isolating one of these agents, or subjecting it to a separate examination. If my pen suddenly rose from my desk and pirouetted in the air, plunged itself in my inkwell and wrote madly on the paper, before relapsing into its customary quiescence, it would be not unreasonable to say that it was 'possessed' by some foreign agent, even if we didn't go so far as to call this agent an 'entelechy' or a poltergeist. And this reasonableness would increase if the disturbances followed a regular pattern, and also passed regularly from one region to another.

136

LINGUISTIC APPROACH TO PSYCHO-PHYSICS

All this has been put in somewhat homely fashion, and could doubtless be developed into long, difficult technicalities in which great play was made with the philosophical notion of 'causality'. We have done no more than make a certain steady consecutiveness and 'belonging together' into a mark of unitary thinghood, while lack of coherence, accompanied by casual interference, were a mark of substantial separateness, a decision based upon tendencies in our language that we have only made definite and explicit.

We hold, therefore, that if each of our stories had its own distinct inner unity and continuity, in which certain marked and sharp 'dints' and deviations could be connected with passages in the other story, we should have reason to adopt that dualistic mind-and-body account that some philosophers have favoured. And this, be it noted, would be so, even if we were only dealing with two *outward* stories, even, for instance, if we found we were in a position to treat men's accounts of their inner experiences as irrelevances of behaviour like the queer conduct of the bewitched pen mentioned above. For there is nothing in the mere difference of 'inward' and 'outward' which should as such point to a difference of agents: were the two as slavishly 'parallel' as certain traditional accounts suppose them to be, it would be extremely queer and perverse to attribute them to different agents.

What then shall we say on this matter, having regard not only to the principles of speaking we have laid down, but also to the empirical facts we want to cover? Plainly our inner story wouldn't *seem* to have that inner unity and completeness which would make it reasonable to credit it to a separate agent: it seems to proceed in fits and snatches, to be punctuated by gaps, to require an indefinite amount of supplementation by *something* before it could figure as an agent's history. Nor do we find anything like the sharp, brave *step-up* between such activities as are held to have no inner inspiration (or no relevant one) and such activities as are said to have one, and only such a sharp step-up could lend colour to our manner of speaking.

We find, instead, something quite different: that processes *without* an inner inspiration, that would, in fact, be called 'merely physical' or 'merely physiological' *lead up* unbrokenly to many of our more significant inner experiences, and that the latter likewise *lead down* smoothly to the former. And we find, further, that while there may be many deep descriptive differences between our spread-out, piecemeal outward living, and our fused, concentrated inner changes, there is none the less a sense in which processes beginning in the one are

LANGUAGE, MIND AND VALUE

constantly being carried over into the other, and continued, as it were, in another manner and medium.

Now I need not give many examples of this very interesting, wholly familiar *lead-up* and *lead-down*: it is indeed strange that experimentation should have been needed to reveal facts so obvious. I shall illustrate *lead-up*, first of all, by the extremely plain fact that it is, for the most part, our unconscious 'bodies' that do all the sorting out and the 'interpreting' of the influences impinging on us from without, thereby giving rise to those 'percepts' which emerge full-fledged before our 'minds'. It isn't, for instance, because a noise in my right ear *seems* louder than a noise in my left ear, or because it *seems* to arrive there earlier, that it seems to me to come from my right: but it is because it *is* physically louder and earlier, that it seems to come from the direction in question. It isn't, likewise, because a paper first seems grey in some shadowy setting that it then—the setting being recognized and discounted—gets taken for white, but it is because our experienced and accomplished body has sized up the whole situation, and has discounted whatever was abnormal and distorting in it, that the paper comes before us as authentically white. It is likewise the unconscious, merely bodily mother of the psychology textbooks, who responds to her baby's slightest whimper (while ignoring the tram-cars), and starts making appropriate movements at the moment that she also wakes up her slumbering 'mind'. It is likewise not because our whole past history has paraded before us, that we have, after some hesitation, picked out the right word or the appropriate action, but it is probably right to attribute this to an obscure massing and shifting of bodily factors such as that which precedes our suddenly acquired, triumphant ability to deal with some hitherto baffling collar-stud.

In all these cases our 'mind' can surely be said to behave like a high-born lady that consumes all sorts of viands in her dining-room, that have come from a kitchen she has never visited, and are handed to her by a 'slavey' that she never notices. And if one wants a good example of *lead-down* one has but to point to the universal fact of silent intent, or, as the psychologists call it, 'mental set': the fact that decisions or instructions consciously entertained lead down insensibly to serene executions, quite undisturbed by any consciousness of purpose, yet not by any means stupid for all that, which go on until some hindrance or some counter-attraction demands that the whole matter should be 'looked into' and our intent consciously reaffirmed.

LINGUISTIC APPROACH TO PSYCHO-PHYSICS

All these facts could be said to show, with the greatest plainness, that pursuit of goals and intelligent self-adjustment are as much present in what we unconsciously do, as in what consciously appears before us, or is felt within us, even if the higher and more difficult forms of self-direction have need of that 'light' of heedfulness that I previously mentioned. And what goes for intelligence and purpose goes also for their absence (or relative absence), for, as Professor Ryle has made plain, things 'done in our heads' may be as aimless and as unintelligent as things done blindly by our hands.

We may note further that what I have called *lead-up* and *lead-down* are evident, also, in the fact that, even in our wholly untutored descriptions of our inward states, we still use the idiom of external action in a setting of circumstances. It is, we say, *as if* we were in this or that position, or before this or that object, and were dealing with it in this or that manner. We may, in fact, say that the characterization of our inner story as 'ghostly' is *doubly* valuable and illuminating: for while it brings out all the deep differences between our outward and our inward manner of being—at least in their extreme phases—the hardness and fullness of the one, and the attenuation and fusion of the other, it none the less also emphasizes that the one is, as it were, nothing but a queer replica and continuation of the other. To sprain one's ankle on a ship's gangway, to live through the vivid appearances and feelings involved in this happening, to imagine vividly what it was like to live through these, to live afterwards through the unillustrated 'nutshell' sense of all that was involved in this: here surely is a ladder leading from the grossly physical to phases more and more 'phantasmal'. I think Professor Ryle manages to strike this spectral note very happily (though he would no doubt detest my 'spectral' language) when he says of our silent soliloquies that they are nothing but 'a flow of pregnant non-sayings'.

The empirical facts being what they are, it would be obviously strained to speak in terms of two agents, a mind and a body, in somewhat casual and external relation to each other. None of the conditions that would justify such a mode of speaking are present. We must, in fact, endorse that perfectly ordinary manner of speaking which treats a *person* as an amphibious being, combining both a fleshly and a ghostly 'side'. It is, in fact, neither proper to confound our lives, nor to divide our person.

Not only must we, therefore, conceive of this single person as straddling two realms, but we must also conceive of him as shifting

LANGUAGE, MIND AND VALUE

his weight regularly from one foot to the other, since the arrest of our fleshly performance generally leads to an intensification of our ghostly activities, whereas the perfection of outward performance (we may say after Heraclitus) is generally purchased at the price of 'soul'. But whether a wiser science will ever find a notion of 'energy' capable of accommodating and accounting for these facts, is something that I leave aside as too difficult for me. The facts don't, however, encourage us to give what is ghostly any uniform priority over the bulky, or the latter over the former. If movements are, at times, merely the overflowing expressions of important inner changes, the latter, likewise, at times merely echo and applaud the former, as when we listen in quiet passive astonishment to our own brilliant utterances.

To speak in terms of something two-sided and amphibious may of course prove fruitful of puzzles. We may be led to look for a mysterious *tertium quid*, endowed with undiscoverable properties, which will hold the two lives or sides together. Or we may begin to search after some 'deeper bond' that will render their connection 'intelligible'. These searchings are metaphysical in the worst sense of the word. We can only be freed from such difficulties by dwelling carefully on those actual connections which lead us to attribute certain outward and inward changes to a single person, by noting how our inner life may be said to carry on, to anticipate, to do duty for and to supplement out outward living, and then realizing clearly that it is only through a confusion that we have been led to look for bonds or binders that would make this unity closer or more genuine. We may, in fact, say that the *lead-up*, the *lead-down* and the 'phantasmal' continuation we have mentioned, simply *are* the relationship between our bodies and our souls.

I have, of course, vastly simplified the issue before me by turning my back deliberately on the whole possibility of saying that those purposive, intelligent outward acts which *don't* seem to have an inner inspiration, really have one, although this latter is of an undiscoverable, 'unconscious' kind. This mode of speaking has, of course, been applied to those preparations, those rummagings, those continuations and those hoardings that I previously dealt with, in which *lead-up* and *lead-down* can be said to consist. Everywhere, if we like, we can see the small, peering eyes and the furrowed brows of vigilant brownies, who, unlike men, never let a matter drop, never acquire skill, never learn to do anything automatically and silently, for this would unfortunately mean that they relegated part of their duties to

140

LINGUISTIC APPROACH TO PSYCHO-PHYSICS

another set of brownies, who might in their turn practise other relegations, and so on indefinitely. And, since brownies have been postulated, we can make them work hard: we can extend their responsibilities to the whole running of the living organism, so that our old dualism will return with novel force, our 'body' being credited with nothing but our most lumpish tendencies, while all order and adjustment spring from the meddling of these unseen 'intelligences'.

Now I don't object on principle to this whole approach, should it really prove better capable of dealing with our facts than any other. I don't abhor the undiscoverable as such, nor do I feel a strong urge to say that all significant talk about it must necessarily be translatable into talk about something else. Provided that the circuit *via* such undiscoverables really represents a shortening of our theoretical path, I am content to let it be. But it appears to me that the theoretical circuit *via these* brownies is lengthy and unprofitable: it does no more than complicate what is already quite intelligible in itself. For, on reflection, we can see no reason why intelligence and purpose should be more closely associated with a ghostly performance than a fleshly one, or why the latter should *derive* its inspiration from the former.

We may, in fact, say of intelligence and purpose that they are radically amphibious: they lie, after all, in the *way* in which we cope with things and situations, and hence can be equally exhibited on the fleshly and spiritual planes. And if we needed to explain our fleshly purpose and intelligence, by postulating a set of ghostly acts behind them, then, as Professor Ryle has convincingly pointed out, we should require another set of ghostly acts behind these latter, to explain *their* purpose and intelligence, and so on indefinitely. If we can perhaps be most highly intelligent when we operate 'in our heads', in that we can then deal simultaneously with a large number of issues, stripped of all concrete irrelevances, yet there are none the less grave perils of confusion in these ghostly dealings, which become apparent when we work them out in practice.

We may note, further, that the only inner life of which we have experience is one that is always agreeably padded by relaxed, unvigilant performances, out of which it emerges and into which it relapses. We can form no conception of that Argus-like scrutiny, that everlasting burrowing and fussing, that we should have to attribute to our brownies. We may point, finally, to that ever accumulating body of facts and observations which points to much the same sort of gradual lead-up and lead-down between the living and the lifeless,

141

LANGUAGE, MIND AND VALUE

that we have already seen between the living and the conscious. For all these reasons I adhere to my amphibious 'person' in preference to an 'entelechy' operating from without, which crowds the interstices of our conscious living with a large number of 'unconscious experiences'.

IV

I see no reason, therefore, for saying anything but that I am a single but two-sided person, having an outward and an inward history: I only hope this meagre mouse will not seem too ridiculous. I, at least, have found it interesting to give birth to it. There are, however, two further issues that I ought to consider, connected with less common-place facts and possibilities than those I have dealt with, and which may have a bearing on our final decision. I must, on the one hand, say something about the feasibility of talking of a 'disembodied' mode of existence, a notion that has been found profitable in dealing with abnormal facts. And I must say something, also, as to the bearing on our recommendations of facts that have been, or that may be yet discovered in regard to our brain, an organ that I haven't yet mentioned, but which is generally regarded as important in the matters now under discussion.

Now in regard to talk about 'disembodied existence', I am sure that very good sense can be given to it, if for no other reason than that Dr Lewy (to say nothing of Professors Moore and Schlick) has thought so. And though we have said that our personal existence reveals itself *both* in the acts and changes of a body, *and* in the way things look and feel from and in that body, still we haven't precluded ourselves from saying that a personal existence of this sort might cease altogether to be an affair of *that* body, or indeed of any body whatever, but might none the less linger on in forms more or less vaguely and dispersedly corporeal, or more purely inward.

I confess, however, that I am not at all clear what I ought to mean by this 'disembodied existence', merely because I *could* mean so many things by it. To live through a long series of cogitative flashes, in which nothing whatever was illustrated or symbolized, and in which one communed with others by a sort of mystical seepage, temporarily extending oneself to embrace portions of their mental history, would be the most truly 'disembodied' manner of being that I can conceive

142

LINGUISTIC APPROACH TO PSYCHO-PHYSICS

of, though some might question whether I really can conceive of it. And since we know of no *noesis* that isn't, in some fashion, an attenuation of our ordinary dealings with the things around us, it is no doubt possible that something of our concrete personal style of living might be carried over into this disembodied state.

But to move among dissolving Swedenborgian landscapes, clothed in some dream-shape alterable at will, and to converse with other phantasms similarly attired, who shared some but not all of one's visionary environment, would be a manner of existence that one might or might not care to call a 'disembodied' one. Whereas to see one's own funeral from a given point in space, though not with actual eyes, or to fling furniture about, though not with actual hands, would be a manner of being differing remarkably little from our present state of 'embodiment'. Quite obviously, our present ways of speaking are ill-suited to conditions in the after-life: all that we can therefore sensibly do is to avoid speaking so rigorously as to make nonsense of modes of speech which may very well prove to have an explanatory or anticipatory value.

I turn, finally, to consider how, if at all, we should let our psycho-physical talk be affected by facts about the happenings in our brains, of which we now only know enough to confuse us, but concerning which we may have better knowledge in the future. Now there is a view concerning our brains according to which they may be compared to perfect, secret *faces*, on which is written, for the eyes of anyone with a key to the cipher, the whole history of our inward feelings and our preparations for action, which are expressed so partially and ambiguously on our fleshly faces. The veil of privacy and secrecy hanging over our inner life is, in fact, on this view, no thicker than our skulls. Not only are we to be thus credited with these perfect, secret faces, but it is also held that everything recorded on them can be explained on principles which obtain elsewhere in the material world, or in the unconscious segment of its living portion, so that *no* reference to what they may be expressing is necessary to explain their changes.

Now this doesn't seem to me at all a plausible theory, and I regard it merely as a product of the verbal difficulties occasioned by our amphibious manner of being, and of the consequent desire to make our outward story self-explanatory and complete, just as the parallel doctrine of 'unconscious states of mind' tries to do the same for our inward story. But the view in question is, without a doubt, an

LANGUAGE, MIND AND VALUE

empirical hypothesis, which may in the future have a great deal of factual confirmation, and it is therefore necessary for us to consider how such confirmation should affect our talk about our twofold personal life.

Now *one* way in which this hypothesis has historically affected speakers has been to make them say that while various unconscious bodily activities may genuinely lead up to important inner states, yet the latter don't genuinely lead on to the former. They are merely idle offshoots of our brain-configurations, which make no difference to our subsequent brain-history, or to our consequent lines of outward action. This theory-cum-way-of-speaking has seemed to some to derogate deeply from our spiritual dignity, though others might find it exhilarating to conceive of their minds as mirrors in which their own irremediable follies may be passively contemplated, much after the manner of the *Manchester Guardian* looking on at the 'notable spectacle of our public death'.

But I really can't see that this supposed situation would make it reasonable to speak in this manner, and to be either humbled or exhilarated thereby: the situation in question might make the use of our inner story *superfluous* in explaining what we outwardly did, but it couldn't, in a significant way, make its use either *illegitimate* or *improper*. We should, in fact, in such a situation, be *as* justified in regarding our brain-states as idle epiphenomena of our inward spiritual condition, as the latter of the former, and we could, if we liked, make that inner spiritual condition bear the whole responsibility for what we subsequently did. The fantastic situation we have imagined would, in fact, put us in a Buridan's ass position, in which it would be *just* as reasonable to take a purely inward, or a purely outward line of explanation, or in which we might proceed along both lines conjointly. The traditional 'parallelists' and 'epiphenomenalists' were in fact being metaphysical in the worst sense of the word, in preferring one manner of speaking to the other, after they had ruled out all possibility of a deciding difference.

I don't myself think so ill of this world as to think it capable of landing me in such embarrassment. I confess that I think that our brain will prove itself, on careful examination, to abound in as many half-formed gestures and ambiguous expressions as our outward countenances. But should we really carry such ideally expressive faces hidden in our skulls, I don't think that this curious fact should be allowed to affect what we say about the relations of our inner and our outer life.

LINGUISTIC APPROACH TO PSYCHO-PHYSICS

I have now completed my treatment of the psycho-physical issue. My results have been ordinary, since this seems to me to be genuinely a case in which the course of philosophical reflection leads us only from the familiar to the familiar. But we *might* have been led by such reflection to a manner of speech differing widely from the ordinary. I think it good, anyhow, to concern ourselves at times with old, large issues, since it is only in their context that we can profitably crawl like beetles over smaller bits of canvas. Just as the old issue of truth, after having been shelved for a decade, came back to us unexpectedly in the relation of a language to another language that talks about it, so will most metaphysical issues return in the guise of questions of linguistic preferability. But they will return with a difference, and perhaps I have been successful in illustrating what this difference is.

VIII

THE NOTION OF INFINITY[1]

(1953)

I

I AM about to introduce a symposium on infinity. I do so, not because I can claim any special intimacy with the infinite, nor yet because I feel myself specially competent to unravel its intricacies, but because I think it all-important that a notion so fundamental should be rescued from the grip of the experts, and should be brought back into general circulation. It is a notion so common and so clear as to lie behind practically every use of the ordinary phrases 'and so on' or 'and so forth', but it is none the less capable of giving rise to vertiginous bewilderments, which may lead, on the one hand, to the mystical multiplication of contradictions, as also, on the other hand, to that voluntary curtailment of our talk and thought on certain matters, which is as ruinous to our ordered thinking. A notion which is at once so tantalizing and so ordinary plainly deserves the perpetual notice of philosophers. Throughout the history of human reflection the fogs of an interesting, and often interested obscurity have surrounded the infinite; they were dispersed for a brief period by the sense-making genius of Cantor, but have since gathered about it with an added, because more wilful, impenetrability. In the growing illiteracy of our time, when the lamp of memory barely sheds its beams beyond the past two decades, and the controversies or discoveries of 1890 or 1910 have been allowed to become as stale and as irrelevant as those of Anselm or Xenocrates, it is well that someone should at times seek to recapture and to revivify some of the positive

[1] The first contribution to a Symposium at the Joint Session of the Aristotelian Society and the Mind Association held at Dublin on July 12, 1953. Published in the Aristotelian Society Supplementary Volume *Berkeley and Modern Problems*.

THE NOTION OF INFINITY

illuminations of the past. It is no doubt regrettable that my own personal grasp of mathematical formulations should so often halt and stumble; I pursue symbolic intricacy in the way of duty, my taste in philosophy being for the gnomically simple. If I make mistakes, there will, however, be many to correct me, and I may hope, also, that, here as elsewhere, sheer myopia and symbolic clumsiness may at times prove the mother of philosophical invention. I must attempt, at any rate, to do what others, better qualified than myself, have so entirely neglected; it is better that someone should discuss this topic with the freedom of philosophy, than that all talk about it should be allowed to flow along those technical channels which, whatever else they may do, never enrich our philosophical understanding.

I shall divide my treatment of infinity into two parts. In the first I shall skim briefly over the historical terrain of western thought about the infinite, so that it may be plain where I propose to come down in this field, and precisely what drifts of thought I intend to reinforce or to combat. In the second part I shall let you have a few of my own personal intuitions on the matter, backed up with an amplifying commentary, which will try to show how our thought about the infinite may be fitted into the general pattern of our thought about number.

I begin, therefore, with my historical perspective, foreshortened as to its remoter phases, of western thought about the infinite. The notion of something so comprehensive (in some respect or another) as to be at least equal to anything we can build up in thought, either by the putting together of parts, or the successive running through of elements or aspects, and which is yet *not* such as to be contained or exhausted in such constructions or resumptions, is a notion of no peculiar difficulty or obscurity, and it is also one that made an early appearance in the clear thought of the Ionians. Here we have successively brought before us, as the 'nature' of the things in our world, a number of august, embracing media, sometimes identified with the homely substances of everyday experience, and sometimes hedged about with negations, which are all infinite in extent, and which are also such that out of their bosom an infinity of worlds can be successively or simultaneously generated. There is nothing, in such a straightforward picture, to suggest that the infinite is *itself* in some manner unexhausted or incomplete, or engaged in some perpetual, restless process of trying to run through, or to sum up, the totality of its parts and phases; it is all there, in majestic, fully-realized

147

LANGUAGE, MIND AND VALUE

plenitude and repose, and it is only we, or the hurrying series of worlds of which we form a part, who are trying vainly to exhaust whatever may be in it. There is also nothing, in such a straightforward picture, which demands that the infinite should itself be in any way exhaustive; the worlds which arise out of its bosom are themselves infinite in number, yet there remains always an infinitude of *other* stuff around them, and outside of them.

What we have called a straightforward picture of the infinite is not, however, one that western thought has found easy to hold. While it may not involve anything intrinsically difficult, and while the only real questions connected with it may be those concerning its precise implications and applications, it has none the less always seemed to abound in contradictions, and to render absurd and self-contradictory any idea in which it could be shown to be present. To speak of it seems to involve exhausting the inexhaustible, than which nothing more absurd could be conceived; it also gives difficulty in that, without being accessible to our imagination, it lacks the happy circumscribability which would render it acceptable to our thought. Hence there has arisen, at an early stage of thinking, a tradition which has tried to substitute for the infinite what we may call the variable finite, the finite which can always be pushed a stage further, without ever achieving *all* the stages or values of which it is capable.

It is this sort of variable finite, always pushing out beyond every bounded unit, or breaking out within it, which confronts us in the Platonic-Pythagorean Unlimited, or, as it was finally called, the Great and Small. As such it is the irrational, evil, essentially formless or flowing principle, which has to be dominated by 'the One' or 'the Limit' in order to give rise to everything intelligible or good. It is the indefinite element in the ideal world, which calls for a first bounding by the One, in order to give rise to that whole range of precise, quantitative patterns, with which the Platonic forms were ultimately identified. It is also the indefinite element in the world of the senses, whose bounding by precise, numerical ratios give rise to whatever is healthful, strong, musical or visibly excellent. In itself, however, it admits only of a contradictious characterization; it is the 'Others', the Great and Small, without any principle of unity or definition in itself. As soon as one seizes a part of it, and attempts to treat it as something definite and single, it will at once begin to evanesce into other parts, and these into other parts without end. And as soon as one imagines it as endowed with beginning, middle and end, one will

148

THE NOTION OF INFINITY

find another beginning emerging before the first beginning, another end emerging after the first end, and another truer middle showing itself within the first middle. I need here only refer to the superb seventh hypothesis of the Platonic *Parmenides* for a full account of the tantalizing and elusive behaviour of the Platonic infinite, whose complex, contradictious characterization is only equalled by the still more complex and contradictious characterization of his indefinite, super-essential One or Good.

The Platonic mysticism passes away in the Aristotelian treatment of the infinite, but the essential features of the Platonic treatment remain. The infinite only exists *after a fashion*; after another fashion it does not exist at all. It never exists in the sense that we ever actually *have* an infinitely large number of parts or elements of anything, nor anything which exceeds all things of limited bigness in its number or its size. The presence of infinity in a field is always something facultative; it means that we *can* go on stretching sizes and numbers in that field as much and as far as we like, that we can always go outside of any given size or number to the one lying beyond it. Whatever else may be true of this infinite, it is wholly incompatible with totality; for something to be infinite means that one *never* can have all of it, only more and more of it. For Aristotle as for Quine it simply makes no sense to speak of an infinite magnitude in connection with our whole cosmos; infinite magnitude applies at best to the *potential* divisibility of a spatial stretch or of a temporal lapse, or to the endless potential augmentation of temporal lapses or numerical aggregates. Even this potential being of the infinite is, however, a rather queer sort of potentiality, for it is not a potentiality that can *ever* be translated into the actual.

The Aristotelian treatment of the infinite is in effect a reductive treatment; our words suggest that infinity is a straightforward qualification of certain actual magnitudes, but those words only really make sense, if we can give them some complex and less obvious restatement. It is this reductive treatment of the infinite which has, in the main, prevailed in post-Renaissance thought. It prevails in Locke when he speaks of our idea of the infinite as an 'endless growing idea', and when he denies that we ever have a positive and distinct idea of infinite magnitude. It prevails in Kant when he circumvents his antinomies by holding that, while there may very well be a *regressus in indefinitum* from one state to previous states, or from a whole to its parts, or from an event to its prior conditions, there

149

LANGUAGE, MIND AND VALUE

cannot ever really be a *regressus in infinitum* which covers all the conditions or all the presuppositions of some actual stage of affairs. It also prevails in Hegel when he cries down his so-called 'bad infinite' as the mere would-be negation of the finite, which latter always crops up again and again, and is never truly superseded; it prevails as much when he cries up the virtues of his 'true infinite', which is merely his bad infinite grown staid and self-complacent, inasmuch as it has come to realize that there can be no other outcome of its whole vain effort at self-transcendence, but itself and itself alone. Nor is it possible to find any straightforward, wholehearted espousal of the infinite in either Leibniz or Spinoza. Spinoza, e.g., altered the whole meaning of infinity by his identification of it with all-embracing, exhaustive *totality*, which is also indivisible unity.

The first attempt to give a non-reductive account of the infinite, in harmony with what our untutored verbal instincts might lead us to put forward, is to be found in the work of Bolzano, and, more fully and finally, in the work of Cantor. The latter managed to show that we can talk consistently about infinity, without needing to translate our talk into talk about the variable finite. He disposed effectively of the many apparent contradictions in straightforward accounts of the infinite which had made such translations seem necessary. He made short work of the supposed contradictions involved in exhausting the inexhaustible, or in completing the everlastingly incomplete, for he showed that while it would be self-contradictory to speak of exhausting an infinite series or assemblage, in the sense of finding some last term to it, yet the very fact that we cannot *thus* exhaust it, means also that we can and do exhaust it in another manner. For if we ask what the number may be of the whole set of terms in some series lacking a final term—and it would be highly unnatural to say that such an assemblage had no number at all—we should be forced to say that it was a number different from, and exceeding the number of any set reachable in the ordered running through of such a class or series. It would be different from any such number, for the very reason that no instance of it could be reached in any such ordered running through, and it would exceed any such reachable number in that a group or whole having this new sort of number would contain parts exemplifying all previous ordinary numbers, while none of these latter would contain parts which exemplified *it*. It is, in short, the number *of* an ordered progression lacking a final term, but it isn't a number anywhere to be found *in* such an ordered progression. It

THE NOTION OF INFINITY

may therefore be said to lie outside of, and beyond the numbers reached in our advance along a progression which lacks a final term, and it may also be called the limit towards which such a series perpetually aspires. But in another sense it does not really lie outside of the whole of such a progressive series for, in having the whole of that series, one automatically *has* an instance of the number in question. One cannot arrive at such a number by the steady stepwise addition of units which Cantor called his *first* principle of the formation of numbers, but one can and does arrive at it by considering *all* the terms reached by such a stepwise procedure, which Cantor called his *second* principle of the formation of numbers.

At the new conceptual level thus attained, the paradoxes attending our former conceptions of the infinite become the truisms stating its essential properties. It becomes plain that an infinite whole can't be increased or reduced by the addition or subtraction of a unit, nor yet of a finite number of such units; it becomes plain, too, that an infinite whole can have *infinite* parts added to it, or taken away from it, while remaining just as large as ever. The most paradoxical property of an infinite whole, that it is possible to take parts from it, which are just as infinite as itself, and which are therefore (on a natural interpretation) equal to itself, was in fact adopted by Dedekind as the defining property of an infinite assemblage. The work of Cantor took away the awe and mystery of the infinite; he taught us to do sums with it; he showed in fact, that there was nothing difficult about it. He himself seemed to enjoy the same sort of hob-nobbing acquaintance with the infinite that some of his Jewish forbears had with the Ancient of Days. And not only did he acquaint us with a single infinite, but he brought into our ken a whole family of infinites, each living above the next on an entirely different floor of the family mansion. In all this he was but developing and giving sense to a notion put forward in a mistaken form by Bolzano: that it is possible for one infinite aggregate to be larger than another.

Hardly, however, had the infinite thus begun to be brought into focus, than the whole picture of it was again blurred. This new blurring was not connected with supposed contradictions in the notion of infinity, but with the whole difficulty of being sure that anything really *was* infinite, or even that we could be clear in our minds what it would be like for something *to be* infinite. Russell, who had done so much to disseminate Cantor's notions, confused them by his extensional account of number, according to which numbers

LANGUAGE, MIND AND VALUE

were to be identified with sets of classes which could be brought into one-one correlation with some chosen class. On such an account it became doubtful, not merely whether the notion of the infinite had an application, but even whether it had a distinguishable content. For unless there were at least *one* actual assemblage in our world having infinitely many members, the class of classes, membership of which would be tantamount to being of such an infinite number, would be simply null, and to be infinite in number would be quite the same as being both five and six in number, or as being anything else which has no application whatever.

At first Russell tried to prove that there *were* certain infinite assemblages, but most of his proofs involved the lumping together of things best treated as of radically different type or level, and so not properly mentionable in a single breath. We were therefore obliged to *assume* the existence of such infinite classes, in order that the whole ordered, mathematical system could be rounded off and made to work. Russell further cast doubt on our power to carry out certain quite commonplace operations upon infinite aggregates; we could not find the product of the numbers of such aggregates, unless we could select terms from them according to a definite and discoverable principle, and it wasn't clear that there always would be such a definite principle. The whole set of possible rearrangements of finite and transfinite series, to which Cantor had assigned numbers of his 'second class', had then to be thrown back into a conceptual melting pot, since it was quite doubtful whether there always would be rules or principles on which such rearrangements could be carried out.

The difficulties raised by Russell were carried a stage further by the verificationists and the intuitionists. For them the infinite had no meaning at all except where there was a rule or principle guiding us through its labyrinth. An assemblage such as that of the points of space, or that of all real numbers, to which no definite principle of arrangement corresponded, should not be said to be infinite in number. Nor would they see sense in a mathematical question to which no *general* method of solution corresponded; a problem that we could solve only by carrying out an infinite number of steps, or by running through an infinity of cases, could not, on their ruling, be mathematically significant. To ask whether there are or are not three successive sevens in the development of π, is to pose a wholly senseless inquiry, even if, embarrassingly, it suddenly acquires significance when someone hits on an instance which verifies it. Here we are

THE NOTION OF INFINITY

back, after a long series of unprofitable windings, at the facultative infinite or variable finite of Aristotle; the infinite can be said to exist only so far as we can apply a rule, or can carry out a procedure, over and over again without let or hindrance; it never exists as something actual and complete, to which our precise route of approach, whether haphazard or systematic, must be indifferent.

The last stage in this gradual obscuration of the infinite is to be found in the interesting article of Quine and Goodman entitled 'Steps toward a Constructive Nominalism'.[1] Having tried at first to prove the existence of certain infinite classes, by methods which involved the relaxation of type-restrictions, and having found such methods treacherous and questionable, Quine was led to conceive a general loathing for the infinite, which was part and parcel of his wider disgust for 'entities of higher order'. For Quine it became supremely dangerous to depart in the smallest degree from a purely syncategorematic or contextual use of predicative expressions, so as to make them even *appear* to be names of peculiar entities. This deep danger existed, to Quine's fine perceptions, even when we merely spoke in *general* fashion about some determination of objects, when we said that an object was of *a certain* shade of brown, or that it would be beautiful *whatever* its colour. To have variables for any sort of determination is to hypostatize such determinations. In a style of speech thus puritanically restricted, there can of course be small room for that freely ranging talk about *all* numbers having certain properties, or about *some* number having a certain property, in which classical arithmetic principally consists; a formula like $(n)(n + n = 2n)$ will at best be a set of meaningless marks from which meaningful formulae can be derived by appropriate substitution and translation. There can, in such a linguistic scheme, be little place for the infinite, whose very definition normally involves the mention of *all* finite or ordinary numbers.

There is yet another reason for Quine's thoroughgoing renunciation of the infinite. He takes with extraordinary seriousness all that the physicists have told us about the limited divisibility of natural things and processes, or about the limited extent of all space or all time. In a cosmos severely limited as our own is thought to be, we can, according to Quine, only manage to *talk* about infinite aggregates in so far as we suppose the existence somewhere of an infinite number of abstract objects, in addition to that finite number of

[1] *Journal of Symbolic Logic*, vol. XII, pp. 105–22.

LANGUAGE, MIND AND VALUE

concrete objects actually present in our cosmos. Nor can we hope to translate statements about the infinitely large, or even about what is merely *very* large, into long conjunctions, or long sets of statements about their individual components. Not only would this take us too long, but we could not actually find the *room* in our world for such statements or sets of statements. Logicians, already so much harassed and badgered, must now submit to yet further restrictions; their notions must not be so many as to require the symbolic service of more than the total number of objects, or empty spaces in our universe. Nor must their sentences ever be so long as to be incapable of being inscribed within our cosmic boundaries; there is no place at all for that indefinite concatenation of expressions into ever longer expressions which is both demanded and permitted in classical syntax. It seems plain that, by a long and circuitous route, we have ended up in a finitism which surpasses even that of Aristotle in its narrow rigour.

II

I have now hurried over the whole historical terrain of thought about the infinite; I descend into the field to make certain personal observations. Some of these are expressions of my own persuasion or intuition, for which I can indeed give reasons, but never wholly adequate or convincing ones. But if Quine and others can be permitted their intuitions, which may exact from them such important sacrifices as that of all abstract objects and with them the infinite, I too may be allowed my own internal promptings, which may lead me to jettison much accepted doctrine.

The first point that I wish to make is that I think that the work of Cantor, and that of his many developers and elucidators, has effectively removed all the serious contradictions in our notion of the actual infinite. We are now past the point at which we could find it absurd to speak about the *whole* of some series lacking a final term, or to say that its number exceeds the numbers that can be reached from zero by a stepwise increase by unity. We are also past the point at which we find it shocking to say that a whole can at times be equal to its proper part, or that it may be impossible at times to reduce or increase a whole by the subtraction or addition of a unit. All such statements obviously involve new and stretched uses of the terms 'whole', 'part', 'number', 'equal' and so forth, and it would be open

154

THE NOTION OF INFINITY

to a determined finitist to deny them application beyond the realm of countable, and therefore finite aggregates. But if we do decide so to employ them, the work of Cantor shows that we can do so without serious contradiction, and without coming into conflict with our former principles, as long as we allow these latter to apply only to things finite. What we still must show is that this whole new extension and enrichment of our talk is in any way profitable, and that we genuinely have something in mind when we round off our language in this manner.

The second point I wish to make is that I don't think we have the smallest reason for thinking that there *is* some actual set of things in our world which is infinitely numerous. There may be such a set, but again there may not. I find no obscurity in the notion that there should be physically minimal objects and happenings in our world, any more than I find it obscure that there should be minimal portions of *experienced* space and time; on such a supposition sets of parts of any finite thing or happening will be finite, not infinite in number. I also find no difficulty in believing that our world may have that closed, re-entrant structure, and that consequent finite extent, with which modern physics credits it. But I do not think the question whether the things in our world are finite or infinite in number, is of any philosophical importance whatever; the philosopher has to ask what it would be for things *to be* infinite in number, and what might be the consequences and the possible applications of this notion, not whether it *has* any actual applications. Philosophers who ignore these questions, because they allow themselves to be bemused by the latest findings of the physicists, are in no better case than their predecessors, who let all their analyses be distorted by the findings of the evolutionary biologists.

This brings me to my third obvious, but important point; that what we mean by infinity, or by any other numerical concept, can never be bound up with the actual contents of our world, nor affected by their numbers, their orderings or the relational bonds that connect them. Being three in number, or being infinitely numerous, would be exactly what they now are, and would carry with them the same body of implied properties, whether our world contained many or few objects, and however these might be connected or varied.

This means that there is something radically unsatisfactory and misleading in an extensional account of number on the lines put forward by Russell; classes or sets may in some sense be the *subjects*

155

LANGUAGE, MIND AND VALUE

of number, but we cannot profitably identify numbers with sets, or with sets of sets of objects that are anywhere present in our world. Though the application of numbers may be to the most purely extensional aspect of things—we may say, with Hegel, to things in their mere otherness and mutual externality—yet it is none the less impossible to talk of them satisfactorily except in an intensional idiom.

Russell maintained that his extensional treatment had the great merit of making the existence of numbers indubitable; the class of trios certainly existed if we could but find a single instance of three objects, whereas the property of being three in number was a metaphysical or Platonic entity, which it was hard for us to lay hold of or to track down. He therefore identified each number with what we should ordinarily call the class of its instances, instances not, however, brought together by virtue of showing forth a common kind or character, but solely by virtue of the possibility of pairing their members, one for one, with the members of other similar instances, a procedure which succeeded, surprisingly, in sorting them out into mutually exclusive classes, while yet involving nothing peculiar in the case of each such class.

But this ingenious analysis has the monstrous consequence that if our world contained no more than 728 objects—and we refused to augment their numbers either by the free manufacture of fictions, or by the introduction of objects from higher levels of discourse—all numbers above 728 would become confounded in a common nothingness, and it would be quite the same to say that certain things were 728, or 1029, or infinite in number. And we could only talk significantly about things having certain high or transfinite numbers, if there *were* things actually exemplifying the numbers in question, a thing which, in the case of the infinite, we could never know or prove. Here we have the old Anselmian situation of essence entailing existence, with the queer added corollary that non-existence entails the annihilation of essence. If this sort of analysis is the only way to steer clear of the difficulties of a metaphysical Platonism, then it is possible to evade such difficulties at too great a price.

The sort of treatment that we call 'intensional' will not, however, profit us much, unless the things said about the infinite, or about other numbers taken in intension, differ profoundly from the things said about the infinite, and about other numbers taken in extension. We cannot bring out the full difference between an intensional and a purely extensional treatment of some subject-matter without pointing

156

THE NOTION OF INFINITY

to *modal* differences; intensional accounts cover what *could* be the case even in circumstances remote from the actual, whereas extensional treatment confine themselves to what actually is the case. Now it is plain that we should not hesitate to apply any of our notions of number to things not in any way actual; there were seven recognized sages in antiquity and four recognized cardinal virtues, but there might very well have been four sages and seven virtues. We should even go farther and say that *being a recognized sage* would maintain its difference from *being a recognized cardinal virtue* even if there were no recognized sages or virtues, and no things at all which were collectively four or seven.

If we like, in this connection, to make use of the highly confusing term 'existence', then we may say that the existence-conditions of things taken in intension differ profoundly from the existence-conditions of things taken in extension; a collection of things may be said to exist when there are at least two or (by a stretch of charity) a single object in that set, whereas a *kind* of thing may be said to exist even when it is only *possible* for there to be things of that sort. It will not, in short, be actual embodiment, nor yet the mere significance of its verbal counterpart, which will constitute existence for an attribute; its existence will consist in the logically possible existence of its instances. Such a manner of speech is, in fact, the one we most frequently adopt; we do not say that a set of salmon-pink objects exists unless there actually are objects of this colour, whereas we should not hesitate to say that there *was* a shade of colour called salmon-pink, if it were merely possible that there should be objects of that shade. The only axiom of infinity that can therefore be tolerated in a philosophical account of number is one which defines the significance, and which asserts the possibility, that certain things should (in their collective capacity) be infinite in number. This is the only sense in which the whole series of natural numbers can be said to exist, and it is in this sense, therefore, that there can be transfinite numbers beyond them.

The intensional treatment we are recommending may be Platonic in that it allows us to speak of 'being infinite in number' just as it allows us to speak of 'being red in colour', but it need not be Platonic in some dubious or noxious sense. To speak in this manner is not really to suppose that, in addition to the ordinary objects in our world, there are also an indefinite number of extraordinary objects. To be red or to be infinitely numerous are not, properly speaking, entities, nor are the words which express them, properly speaking, names. They are, if one so likes to put it, merely sorts of things, of which sorts things may, in their individual or their collective capacity, be. Their verbal expressions merely tell us what sort of thing we have before us, and whether of the same, or of a different sort from other things.

We may here briefly advert to Quine's queer doctrine that to speak *generally* of the character of some object is to commit ourselves to an unwarrantable ontology, that quantification necessarily goes hand in hand with reification. Because the statement 'Some men are amorous' can, with a certain amount of creaking, be transformed into the statement 'There are amorous men', it is therefore assumed that any and every use of 'some', 'every', 'a certain' 'any' and so forth, must necessarily involve an assumption of existence, and that not in an innocent and translatable, but in some dubious and noxious sense. There is only confusion in this doctrine. A man who says that something is of some colour or other is not reifying colours, any more than a man who says that he will find his way *somehow* to London need be reifying manners. Nor is one practising reification if one defines *being infinite in number* in terms of having proper parts which are of *every* natural number, and if one then goes on to define the latter in some form of the accepted rigmarole which amounts to saying that they are the total progeny which can be generated out of *being nought in number*, through repeated fecundation of this notion and of its offspring, by the relation of *being one more in number*.

We may note further that not only are the phrases 'being three in number' or 'being infinitely numerous' not necessarily to be taken as names of peculiar entities; it is not even necessary to take them as *applying* to such entities. We may here repudiate Frege's doctrine that it is to class-concepts alone that numerical predicates can be properly said to pertain, that it is *being a recognized sage in antiquity* that is seven in number, and not Thales and his confrères. This view is mistaken for the double reason that, if there is a sense in which *being an ancient sage* can have number, then it will be one in number and not seven, and also because the exemplification of number by a set of things does not at all depend upon their being of a common sort of character. Of *some* sort each of a number of things must undoubtedly be, since it is only as exemplifying a sort that a thing can be said to be a thing at all, but it is by no means necessary that the things which collectively are of a given number should be homo-

158

THE NOTION OF INFINITY

geneous rather than heterogeneous. My arm, your toothbrush and Quavam es Sultaneh are three in number, and they are as much three in number as are the three Norns or the three Persons of the Trinity, but it is mere artificiality to demand that they should therefore be reduced to some common denomination. It is further merely *our* difficulty that we cannot refer to things having certain large or transfinite numbers, except as being all the cases of a common sort or kind.

We may note, further, that we have no need to say that it is to classes or sets that numbers pertain, if by 'classes' or 'sets' are meant, not things in the plural, but mysterious higher-order compartments into which things may be herded or concentrated. Quite obviously it is to *things in the plural* that numbers are normally applicable, even if, in our charity, and for verbal convenience, we also extend this privilege to things taken in the singular, or even to nothing whatever. It is not my pen singly, nor your arm singly, nor Quavam es Sultaneh singly, that is three in number, nor yet any higher-order unity that these objects may form. They are so *collectively* only in the sense that they are so co-operatively; we must not, except for mere verbal convenience, confuse the collective possession of a property by things in the plural, with the non-collective possession of a property by some single entity called a collection. In uttering these forgotten truisms I am not, of course, saying that, in addition to being many, things may not also be multiply many, or multiply multiply many, and so on indefinitely, and that, from the standpoint of such multiplied manifoldness, what is simply manifold may not rightly be treated as unitary. Nor am I casting scorn on any of the convenient, if misleading, devices and distinctions of the logic of classes, for which my respect is immeasurable.

There are, no doubt, perplexing peculiarities in the grammar of numerical statements—the *joint* ownership of numerical predicates is particularly teasing—which suggest a recourse to further reductions. We find it illuminating to hold that numerical predicates 'aren't really predicates at all', any more than existence 'really' is a predicate, or diversity 'really' a relation between objects. To say that something of a certain sort exists is not 'really' to say that this object has a predicate; it is merely to say that one *has* an object of the first sort in question. In the same way to say that an object and an object are diverse, is not 'really' to point to a relation between them, but merely to say that one has *objects*, as distinct from *an* object, to deal with. In much the same way to attribute numbers to objects, is in a sense,

159

LANGUAGE, MIND AND VALUE

merely to give an exact specification of their diversity, to indicate with precision *what* objects we have before us for characterization, without saying *anything* about their kind or character. Quite plainly to say that one has four things before one, is not different from saying that one has something of an unspecified sort before one, and something else of an unspecified sort, and something else of an unspecified sort, and yet again something else of an unspecified sort. And if one possessed a set of co-ordinated pens, such as those with which it was fabled President Roosevelt used to sign cheques under the New Deal, and if the dimensions of our universe allowed such a set of pens to be infinite, rather than finite in number, then it would be perfectly easy to write down a specification of diversity which would amount to the attribution of a transfinite number. All this is brought out clearly in Tarski's illuminating notation, where we express number by special variants of the existential operator, under whose inverted E various numerical subscripts are written. But if numbers are thereby shown 'not really' to be properties, any more than they really can be considered as classes, our treatment of them remains intensional, since their 'existence' will amount to no more than the mere possibility of a certain specified diversity, of which their 'instances' will be actual realizations.

III

We have strayed long and far into the general philosophy of number, a procedure necessitated by the technical barnacles which have been allowed to encrust every inch of the subject; we may now return to the narrower limits of infinity. We have disposed of the general, threshold difficulties which concern the notion, but we have yet to find sufficient motive for framing it, or an adequate guarantee that we can attach more than an empty, syntactical meaning to the terms that seem to stand for it. We have said that the only sense in which the existence of infinite numbers can be philosophically significant, is the sense in which it is logically *possible* for things to be infinitely numerous, in other words, the sense in which it is logically possible for them to be of a number greater than, and different from any that can be elicited out of the directly showable numbers, through repeated use of the notion 'greater by unity'.

We here come face to face with a doctrine that has acquired much

THE NOTION OF INFINITY

recent authority; that modal distinctions merely reflect arbitrary linguistic choices, and that it is *we* who, by determining what we will, or won't, or may say in certain circumstances, also fix the bounds of the necessary and the possible. On such a view it would be more good to replace all ordinary, first-order talk about what might or must or couldn't be the case, by a corresponding metalinguistic set of verbal prescriptions, permissions and prohibitions; our straightforward talk about objects could then be left in extensional purity. On this view it would merely depend on a linguistic fiat whether it was or was not possible for there to be infinitely many objects. This whole approach to modality may, however, be described as unrealistic, if not frivolous. It ignores the fact that our decisions to speak in one way rather than another are by no means arbitrary, but profoundly motivated, and that they depend not merely on personal habit or inclination, but on our deep intercourse with, and repeated turning to, the matter on hand. We may, if we like, say that there is a 'lie of the land' in the realm of essence, just as there undoubtedly is a 'lie of the land' in the realm of existence. This 'lie of the land' never *forces* us to do linguistic road-making or bridge-building in a given manner, but it none the less makes it easier and more 'natural' to proceed in one manner rather than another. It is not unlike Hume's 'gentle force' of association, which while it does not compel us to say one thing to the exclusion of others, none the less sets bounds to our linguistic liberty, and in the end 'everywhere prevails'.

Applying these thoughts in the field of numbers, it would no doubt have been possible for us to have called a halt in our formation of numerical notions after the number Ten (as Plato and the Pythagoreans are reported to have done); we could then have refused to predicate number of the Apostles, or of the States of the American Union. Such a decision would, however, be arbitrary in a vicious sense; it would have involved a wanton refusal, not based on differences in the material on hand, to carry on with a certain general procedure. We are subject to a rational obligation, not at all minatory and coercive, but insistently, if mildly hortatory, which urges us always to leave room in our thought and language for sets of things exemplifying an unending series of natural numbers, each arising out of its predecessor when an aggregate is increased by a unit. And being obliged to admit all these natural numbers, we are also obliged to admit the possibility of aggregates which have *parts* such that *each* of the natural numbers will be exemplified in *some* of such parts, and

LANGUAGE, MIND AND VALUE

which can't therefore themselves be of *any* of the ordinary natural numbers. And since it would be highly unnatural to say that they weren't of any number at all, we are urged to say that they are of a number different from, and greater than, any of the natural numbers.

We might indeed come to admit the existence of such transfinite numbers by mere reflection on the existence of the ordinary natural number series; this latter series exists in the only sense in which numbers can be said to exist at all, and hence the former also exists, even if at a higher level of discourse, as the number *of* the latter. (We may then be led, by precisely similar considerations, to concede numbers to aggregates of aggregates, or to aggregates of ordered aggregates, much more intricately organized than are simple progressions; we shall then also be led, by Cantor's arguments, to accord other, higher kinds of infinite number to such aggregates.) In all this process of extending our notions, we might stop short where we wished, but it would be highly unnatural to stop short anywhere. We were, in a sense, committed to the whole indefinitely ascending hierarchy, on the occasion when we first passed in thought or experience from a unit to a couple, or from a couple to a triad. Those who, like Quine, seek to check the natural increase of the numerical population so as never to exceed the resources of our actual universe, commit a fault worse than that strangulation of births condemned by the Church. They commit the fault practised by all unjust judges and idolaters since the beginning of the world: that of undue deference to the powers that be.

We have not, however, given a satisfactory justification of our introduction of the infinite, as long as it merely serves as some great gilt cupola rounding off a conceptual edifice, not itself made of solid materials nor resting on solid underpinning, so as to permit of circumambulation or closer examination. The standing objection to the infinite is, after all, that it is impossible to produce an instance of it, as one can very well produce instances of lesser numbers. Even if such an instance were forthcoming, we could never be sure that it *was* infinite; we should need all time to correlate its members, one for one, with the finite inductive numerals, and should, therefore, have neither occasion nor need to speak of a number lying beyond all natural numbers. These considerations, as well as a large number of fallacious ones, have led philosophers in all ages to attempt reductive analyses of the infinite in terms of the variable finite, and to condemn other ways of speaking as metaphysical *flatus vocis*.

THE NOTION OF INFINITY

Against all such tendencies and difficulties I should like to take a stand; I want to maintain, on grounds that are themselves intuitive, that though the infinite may be for us no more than a concept, it might also very well have been an intuition, that it is, in fact, no more than accidental infirmity that we have to grope and gesture after it as we actually do. I also wish to maintain that our difficulty in exhibiting the infinite isn't really the difficulty of exhibiting something quite unlike anything we have ever seen and known; in a sense, its exhibition would involve nothing novel, and we know exactly what it would be like. It is, in fact, no more inaccessible to imagination or sense-perception than any other highly complex object or property. We may here point out that not all instances of number are known for what they are by that step-by-step procedure known as counting; there are many lower degrees of number that can be recognized and exhibited *non*-successively. We can see at a glance, and can plainly recognize, such inferior grades of number as unity, duality, triplicity and so forth; shepherds, company commanders and other practised persons carry this sort of immediate discrimination much farther. We can also sometimes see at a glance how a certain quartet is made up out of two couples, or how a group of eight consists of parts which are respectively five and three in number. What then is the fundamental difficulty in supposing that such a non-counting, non-successive apprehension of number might not be indefinitely extended, so that one might see at a glance how *each* of the natural numbers was exemplified in *some* part of an assemblage before us, and could therefore also recognize at a glance the presence of that first simple infinity which sums up them all? I can see no difficulty in the supposition.

It is plain, further, that, even where our apprehension of number *is* successive, it may none the less fall wholly within the present (which won't deserve any qualification of 'specious', since it is the only present we can understand or know). What then is the difficulty in supposing that our present faculties of time-discrimination might be so indefinitely refined and sharpened, as to take in, within the limits of the present, one of those infinitely numerous, indefinitely diminishing Zenonian series, to which our present poor capacities give an air of paradox and absurdity? And what further difficulty could there be in supposing that our sense of what is actual and present might not be so infinitely extended, as *never* to break up into any succession of disjoined phases, only linked to each other by

163

LANGUAGE, MIND AND VALUE

memory or anticipation? If this were the case, we might certainly enjoy an unending counting apprehension, which would also be, throughout its *undivided* extent, an apprehension of the actual infinite. If anyone doubts whether I really know what I mean by the alternatives I am putting forward, I confess I can't convince him that I I do know it; I am in the position of Hume when he tells us that he knows what a certain intermediate shade of grey is like, of which he cannot produce an instance. And if it be argued that I *cannot* know what I mean since I cannot *illustrate* this meaning, then I should answer that the fact that I *do* know what I mean shows that power to illustrate is not necessary for such knowledge.

I shall conclude my contribution by saying that I see no difficulty, apart from the purely human difficulties I have mentioned, in the making of an infinite number of arbitrary selections from some aggregate before us, or in the carrying out of an infinite set of arbitrary pairings among the terms of two such aggregates. There can therefore be no reason, apart from human infirmity, why we should not be able to refer to some infinite set of objects except as being of a common sort or kind, or why we should not be able to predicate equality between two such aggregates except by virtue of a specifiable one-one relation among their members. Nor is there any but an accidental human reason why we should not be able to order a transfinite aggregate except by means of a specifiable serial relation. The bearing of all this on the Theorem of Zermelo, on the Multiplicative Axiom, and on the equality or inequality of certain transfinite numbers, may be left to others more competent to determine. But I see no reason why an infinite aggregate, arranged as are the points in the continuum, or consisting of all the series belonging to Cantor's second class, should not, like some simply infinite progression, become a direct object of intuitive apprehension. I also have no reason to doubt that it might be perfectly possible to carry out in a single flash of vision, some calculation involving a transfinite number of steps, and that it would then be possible to write the result down by means of an infinite series of simultaneously functioning pens. It would then be quite definite whether there were or were not three successive sevens in the development of π, and the Law of Excluded Middle would apply in *this* field without any restriction whatever.

IX

THE JUSTIFICATION OF ATTITUDES[1]
(1954)

I

I AM going this evening to discuss a subject of some obscurity: the sense in which, as we say, people are more or less *justified* in having attitudes of certain sorts and of certain degrees of intensity towards objects and situations of certain sorts, and in certain typical constellations of circumstances. It is obvious that talk of this sort is widespread and well-established: we have no hesitation in saying that someone is showing a thoroughly warranted attitude of amazement or anger or shame in a certain situation, or that he is manifesting such an attitude in a proper and suitable degree, whereas, in other cases, we have no hesitation in finding an attitude bizarre, uncalled for, out of place, unwarranted, or at least of quite an inappropriate quality or intensity. Our use of such pejorative and laudatory qualifications is by no means confined to attitudes of a pretentious cast, in which rational reflection plays a considerable part, and which are informed by various lofty aspirations. It may be possible to be justified or unjustified in a deliberate decision, a moral valuation or a critical aesthetic preference, but it is just as possible to be justified or unjustified in a transient spasm of envy, of jealousy, of vindictive wrath or of tremulous self-abasement. Ordinary speech undoubtedly recognizes a propriety and a validity in our emotional and other attitudes which has seemed very questionable to philosophers: our task this evening is to look into our usage on this point, and see whether ordinary speech may not have a better justification for talking about the justification of attitudes than many philosophers have supposed.

[1] Based on papers given at the Cambridge Moral Sciences Club and at University College, London. Published in *Mind*, January 1954.

LANGUAGE, MIND AND VALUE

The theme I am going to discuss is one that has interested me ever since I read Brentano's *Vom Ursprung sittlicher Erkenntnis*, a work which first put forward the doctrine of an inner moment of *Berechtigung* in our emotional attitudes, something analogous to, but different from the *Evidenz* that informs certain of our judgements. It is also a doctrine interestingly developed in Meinong's neglected theory of emotional presentation, as in Scheler's elaborate emotional *a priori* or 'logic of the heart', which builds a huge structure upon an exciting phrase of Pascal's. From thence it has spread into an underworld of influential but badly written books, which I shall not here try to enumerate. But my own poor attempts to contribute to this 'logic of the heart' seem to have fallen on to a singularly stony and unreceptive soil: I don't seem to have convinced anyone that there is something really worth while and illuminating to be said on the matter. I therefore return to the attack, though I shall deal with my topic in a rather different manner than heretofore.

II

Before discussing the appropriateness of attitudes, I shall say something about the bare bones of my subject, the degree of formal complexity that it involves. It is plain that we normally have *three* things to inquire into in discussing the appropriateness of an attitude, the *sort* of attitude under consideration, in which I wish to include both its characteristic pattern or make-up, and also its intensity, the *object* or *objects* of our attitude, the sort of things with which it is concerned or upon which it discharges itself, and lastly the whole *background of circumstances* in which an attitude arises, whether this be actual and present, or merely imagined and foreshadowed. It seems clear that we sometimes do recognize cases of appropriateness in attitude which have a degree of logical complexity less than this. Thus the Stoics and many other detached persons have held that there was some attitude of apathy or serene good cheer or what not, which is *always* appropriate whatever our object, and whatever the circumstances; this means that the attitude in question is justifiable *per se*, without regard to anything external. In the same way, some have held that we ought to adopt *some* attitude, it does not matter what, towards certain important objects: everything can be tolerated except that Laodicean mean which is really the absence of any attitude at all. And

166

THE JUSTIFICATION OF ATTITUDES

many would hold, of course, that there are attitudes to certain solemn duties, or to certain moral enormities, which are always justifiable or unjustifiable, without *any* consideration of circumstances. But it seems plain that the instances we have adduced, if they are genuine instances at all, are all either eccentric or degenerate: the justifications that we normally recognize are always justifications of attitudes more or less definite in type and intensity, towards objects more or less definite in character, in circumstances similarly definite.

We may note, further, that the justifications we acknowledge are themselves capable of degree: they have an upper limit in *complete justification*, from which they may fall short in a large number of distinct degrees. And we may note, further, that there is an ambiguity in the word 'unjustified' which connotes such falling short: it may be merely *privative* in meaning, pointing to some absence or partial absence of positive justification, or it may, on the other hand, express a sort of *counter*-justification or justification in reverse. An attitude of collapsing mirth will be unjustified in the former sense by the fact that it is spring and that I am walking agreeably by the Cam: it will be unjustified in the latter sense by the fact that I find myself in Westminster Abbey, and that the body of some sainted king is the main object in the proceedings.

All this rehearsal of mere grammar is too Aristotelian and too Meinongian to be further pursued: we must try to say something about the analysis of the factors involved in such justificatory situations. In regard to attitudes, we accept an analysis which identifies them, in part at least, with certain more or less definite *policies of action*, policies which could, for instance, be characterized as policies of withdrawal, of self-obliteration, of aggressive lashing out, of nauseated expulsion, of tranquil basking, or luxuriant gloating, of prurient exploration, of limp breakdown and so forth, and which cover in their range of expression a vast number of fully fledged performances, as well as countless variously truncated symbolic gestures.

This does not mean that the attitudes in question may not be *introspectively* as well as extraspectively evident, for those about to behave in any out of a certain range of possible ways, are also, for the most part, ready for the varied experiences which make up the inner or felt side of such behaviour. The readiness for such experiences, as well as the readiness for certain sorts of action, give meaning to the reports that they then utter. The same words 'I am

LANGUAGE, MIND AND VALUE

furious' are at once a betrayal of our readiness for certain smashing and retaliatory acts and gestures, as well as of our readiness for the varied experiences which are what we feel like when such acts and gestures are executed. The only thing I am flatly denying, as a supposition profitless and unintelligible, is the doctrine that there are certain unanalysable nuances of inner mood corresponding to our various attitudinal names. I repudiate this because it makes nonsense of the whole connection between attitudes as we feel them, and attitudes as they show themselves in action, which has then to be treated either as an extraordinary empirical accident, or as yet another *ad hoc* case of the synthetic *a priori*. I repudiate it also, because it is false to the whole range of our normal introspective diction, in which a man spontaneously describes his attitude in such words as: 'I felt ready to burst', 'I felt ready to collapse', 'ready to swear', and so forth.

If we thus connect attitudes, in part at least, with peculiar active readinesses, we may pass on to that entirely traditional conception of their relation to their objects which looks upon this relation as *causal*, the object in its setting of circumstances being that which provokes, occasions or arouses some attitude in us. To this we must add the obvious emendation that it isn't really the object as such, which may be remote, inaccessible or even non-existent, but rather our own thought of, or belief in, such an object which evokes the given attitude. It will, however, be plain, on reflection, that causation alone isn't sufficient to explain a relation of genuine *concern* with an object: otherwise the mere fact that my wife has annoyed me at breakfast, and that I vent my wrath on an unoffending student, will mean that my wrath is in this case directed to my wife. The relation of concern between attitude and object is in no sense mystical or hard to understand: it involves no more than that the actions for which we are prepared, and for which we feel ourselves prepared, are all actions *physically* bound up with a certain object. Thus my passionate love for you is a readiness for embraces and caresses to be lavished, not on dogs or mistresses or old furniture or saintly relics, but on you, it is a readiness for protective poses or clinging poses or mastering poses or surrendering poses, not connected promiscuously with persons in general, but exclusively with you. In the same way the attitude expressed by 'What couldn't I do to a Worthington' (or 'a beefsteak', or 'a brace of partridges' or 'an Abyssinian village') is not at all mysteriously connected with its object. There is in fact no problem more completely gratuitous than the one somewhere raised

168

THE JUSTIFICATION OF ATTITUDES

by Professor Broad, as to how, if we are thinking of two objects simultaneously, and experiencing distinct attitudes to each of them, we can be at all sure which attitude is directed to what object, that we are not perhaps really pitying a torturer and condemning his victim when we seem to ourselves to be doing the opposite. If there is any exposure of the utter inadequacy of the inner-quality theory of attitudes, it lies in the sort of example we have cited.

III

So far there is little in our account of the relation of attitudes to their objects and objective conditions, which leaves scope for the notion of a justifiability or an appropriateness of such attitudes. The mere fact that a policy is excited or modified by our thought of certain things and circumstances, and that this policy itself issues in acts physically bound up with such objects, will not give sense to the assertion that the policy in question was *justified* by the character of its objects and circumstances, or that it was *appropriate* to them. At best we could predicate non-justification of an attitude in a derivative sense, if the attitude was founded on false opinion, on some mistaken view of its object. If I love you for your kindness, purity and personal fondness for me, and you turn out to be hard of heart, libidinous and incapable of personal attachment, then my love and devotion will be to this extent unjustified, that they are founded on false assumptions: if I choose, however, to love you for your Dolores-like qualities, there seems no plain sense in which such a love can be unjustified. The justification we are considering is in fact only a justification in so far as the *real* state of things is taken into account: what we should *like* to give a sense to is a justification for loving people who *seem* to us kind, pure and fond of us, not for the mere belief that people really *have* the properties that determine us to love them.

So far as we can see, such a justification is not at all easy to come by, unless our statement that a certain attitude is justified is merely an expression of a further attitude of recommendation or sponsorship which is directed to the first attitude. Doubtless there are occasions on which this is all there is to the matter, but these are not the cases we are now considering. It would not even seem, *prima facie*, that men uniformly have similar attitudes to the same objects in the same circumstances, and much less that they *must* do so. We could, with

LANGUAGE, MIND AND VALUE

a little effort, follow Francis Galton, and attach our emotions to the most ludicrously inappropriate objects: we could learn to sweat with fear before a horse, or to direct our anger to things bald or snub-nosed or viviparous or parallelepipedal; we might teach ourselves to feel guilt whenever we blew our noses or whenever anyone else did so. Any sentiment could thus come to be attached to any object, and the whole issue of rationality or justifiability would become a wholly confused and senseless one.

There is, however, one obvious way in which we can give our attitudes a genuine justifiability or unjustifiability, and that is to make it part of their *definition* or *description* to be concerned with objects presumed to be of certain sorts, and presumed also to be surrounded by certain types of circumstances. We can thus, by a mere exercise of the sovereign rights of Humpty Dumpty, make it part of what we mean by certain attitudinal names that the attitudes named by them should be capable of being excited by the thought of certain objects, and that they should also terminate in acts physically con-nected with such objects: we can also make it part of what we mean by certain attitudes that they should be strengthened or weakened by an idea of, or by a belief in, certain typical circumstances or consequences. All this means that we can make it 'of the essence' of certain sorts of attitudes that they should be amenable to certain kinds of reasons and counter-reasons, by means of which they may be confirmed or tested, whereas other reasons, however weighty and impressive, will not contribute a jot to such justification or testing. We can, if we like, say that certain attitudes involve judgements or supposals, by the truth or falsehood of which they may be validated or invalidated: this would, however, be to recur to that old intel-lectualistic tradition according to which fear always involves a con-fused judgement of danger, desire a confused judgement of profit, and so on. Quite obviously, this would involve a particularly bad use of the much abused word 'judgement', since nothing seems more utterly absent from many of our emotional attitudes than a considered pronouncement on, or assessment of anything.

There would, however, be less objection to our following a reputable Austrian tradition, which says that our attitudes have certain cognitive *presuppositions*, especially if we meant by this latter that they are such as to respond to certain presented features of objects, and to be modified by certain characteristic considerations. The having of such presuppositions would *not* need to be anything actual

170

nor discoverable by introspection: it would show itself rather in the whole pattern of reflection, the whole marshalling of reasons and counter-reasons, by means of which such attitudes would be confirmed or tested. The presuppositions in question could be said to weigh heavily in our attitude according as certain discoveries led to a considerable modification in our policies, or according to the low degree of confidence in a possibility which was sufficient to effect such a modification. If one possibility dimly entertained made a much bigger difference to our policies, than another confidently believed or known, then there might be said to be a much stronger presumption of the former possibility in our attitude than of the latter. Our attitude would always essentially be an attitude *towards* this or that possibility, and it would lose its whole sense and its *raison d'être* if the possibility in question proved really chimerical. It will be noted that we avoid circularity in the account we are giving by speaking of the modifications of *attitudinal policy* effected by the discoveries which correspond to certain cognitive presuppositions: if we said that *the attitude itself* was modified by such discoveries, we should be forgetting that the presuppositions in question were a part of itself.

IV

A question now presents itself which is itself a question of justification: Are we justified in incorporating into what we mean by having certain attitudes, the presence of presuppositions which enable us to attribute justifiability to the attitudes in question? Isn't this merely an elaborate method of cheating? Aren't we trying to give an impression of rigour and objectivity, after everything questionable has been smuggled, Spinoza-fashion, into our axioms and definitions? Isn't our procedure like trying to prove that men can't die, by simply deciding that, if any of our friends or acquaintances does manage to pass away, we shall meet the situation by ruling him not to have been a man? It is true that physics is honeycombed by similar proceedings, which confer the august flavour of the *a priori* on certain purely contingent causal relations, but the bad philosophy thus engendered makes them very much *not* to be recommended.

Stevenson has, in fact, developed two techniques, one that does, and one that does not, incorporate certain objective presuppositions into the meaning of the name for an attitude, in his two distinct

LANGUAGE, MIND AND VALUE

models for the meaning of 'good'. In the one model the use of 'good' merely says that we have a certain policy of approval, and also expresses a wish to communicate such a policy to others: we may then support our utterance with any reasons which actually prove effective in propagating this policy. In the other model, the content of certain reasons becomes part of the meaning of the word 'good', so that it becomes analytically true that it is good to promote the greatest happiness of the greatest number, or to mortify the flesh, or to assimilate oneself to God, and so forth. By practising the incorporation in question one then lends covert support to the ideals of Christianity, or of democracy, or of asceticism, or of some other 'ism': one redirects the attitudes connected with the word 'good' to the peculiar objects one puts in one's definition. Stevenson calls the device embodied in this second model that of 'persuasive definition', and though he *says* that there is nothing discreditable about it, his treatment is such as to attach a definite stigma to it. It creates an illusory appearance of objectivity and validity where no such objectivity is really present: in so doing it sins against those analytic values to which Stevenson and those who think like him are so exclusively devoted. For while it is theoretically just as open to a man to reject some definition of 'good', as to reject any particular reason we bring forward for saying that something is good, yet the whole process of persuasive definition makes such a rejection more difficult: it tricks a man into thinking that he is committed to saying something that he isn't really bound to say at all, and it makes it seem absurd to deny something, which he really can deny with impunity. Is there any good reason why we should thus cover up an arbitrary choice or an empirical connection, by words that give them this flavour of *a priori* necessity?

It seems to me that there are two reasons why we should *sometimes* do this. The first is the fact that there is an extraordinarily close empirical connection between certain typical policies of action and certain features of objects that are their normal excitants. It simply is not the case, for instance, that people are very often in a mood in which they are disposed to lash out indiscriminately at *any* and *every* object, though Malays and maniacs may occasionally do so: people normally lash out only at *provocative* objects, and though it isn't easy, it is by no means impossible to give a comprehensive account of the varied forms of obstruction, resistance, intrusion, persecution, effrontery, baiting, belittling, taunting, flouting and so forth in which

172

THE JUSTIFICATION OF ATTITUDES

provocation may be held to consist. It is *sub specie provocationis* that objects anger us or annoy us, and not merely because they are loud or persistent or unfriendly or immovable or what not.

It is, moreover, an empirical fact that, wherever we are in a state which allows us to be influenced by factual considerations, our lashing out policy does tend to be damped down if it becomes really plain that there is nothing provocative in the thing or situation before us, that no one is really obstructing, resisting, baiting, flouting or lording it over us, whereas it may be reinforced if it becomes plain that someone or something is genuinely being provocative. A creature which, when it does lash out at anything, *never* pays the slightest heed to the sort of thing it is lashing out at, and which never cares whether anything is or is not being provocative, would be a rare bird altogether, and is certainly not one that I myself have met or heard of.

Much the same might be said of our other attitudes: the varied forms of mourning grief, with their policy of prostration, sinking, retardation, indifference to immediate calls, and unpractical dwelling on things past and done for, is connected, almost invariably, with the destruction, removal, degradation or injury of something we have regarded with another attitude known as cherishing affection: I have yet to hear of a man who grieved over something that he did not cherish, or that he didn't imagine to be lowered, or lost, or injured, or destroyed, and whose grief was not at all weakened by the discovery that the thing in question wasn't really harmed at all, or by a change of heart which made it no longer seem worthy of his affection. Even the lunatics in their asylums grieve over things marvellously precious, that have been sadly sullied or irreparably impaired, though they might be hard put to it to say exactly what they are thus grieving over. So much is this so that Dr Ewing has somewhere suggested that we must have a glimmer of *a priori* insight into the tendency of certain types of situation to awaken certain attitudes in us.

We may now ask ourselves a question: granted that certain policies of action almost invariably go together with certain objective presuppositions and presumptions, and are regularly affected by certain discoveries, is it none the less our linguistic duty to provide for the mere possibility that there might be beings otherwise constituted than ourselves, and should we therefore refuse to incorporate into the meaning of our attitudinal names a reference to such objective presuppositions as would lend them an impersonal validity? I can't for

LANGUAGE, MIND AND VALUE

the life of me see why we should be obliged to do so. It runs counter to our normal linguistic policies that we should refuse to cover with a single blanketing name features that almost invariably go together, and that we should take elaborate pains to provide for contingencies that aren't ever likely to arise, and which are, in some cases, merely logical possibilities. Surely, if we must have words to cover such strange contingencies, they should be queer words belonging to the technical vocabulary of philosophers, and not ordinary words whose purpose is so different? We have, for instance, well-established ways of talking about those sounds which, in our experience, invariably arise in connection with vibrating objects and media: should we also feel bound to provide for those other logically possible 'sounds and sweet airs' which are without concrete source or provenance whatsoever? Surely it would be highly misleading to provide ordinary linguistic pigeonholes for situations that seldom or never arise? It might lead us to think that what was infrequent or even wholly non-existent, was quite the regular run of things. And it is plain, in fact, that the way in which many modern philosophers *have* chosen to talk about their feelings, has blinded their eyes to many obvious truths about them.

But there is yet another reason why we should *not* refuse (in certain cases at least) to incorporate certain characteristic claims and presuppositions into the meaning of our attitudinal names, and that is the fact that such claims and presuppositions are *in fact* firmly incorporated into those meanings, and that we should be using such names in a wholly new and confusing sense if we tried to leave such presuppositions out. Thus it is certainly part of what we ordinarily mean by 'jealousy' that it should be directed to someone enjoying favours from someone that we should very much prefer were directed to ourselves. To talk of a jealousy that one might direct to the number of particles in the universe, or to the restrictive practices of the Board of Trade, would be to use the word in a wholly meaningless or self-contradictory fashion. It is likewise part of what we ordinarily mean by 'ethical' or 'moral' approval, that it should proceed according to rule, and that it should be directed to the free acts of persons, and to what are regarded as their bearing upon certain other personal interests: it simply would not be clear what was meant by an ethical approval directed to the weather, or to one's fiancée's charming ways, or to the use of thatch in covering houses. The whole proposal that we should leave out all presuppositional meaning in laying down the

THE JUSTIFICATION OF ATTITUDES

meaning of an attitudinal name like 'jealousy' or 'ethical feeling', would have highly inconvenient consequences. It might lead us to think that there was something unique and unanalysable about the feelings in question, than which nothing can be farther from the case. And it might also lead us to think that it was a remarkable empirical coincidence, or a plain case of the synthetic *a priori*, that certain attitudes were so uniformly connected with certain sorts of objective circumstance. It would seem a wonder that men could feel ethical approval only of voluntary acts, or that they never were jealous except in cases where love was involved. And if we did at times succeed in banishing all this presuppositional meaning from our attitudinal names, we might still find ourselves slipping back into the old senses at other times. Thus even Stevenson, who deliberately uses the word 'ethical' to cover our approval of a beefsteak or a bedstead, as much as of the social aspects of voluntary activity, none the less chooses practically all his examples from the latter sphere, and has a long chapter on avoidability which is entirely out of place if 'ethical approval' is to mean just what he wants it to mean. For we don't refuse to approve of a graceful carriage, nor to disapprove of epilepsy, and to express our approval or our disapproval in the use of the terms 'good' and 'bad', merely because the conditions in question are unavoidable, and are not to be altered by personal choice or suasion. We certainly call a graceful carriage a good thing, and epilepsy a bad thing, and we invite the world to share this preference, even if we think that neither condition will be modified by our judgements. It is only that special sort of approval which the ordinary man (not Stevenson) calls 'ethical' or 'moral', which is confined to cases of avoidable activity, and this special sort of approval Stevenson declares to be wholly lacking in theoretical interest, inasmuch as it exhibits no peculiar methodological features. By using the term 'ethics' in the title of his book, Stevenson has deceived himself and others into thinking that he has made an important contribution to ethical literature, whereas he has in fact ignored or minimized practically all the distinctive features of ethical methodology. If proof is required that it is a bad thing to use attitudinal names in a radically new and presuppositionless manner, it is to be found in the extra-ordinary confusions which surround Stevenson's treatment and influence. It was important that such a book should have been written: it is also important that the performance should not be repeated.

175

LANGUAGE, MIND AND VALUE

V

If we then hold that it is sometimes right and proper to incorporate certain objective presuppositions into the meaning of our attitudinal names, the question arises *when* it is important to do so. Here I have no general recommendation to make. The advisability depends on the extent to which, in fact, certain presuppositions and aspirations normally go together with certain attitudinal policies, so as to constitute an important standing concomitance that deserves special linguistic recognition; it also depends on the extent to which such standing concomitances have *in fact* been recognized in our language. Different recommendations would be appropriate in different cases. In the attitudes covered by such names as 'envy', 'contempt', 'admiration', 'reverence' and so forth, there are fairly clear-cut presuppositions, connected with the notions of superiority and inferiority, which it would be absurd to leave out: so uniform, in fact, are they, that there would be small point even in trying to distinguish between different species of such attitudes. But in other cases attitudinal names cover much vaguer presuppositions and much wider variation in policy, and here many quite different recommendations would be equally legitimate.

I don't, however, wish to range over the whole field of possible human attitudes, but rather to say something about a certain family of attitudes, once highly regarded but now somewhat neglected, which seem to me of very central importance in the regulation and direction of human life. These are the attitudes that one might group together under such vague titles as 'reasonable', 'dispassionate', 'impartial', 'disinterested' and the like: they represent, in some sense, a determined attempt to steer our attitudinal policies *away* from anything that is merely personal, contingent, arbitrary, provisional or ill-considered. I shall avoid the vagueness and the associative richness of old words, and shall refer to them all as 'Butlerian attitudes', since they have many of the characteristics attributed by Butler to his conscience. Perhaps I should here conflate the two major moralists of the eighteenth century, and refer to them all as Butlerian-Smithian attitudes: what I mean by such attitudes will not, however, be impenetrably obscure, nor will it be doubted that they form an all-important segment in our attitudinal life.

By Butlerian attitudes I mean attitudes that are either entirely of higher order, or which involve higher-order components: to preside

176

THE JUSTIFICATION OF ATTITUDES

and govern is part of their 'idea', they are not so much concerned with external situations as with our policies towards these latter, which they always seek to organize and to bring into line.

In so far as my attitude is Butlerian, I demand that my first-order policies falling within a certain segment should be all subject to certain general prescriptions; and in so far as I opt for some definite policy, I may be said, further, to claim implicitly that this policy *is* in harmony with the prescriptions in question. In so far as my attitude is Butlerian I am prepared, further, to organize *other* people's policies and activities as much as my own: my prescriptions might be put in the first person plural in some such form of words as 'Let us all be thus and thus disposed to such and such objects in this or that sort of situation'. It is not of course needful that these claims and demands should be voiced in my overt utterances: they will show themselves rather in the way in which I bully myself and others whenever I note some sign of backsliding or halfheartedness, as well as in the way in which I seek to modify such policies as are plainly at variance with the prescriptions in question.

We may, in the second place, make it part of what we are to mean by a Butlerian attitude, that it should always be, in however small a way, a principle of reflection; that it should yield itself to the arbitrament of facts, and to such probabilities as arise out of those facts, and that it should do so without reserve, and that it should also be unwilling to rest until it has pushed its inquisition into such facts and probabilities to the utmost limit of what is available and accessible. In so far as my attitude is a Butlerian one, it can never be indifferent to me whether I can or cannot give reasons for my policies, nor can I ever feel justified in adopting a policy which I don't implicitly claim would still be my policy after the fullest dwelling on the available data.

We may, in the third place, make it part of the meaning of a Butlerian attitude, that it seeks to proceed in a manner which is *general* or *impartial* as between case and case, or as between occasion and occasion, or as between person and person: as I have said, I am here conflating Smith with Butler, and perhaps adding a spice of Kant to the mixture. Now I don't want to suggest that Butlerian attitudes are anything peculiarly clear-cut and uniform in human experience and behaviour, much less that I have characterized them in a wholly luminous and unambiguous fashion. Quite plainly many of our attitudes are only approximately Butlerian, e.g. the attitude

M

LANGUAGE, MIND AND VALUE

of a chairman pronouncing some authoritative ruling, or that of a tribesman speaking to and for his tribe. And many of our attitudes only satisfy *some* Butlerian conditions: if I try, e.g., to impose some purely personal policy on the world at large, or if I turn my back deliberately upon certain large ranges of fact. There are also very many quite different kinds of Butlerian attitude, which correspond to the different ways or senses in which one might try to be unbiassed or impartial. There is an impartiality of universalized bias which subordinates everything to some arbitrarily chosen occasion, person, position, or point of view; there is, likewise, a negatively indifferent species of impartiality, which hands out a blank charter of liberty and equality to every occasion, position, person and point of view (as in the Protagorean attitude to sense-perception, or as in the *laissez-faire* attitude to our economic activities). There are also all those countless forms of impartiality which accept definite but wholly different standards of parity, in their assessment and grading of occasions, positions, persons and points of view. It is certainly impossible to exhaust the ways or senses in which a man's attitude might be said to be impartial, nor is it even the case that all these ways tend uniformly, in every field of discussion, to one single limit of absolute or maximal impartiality. It seems clear, however, that we do meet with Butlerian attitudes, of different kinds and of different degrees of stringency, in many fields of human activity, and that we even at times feel ourselves in a position to say of one such attitude that it is *more* Butlerian than another. Thus the impartiality which adopts *some* positive general standard in the assessment of its objects, would appear to be more genuinely Butlerian, more free from arbitrary partiality, than one which is merely negatively indifferent to those objects, or which makes everything centre about some arbitrarily chosen individual fulcrum.

However this may be, there are undoubtedly attitudes in the ethical field that one might call attitudes of Butlerian conscientiousness: in these there is a studied attempt to achieve general law-giving, complete openness to facts and probabilities, as well as complete neutrality and unbiassed impartiality in regard to personal interests, however vague and ambiguous this last requirement may turn out to be. There are likewise, in the theoretical sphere, attitudes of reasoned expectation, which are in every respect Butlerian, even though their impartiality shows itself in regard to characters and alternatives, to frequencies of occurrence and to ranges of possible variation, rather

THE JUSTIFICATION OF ATTITUDES

than in regard to persons and their interests. And it would not be hard to point to cases of Butlerian disinterestedness in the aesthetic sphere, as well as to instances of Butlerian religiosity. Now in so far as a Butlerian component enters into some attitude, that attitude becomes liable to counter-justification as soon as we can discover in it any lack of general applicability, any ignoring of available data, or any trace of bias and partiality. That such conditions involve a great deal that is vague and of manifold interpretation, makes no difference to the fact that we often can and do apply them.

VI

It is not, however, my aim to blaze a trail through the jungle of Butlerian attitudes: I wish rather to raise one general point of method. I wish to ask whether we are justified in having special terms in our language to stand for Butlerian attitudes, and whether we are also justified in making use of these *same* terms, perhaps with superadded qualifications, for attitudes that fall short of Butlerian standards in a number of ways. Should we, for instance, follow traditional moral philosophers in making use of the term 'moral consciousness' to stand for a family of rather stringent Butlerian attitudes, and then also employing the same term, perhaps with some qualification such as 'undeveloped' or 'distorted', of the attitudes expressed in certain of the prescriptions of Nietzsche, or in the exhortations of the Mau Mau or similar movements. Or should we simply throw this traditional approach overboard, and adopt another quite different policy, that might be called a policy of 'minimum meaning', according to which we shall give our attitudinal names only such meaning as is genuinely common to the whole range of instances of their use, which means in this case that we should decline to see anything fundamental or distinctive in the peculiar features of Butlerian attitudes? It seems to me that there is a great deal to be said on either side.

In favour of the policy of minimum meaning, it may be argued that the traditional policy tends to warp our view of the wide variety of attitudes, some non-Butlerian and some only partially Butlerian, which are covered by such names as 'ethical', 'aesthetic', 'religious', 'scientific' and the like. It sees them all merely as leading up to members of one narrow class of attitudes, themselves in many ways the product of artificial sophistication: it warps our view even of

LANGUAGE, MIND AND VALUE

the variety within that narrow class itself. It may, in the second place, be argued that our procedure amounts to a form of dishonest propaganda: we try to trick people into adopting certain attitudes, not by frank advocacy nor by open suasion, but by persuading them that they have always covertly accepted them. It may be objected, further, that the traditional policy really makes it unjustifiable to predicate unjustifiability of such attitudes as lie behind the quasi-moral adjurations of the Mau Mau or the prescriptions of Nietzsche. Such persons certainly were not trying to be Butlerian, so we can't rebuke them for failing to be so. At best we can say that their utterances aren't really moral utterances at all, but this is not to say that they are either unjustifiable or immoral. And a final objection is that, if we continue to pack more and more presuppositional meaning into our attitudinal names, we may end in a position in which no attitude can be called moral which does not accord with a particular moral code, no attitude be called aesthetic or scientific which does not obey certain narrow canons, and so on in other cases. Here surely we may see the apogee of arbitrary unreason madly posing as reason.

Despite all these weighty arguments, I still think that a good case can be made out for the traditional policy. I think it plain that the existence of Butlerian attitudes should be emphatically recognized in our language: without doubt we should have special words to stand for them. The passage from such attitudes as are merely personal and capricious, to those which try to legislate for all and which address themselves to all, and which endeavour to take impartial account of every fact, every possibility, every interest and every point of view, is surely a step of immense moment: traditional philosophers were not wrong in seeing in it the principal difference between man and other creatures. Man certainly may be said to be a Butlerian animal. And we may say, further, that, in a sense, *reasoned argument* upon matters of aesthetic, scientific, religious or ethical acceptability, can only begin once this big step has been taken: before that there can be nothing but wrangling, and interchange of propaganda. To have no special name for the big step in question may lead to the regrettable consequence that we shall cease to be alive to its momentous character, and that we shall feel that the question 'Shall I be Butlerian or not?' is really one that can come before us for rational decision. Whereas Butlerian attitudes are just those attitudes in which we try to do and be all those things in which being reasonable can be held to consist, so that it would be absurd to treat the adoption

180

THE JUSTIFICATION OF ATTITUDES

of a Butlerian attitude as something that could be rationally debated or decided. Only at the Butlerian level can there be reasons, below that there are merely causes. Nor is there a danger that by packing too much presuppositional meaning into an attitudinal name, we shall end by giving unwarranted sanction to some narrow canon. The ideas of impartiality and disinterestedness are the exact antithesis of everything that is narrow, and they are also so happily vague, and so capable of diverse interpretation, as to leave room for an indefinite amount of argument and adjustment even on a Butlerian plane.

I think, further, that it would be possible to defend the traditional policy of applying one and the same name to certain stringently Butlerian attitudes, and also, in a qualified sense, to attitudes that are only approximately like them. This is because Butlerian attitudes can be said to exist 'in germ' even in our most ordinary daily commerce with objects, as well as in every conversation, or in every practical dealing with our fellows. In all such intercourse we must, in a sense, put ourselves into a position which is neutral as between ourselves and others, and from such an elementary grade of impersonality we can be pushed, along natural grooves of persuadability and analogy, into almost any pitch of Butlerian stringency. It is not, therefore, nonsense to say that our attitudes always are implicitly Butlerian, since there is this natural slide or slope which leads us on, even from the most passing and personal of attitudes, to the most strenuously and stringently Butlerian ones. We reason with Nietzsche and the Mau Mau, and we condemn their policies from a Butlerian standpoint, precisely because their attitudes are ready to pass over, by slow stages and from many small beginnings, into fully-fledged Butlerian ones. And if we ignore the important natural slide in question, we may be led, quite monstrously, to attribute the prestige of Butlerian attitudes to the contingent instruction of our parents, or to the fortuitous example of such 'innovators' as Buddha or Jesus. Whereas the roots of Butlerian attitudes lie much deeper: they could not be absent from a practical or social being. It will be well, however, to make plain, whenever we use an attitudinal name, in precisely what sense we are speaking, since Butlerian attitudes have no need of verbal subterfuges in order to gain a hold upon reflective and socially minded persons.

X

THE LOGIC OF *BEWUSSTSEINSLAGEN*[1]

(1955)

I

As THE title of my paper may be perplexing to some, I shall begin
with a few words of elucidation. The word *'Bewusstseinslage'* is a
technical term which was brought into psychology in the early years
of this century by the Würzburg psychologists Mayer, Orth and
Marbe: it was translated as 'Conscious Attitude' by Titchener, and
has been more recently translated as 'State of Consciousness' by
Humphrey. Both of these translations seem to me to be too general
and too ordinary: I shall therefore continue to make use of the
German term *'Bewusstseinslage'*, and, when I want to translate it,
shall adopt the unusual rendering 'Posture of Consciousness'. By the
term *'Bewusstseinslage'* the Würzburg psychologists meant to pick
out, to baptize and to characterize a new mental element, an irreducible variant of experience which could be added on to the elementary feelings and sensations previously distinguished by Wundt, very
much as the recently discovered rare gases—Argon, Krypton, Neon
and Xenon—had been added to the previously listed chemical
elements. Like their chemical fellows, these new mental elements were
inert, secret, novel and strange: they were hard to isolate and to
characterize. They revealed themselves only through residual phenomena, and they were credited with an *Unanschaulichkeit*, an 'unsee-
ability' or impalpability, which was not at all unlike the negative
aspect of the rare gases. At a later date these *Bewusstseinslagen* were
replaced in the writings of certain Würzburg psychologists (particularly in those of Ach) by a new category of *Bewusstheiten*: these

---

[1] This paper was read at the Cambridge Moral Sciences Club and the Oxford
Philosophical Society and has been left in its original conversational form.
Published in the *Philosophical Quarterly*, April 1955.

182

THE LOGIC OF 'BEWUSSTSEINSLAGEN'

latter one may translate as 'Nutshell Consciousnesses', as 'Condensed Awarenesses' or simply as 'Knowings'. The relation of these *Bewusstheiten* to the previously distinguished *Bewusstseinslagen* was not, however, made perfectly clear: at times *Bewusstheiten* were regarded as a peculiar subspecies of *Bewusstseinslagen*, at times the reverse was held to be the case. At a still later date both categories were merged under the misleading and colourless name of *Gedanken* or 'thoughts'. It is not, however, our business to follow the elaborate distinctions drawn among all these impalpables, nor to discuss the relations that may obtain among them: for our purposes the conveniently strange blanket term *Bewusstseinslage* will do for them all.

Bewusstseinslagen may in some cases be described as involving a *broad* awareness of some complex whole or content, or of some complex attitude on our own part, or of a wide range of alternatives, in which there is little or no discrimination of parts or details, and in which few or none of such parts or details are present either in sensory or imaginal form. It is natural to predicate 'vagueness' of such Postures of Consciousness: they also invite non-cognitive designations such as 'Feelings', 'Sentiments', 'Colourings of Consciousness'. But there are other *Bewusstseinslagen* which are narrow in range and clear in intent, and which are therefore much less readily describable in affective terms. In these some single circumstance which concerns either ourselves or the world, comes pointedly before us, with little beyond the most sketchy sensuous or imaginal wrappings; these pointed experiences rather fit the designation of *Bewusstheiten*, of 'Consciousnesses' or 'Knowings'. In either case, it is the teasing conjunction of a great deal of highly definite, significant content, which somehow makes its impact on the subject, with an almost total absence of illustrative or symbolic imagery, which constitutes the distinguishing mark of the experiences in question. The general theory was put forward by Ach that all such states were the reflection in consciousness of innumerable dispositions left behind them by past experience, dispositions which, if *fully* aroused, would give rise to sensations or imagery, but whose *sub*-arousal only gave rise to certain modifications of experience, which could at best be said to *correspond* to sensations or images. Such *Bewusstseinslagen* were at times *forward-looking*, as in our consciousness of Meaning or of Tendency: at other times they were *backward-looking*, as in our consciousness of Determination or Relation. It would be neither possible nor profitable to run through the intricate classifications and hypotheses, or through

LANGUAGE, MIND AND VALUE

the protocols and the experimental material in this astonishing literature. One can get all, and more than all, that one wants in Titchener's *Experimental Psychology of the Thought-Processes* or in Humphrey's book entitled *Thinking*.

If anyone now wants examples of *Bewusstseinslagen*, I can do no better than quote from a striking passage in Titchener's *Text-book of Psychology* (p. 506). Titchener writes: 'We may have under the guise of attitude [i.e. of *Bewusstseinslage*] the consciousness that something is real, that it is lasting a long time, that it is over more quickly than we had expected, that it is the same as what came before, that it is compatible with some other thing, that it makes sense, that it is novel, that it is on the tip of the tongue, that it will be difficult, that we need not do it, that we are not ready for it, that we can do it if we try, that we have made a mess of it, and so on. Or on the emotive side we may feel that we approve, that we dissent, that we are saved, that we have been tricked, that the whole thing is trivial, that at all events we have done our share, that we should like to swear, that it is rather interesting after all, that no one has the right to treat us like this, that we may as well go through with it, and so on again. There seems literally no end, till we have exhausted the resources of the language, to the catalogue of conscious attitudes [i.e. of *Bewusstseinslagen*].' We may note, in passing, how closely many of these examples are connected with the artificial tasks set in the psychological laboratory: it was there, and not in any uncontrolled setting, that *Bewusstseinslagen* first made their appearance, and forced themselves on their unwilling observers and reporters. Titchener's last remark, as to the inexhaustible variety of *Bewusstseinslagen*, is also very interesting. Wittgenstein somewhere asks whether there could be an experience characteristic of pointing to a piece in a game *as a piece in a game*: I have no doubt at all that there are *Bewusstseinslagen* with precisely this content.

Bewusstseinslagen often occur very richly in dreams, where the rapid change of scene forestalls their expansion into words or pictures. I shall give you two examples from my own recent dream-life. I dreamt that some people, whom I had met in my usual dim dream-room (which resembles a school-room and is set on a rising hillside), had accused me of quarrelling with a certain lady, whose identity was clear only within the context of the dream. I protested that I had not quarrelled with her, and ended my protest with the French sentence '*Je ne mens pas*'. I then experienced the most vivid possible

184

Bewusstseinslage to the effect that it was foolish to have uttered those words, since they could only serve to awaken doubt in my auditors' minds. Immediately afterwards I found myself involved in a discussion of the conduct of the same lady with two persons, both French but of opposite sex, who were undoubtedly her servants. I then saw the lady herself looking down on me from a verandah above and smiling somewhat cynically. I experienced a second very vivid *Bewusstseinslage* whose content might be phrased in the words that she had every right to regard me with contempt, since I had gossiped about her in this caddish fashion. I quote these examples merely because they evince an overwhelming disparity between richness of significance and extreme poverty of imaginal development: one could say that ninety-nine parts of what was in them was neither illustrated nor symbolized at all. I shall here leave out of account the whole question of the difference between those *Bewusstseinslagen* which seem, as it were, to be parasitic upon sense-given or quasi-sense-given contents, and which hang about these latter like an 'atmosphere', and those other sturdier Postures of Consciousness, which can (it is claimed) stand entirely on their own legs, without sensory crutches to support or steady them. I do so, because the question of the existence of these latter is no simple question of fact: it depends on the account that one gives of the relation of 'standing for', 'illustrating', 'representing' or 'expressing', which obtains between palpable data and *Bewusstseinslagen*, whether it can be affirmatively answered or not.

II

I have not, however, dragged up this notion of *Bewusstseinslagen* from the somewhat mildewed archives of psychology without a pressing and a contemporary reason for doing so. *Bewusstseinslagen* are, of course, a notion constantly mirrored in unreflective talk—we are constantly talking of experiences which condense this or that 'as in a nutshell' or of the 'indefinable suggestiveness' of this or that object, place or passage—but they represent a notion to which philosophers have perpetually had recourse. This is involved in the Platonic and the Aristotelian accounts of thinking, in which the stuff of sense or imagery may help, but cannot constitute the act of thought. In modern times it has been picturesquely put forward by James in his account of the 'free water' which runs its course among sensory and imaginal pailfuls, and it was also clearly and explicitly defended in Stout's doctrine of 'implicit apprehension', long before it made its scientific début in the Würzburg laboratories.

My main reason for occupying myself with the notion is not, however, its remoter history, but the fact that it figures so largely in recent philosophical writing. It may almost be said to be the main topic of Wittgenstein's *Philosophische Untersuchungen*, particularly in its latter portions, as where he dwells on the varying 'looks' that can be put on a face or drawing, or as where he speaks of words as being surrounded by a 'corona of lightly indicated uses'. It is dealt with implicitly in a great deal that Ryle has to say about moods and emotions in the *Concept of Mind*. It has also casually been brought forward at several points in Price's *Thinking and Experience*, as where he speaks, like Ach, of a sub-activation of our verbal and imaginal capacities which imparts a 'felt flavour' to our words, or a 'characteristic feel' to our images, or as where he brings in 'feelings of tendency' corresponding to various lines of verbal or imaginal development. I am concerned, not so much with the facts of the case, as with the *logic* of these curious expressions, to which laymen and philosophers seem alike so readily and so unthinkingly to have recourse.

Why in the world should we speak of feelings as being 'characteristic' when we cannot say at all in what their being characteristic can consist? And why in the world should we want to speak of them as being feelings *of* this or that situation, or *of* this or that activity, when it seems repugnant to their nature as feelings to be *of* anything whatever? Do they come with labels pasted on their faces to tell us *of* what they are? And why above all should we want to speak of some of them as feelings *of tendency*, where, in addition to the difficulty of making them feelings of anything, we have the enormous added difficulty of making them feelings of something *merely dispositional*, of what is, in common parlance, just nothing at all? Shall symbols whose cash-value is so doubtful in logic stand for simple realities in the sphere of psychology? Even Hume that arch-enemy of impalpables does not hesitate to have resort to a feeling of tendency: he says without scruple that we *feel* 'a determination of the mind' to pass from one object to its usual attendant.

Now I wish to find out why we all slip so easily into making use of these curious expressions, which may, from a certain point of view,

THE LOGIC OF 'BEWUSSTSEINSLAGEN'

be both natural and obvious, while yet, from another point of view, they can readily be made to seem both queer and unnatural. I also want to consider whether they belong to a healthy and useful, or to a misleading and pathological section of our language. Wittgenstein has a great deal to say on the topic in the *Investigations*. He does not seem to me, however, to have considered the matter in a really rounded manner, nor can I feel either happy or clear as to the outcome of what he says.

Questions about *Bewusstseinslagen* were, of course, raised and discussed in the early naïve days of philosophy and psychology in the form of straightforward questions of existence: "Are there imageless thoughts?', 'Is there an imageless component in our thoughts?' and so forth. It was assumed that such straightforward questions of existence could be answered by an equally straightforward use of inner observation: we could, by looking into and examining our minds, decide whether they did or did not include imageless acts or components. The same questions are sometimes still asked and answered in this primitive fashion in our own day and age, even though the sophisticated proponent now realizes full well that he is merely putting forward a linguistic edict, which he hopes that his auditors will accept without question, and without troubling him to provide reasons or abolish counter-reasons.

Such ways of dealing with the sort of question before us are, however, profoundly unsatisfactory. For questions about the inner make-up of experience are by no means questions that we can test or settle by observing peculiar data: they are settled, where they can be settled, by the fact that people spontaneously make use of certain expressions, which are drawn from the ordinary talk about objects around them, to express certain non-public accompaniments of their public activities, and that other people evince their understanding of the expressions in question, by adopting them to express similar non-public accompaniments of their own. Apart from such a spontaneous transference of expressions out of public into private settings, and apart from all this ready give-and-take of transferred expressions among different speakers—we must not, be it noted, speak of 'metaphors' in this connection, since there are no straightforwardly descriptive expressions to which one might oppose them—there can be neither propriety nor correctness in our talk about the inner life. We do, however, find that transferred expressions are very often acceptable to others, and it is in terms of such acceptable trans-

LANGUAGE, MIND AND VALUE

ferred expressions that talk about the inner life must of necessity proceed.

One cannot, therefore, condemn talk in terms of *Bewussteinslagen* on the score that such states are not observable, or that it is only owing to an illusion or a misperception that we imagine them to be there. The notion of illusion could, in fact, have none but an indirect or transferred application to the data of the inner life. Nor can we condemn talk in terms of *Bewusstseinslagen* on the score that it would be absurd or self-contradictory to speak of *other* objects as we speak about our inner states. Professor Mace is therefore wrong when, in a review of Humphrey's book that makes most of the points I have just been raising, he remarks on the 'enormity' of the Würzburg discoveries, and maintains that the facts, *as reported by them*, are incredible. I myself find it incredible that *any* fact should be incredible, *however* one may choose to report it. The fact that we do at times express what is taking place in us in terms of *Bewusstseinslagen*, and that other people find such talk as apt as we do, and that we continue to find it apt when we choose our words quite carefully: all these are a sufficient, and in fact our only possible warrant, for saying that *Bewusstseinslagen* exist, and that they are correctly described by those who say they have them.

The only question that can be legitimately raised in this connection is whether it is or is not *desirable* that we should speak in terms of *Bewusstseinslagen*, whether such talk may not create a confusing picture of experience, which leads us on to ask empty or preposterous questions, and whether one cannot replace it by an alternative form of speaking, which will prove less stupefying in its general effect. That this is the issue is, in effect, admitted by Titchener, when he holds that the question is not one of the existence or the non-existence of the experiences called *Bewusstseinslagen*, but merely of the precise *analysis* of these tantalizing states. And it is, of course, open to anyone to prefer the analyses of Clarke, Pyle, Okabe and Titchener, to more natural talk in terms of *Bewusstseinslagen*. But if we do decide that we ought or ought not to speak in terms of *Bewusstseinslagen*, we should make our decision against a background of reasons and counter-reasons: edicts are wholly out of place in an issue like this. I shall therefore begin by considering various important objections to the notion of *Bewusstseinslagen*, after which I shall consider various counter-reasons in its favour. Thereafter my present preferences in this matter will have become perfectly plain.

THE LOGIC OF 'BEWUSSTSEINSLAGEN'

III

I shall now marshal several reasons, some obvious and some recondite, *against* talk in terms of *Bewusstseinslagen*. The first of these lies in the general undesirability of employing mystical, extravagant and apparently contradictory expressions, which demoralize understanding and corrupt inference. A mode of speaking should not *sound* absurd, otherwise it may very well lead to abuses which really *are* absurd. So though we may describe the facts of our inner life in what terms we please—and can succeed in making intelligible to others—it is to be preferred that we should describe them, as nearly as we can, in terms functioning in the well-understood ways in which they also function in ordinary public contexts. Now our talk about *Bewusstseinslagen* seems at once to suggest that *nothing at all* is contained in certain experiences, while at the same time suggesting that *a very great deal* is contained in them; expressions connoting extreme vacuity alternate regularly with expressions connoting superabundant fulness. And the whole situation is rendered doubly difficult by the fact that what is thus held to be present in an extraordinary fashion, is also frequently something that *might* be present to our senses. Now a conjunction of presence with absence may be hard to stomach, even within the limits of a mystical treatise, but it seems vastly more difficult to stomach the *non*-sensuous presence of a sensible quality. There are, therefore, enormities in the Würzburg way of speaking, even if, as suggested above, the Cornell way may prove even more enormous.

A second weighty objection to talk in terms of *Bewusstseinslagen* is that it seems to obliterate, and to make nonsense of, the all-important distinction between the thoughts that are *mere* thoughts—whether they be unrealized meanings or unfulfilled intentions—and the thoughts which are 'fulfilled', 'realized', 'carried out', 'executed' in terms of objects, actions or imagery. It is surely a basic point in the grammar of 'thoughts' that they always stand opposed to states which will 'carry them out' or 'fulfil' them. The practical intention stands opposed to the *execution* of whatever is planned. The expectation stands opposed to the actual *confrontation* with whatever it had looked for. The mere meaning or understanding stands opposed to the concrete carrying out in sensuous materials, or, failing that, in the materials of fantasy. The artistic inspiration stands opposed to the production and enjoyment of the work of art. We may say, in general, that the perfection of thought lies in something more than mere

189

LANGUAGE, MIND AND VALUE

thought: that cogitation by its very nature points to a more than cogitative fulfilment. Now the doctrine of *Bewusstseinslagen* seems to obscure this basic point in logical grammar: it incorporates and encapsulates in the thought what can only be deployed in the actual fulfilment. But if everything can be present in a *Bewusstseinslage* which is also carried out or realized in an action, a product or an image, then there can be absolutely no *achievement* in proceeding from the former to the latter. There can, in fact, be nothing but a deterioration, since a *Bewusstseinslage* is thought to be capable of embracing more details, and a wider range of alternatives, than can ever be worked out in anything serial or concrete. Nothing can, however, be plainer than that a thought without intuitive fulfilment is in some sense vain and empty, and that it is only in executing or unpacking or imparting them, that we really know the full content of our thoughts.

There are, in the third place, many profound difficulties in regard to the whole *relation* of a *Bewusstseinslage* to the objects, acts and images which represent what we have called its unpacking, its execution or its fulfilment. Shall we hold that the relation in question is something merely contingent and empirical? Is it merely the case that a *Bewusstseinslage* of given quality regularly unfolds itself into a given train of acts, things and images, until, by sheer dint of custom, it appears to be the natural precursor of the latter? Is it merely like the 'aura' of the epileptic which has come by association to portend an oncoming seizure? If this is the case, a *Bewusstseinslage* of *any* quality might have been associated with *any* sort of fulfilling outcome. There may be wholly different *Bewusstseinslagen* which connect with the same objects, acts and images in different individuals, and there may even be persons in whom there is no *Bewusstseinslage* to fit a given reference. On such assumptions *Bewusstseinslagen* become wholly trivial features of our private economy: they fall into much the same category as number-forms, of which some people make regular use, but of which other people make no use at all, and of which they are astonished to hear. There will then not be the slightest conceivable scientific or philosophical interest in knowing that anyone experiences *Bewusstseinslagen*, nor what they are like. And there will also be the further difficulty that it will be impossible to say anything intelligible or communicable in regard to their quality: they will be like the 'beetles' mentioned by Wittgenstein in the *Investigations*, which each man keeps in a private box, and concerning which it is

THE LOGIC OF 'BEWUSSTSEINSLAGEN'

senseless to ask whether they are the same or different, or whether they vary or are constant.

We may, on the other hand, prefer to say that there is something necessary, something non-empirical or *a priori*, in the relation of a *Bewusstseinslage* to the things that fulfil it. One would not hold, of course, that a *Bewusstseinslage need* unfold or unpack itself at all, but only that, *if* it does so unfold or unpack itself, it must necessarily do so in items falling within a given range, and that it *cannot* do so in items lying outside this range. It is then not at all an accident that the sights, sounds and manifold impressions that I have known during a performance of *Tristan und Isolde* should condense into just this rich *Bewusstseinslage* that I have on the threshold of Covent Garden: there would have been no sense in supposing that the same *Bewusstseinslage* could have been left behind it by a performance of *Der Rosenkavalier* or by a performance of *The Boy Friend*. In the same way a readiness to fume will correspond to one kind of *Bewusstseinslage*, whereas a readiness to laugh or to sneeze will of necessity correspond to another.

But if we say all this—which certainly seems an entirely tempting and natural thing to say—we are assailed with yet another deep difficulty. Shall we say that the necessity we have postulated is a case of analytic or that it is a case of synthetic necessity? The former alternative is by far the more attractive, yet it remains difficult to see how something that can only be described in a welter of negatives can be analytically connected with something that one describes in most highly positive and concrete terms. Whereas, if one adopts the second alternative, one is involved in all the general obscurity of the synthetic *a priori*. Nor will it give us what we want, since the relation of a thought to its fulfilment is not at all like the relation of a relation to its converse, or the relation of a hue to other hues.

We may, in the last place, object to talk in terms of *Bewusstseinslagen* in that it suggests that we can independently determine what is *in* a *Bewusstseinslage*, and then set it side by side with its corresponding fulfilment. Whereas we only really pin down the content of a *Bewusstseinslage*, we only discover what may really be involved in it, by letting it pass over into the acts, objects or pictures which represent its unfolding or its carrying out. Thus it is only when the old lady develops all the associations, quotations, anecdotes and pictures which are for her part and parcel of the meaning of the blessed word 'Mesopotamia' that we can have an inkling of the sort of *Bewusstseinslage* she connects with the word. And the astonishing thing is that, once she has carried on this development to a sufficient extent, there is no longer anything of mystery attaching to her *Bewusstseinslage*; the ineffable and the incommunicable has become precisely delimited and known. The doctrine therefore lies ready to hand that a *Bewusstseinslage* is only *said* to be a *Bewusstseinslage of* this or that, because this or that emerges into consciousness when the *Bewusstseinslage* passes away.

The *Bewusstseinslage* then becomes a misleading notion begotten of our over-readiness to read into a phase of experience what can at best be present in it in dispositional form, whose actual emergence would in fact disrupt the phase of experience in question. This doctrine seems to yield the key to the phenomena in our field: it seems to explain all that is puzzling and anomalous in our talk about *Bewusstseinslagen*. It explains why we tend to talk of them in terms which alternate between vacuity and superabundant plenitude. For plainly what is dispositionally present may, in one sense, be most rich and varied in its content, while in another sense it will always be just nothing at all. The doctrine explains also why we should regard certain things, acts and pictures as constituting the unfolding, the inevitable unpacking of a *Bewusstseinslage*. A disposition must obviously unfold or unpack itself into the things of which it is the disposition. The doctrine also explains why we are so bent on finding some analytically necessary connection between a *Bewusstseinslage* and whatever fulfils it: there *is* an analytically necessary connection between a disposition and the things of which it is the disposition.

The solution we have reached seems quite dazzling in its illumination: it dissolves into pure grammar so many seeming queernesses of fact. And not only is it thus intrinsically dazzling: it also gathers in reflected light from much competent authority. It may claim the support of Titchener when he holds that the Würzburg doctrine of *Bewusstseinslagen* is only yet another case of the 'Stimulus Error', of the systematic confusion between the 'existential content' of experience, and the psychologically irrelevant 'meaning' we so readily put upon it. It may also claim the support of Wittgenstein, when he says, for instance, that we should never speak of Understanding as a mental process, and that it is only to such things as the coming on or the going off of a pain, or the hearing of a tune or sentence, that we should apply the term 'mental process'. The doctrine also may claim the support of Ryle in the *Concept of Mind*, when he says of

THE LOGIC OF 'BEWUSSTSEINSLAGEN'

a man's reported emotions of dismay, anger and so forth, that they represent no more than fallible *diagnoses* which have been put upon certain of his pangs, throbs, thrills and primitive feelings.

IV

I have now cited enough authorities and have given sufficient reasons why we should *not* talk in terms of *Bewusstseinslagen*: I shall proceed to give reasons why I none the less think we *should* do so. My first, most weighty reason is that talk in terms of *Bewusstseinslagen* is a widespread and spontaneous product, that it comes as natural to children and to uninstructed persons as it does to philosophers, and that it is in fact merely the adoption of sophisticated rules and dogmas which leads people to reject it or to reconstrue it. Not for nothing was it objected to the first introducers of *Bewusstseinslagen* that they were forsaking that purged *Beschreibung* which should be so solely characteristic of the laboratory protocol, for that unpurged natural *Kundgabe* which was characteristic of ordinary talk and life. I have said before that there can be absolutely no standard of correctness in regard to the use of inner-life expressions beyond the fact that we do find it fit and proper to employ them. We can no more call it monstrous or improper or self-contradictory to speak of our experiences in terms of pregnant vacuity or of nutshell containment, than we can call it monstrous to predicate 'leanness' of Tuesday or 'plumpness' of Wednesday, to quote one of Wittgenstein's illuminating examples. There is, in fact, less whimsicality and less personal idiosyncrasy in the former than in the latter. We shall only go astray if we think that inner-life expressions arise in the same way, and are governed by the same rules, as are outer-life expressions, and that, surely, is an elementary error.

A second weighty reason for persisting in talking in terms of *Bewusstseinslagen* is that we continue to want to talk in these terms, and that we feel baulked and frustrated if restrained from doing so, even after reading and pondering all that Titchener, Ryle and Wittgenstein have to say on the matter, and even after oscillating ourselves for years between different attitudes in regard to it. We feel that such talk manages to *hit* off something in our inner life, that it is satisfying, fitting and appropriate, whereas talk in other terms seems to miss out something crucial and characteristic, and to warp the

LANGUAGE, MIND AND VALUE

whole picture of experience. And if it is odd and paradoxical to talk in terms of nutshell concentration, surely it is still more odd and paradoxical to say, with Clarke and Titchener, that the *very same experience* which, from one point of view, is no more than a simple flash of kinaesthesis, may none the less, from another point of view, be a complex conscious attitude, that what is, in one regard, no more than 'a noticeable sense of breathlessness', is also, in another regard, a pregnant consciousness of infinity? We have, moreover, an over-whelming shrinking from all *dispositional* accounts of *Bewusstseins-lagen*. We feel that, while a *Bewusstseinslage* may very well be the *punctum saliens* of a large number of dispositions, yet the things we say are *in* it are not merely *ready* to be precipitated, that they are, in some perfectly definite and intelligible fashion, *there*. We are strengthened in this objection by the crucially important fact that we do *not* always claim to be having *Bewusstseinslagen* in situations where we are ready for certain acts, pictures, words or states of affairs. We may be wholly ready for a range of such items, in that they come forth without difficulty and are greeted without surprise, without being willing to say that we are experiencing anything remotely like a *Bewusstseinslage*. It is only in the transitional situa-tions when details are fading but have not as yet completely faded, or when details are assembling but are not as yet completely assembled, or when details are familiar but are not as yet completely familiar, that we feel impelled to speak in terms of *Bewusstseinslagen*. And the tense and mood in which we want to speak of them are the present indicative: we cannot be fobbed off with anything future or con-ditional or subjunctive.

A third weighty reason for wanting to go on talking in terms of *Bewusstseinslagen*, is that those who object to our doing so follow a line not at all unlike the line of those who want us to give up saying that we have to do with chairs and tables, in favour of saying that we have only 'really' to do with sense-data and images, out of which talk about chairs and tables must be 'logically constructed'. This policy is, however, extremely topsy-turvy: it attempts to found talk which is of plain, direct and obvious import, upon talk which, however legitimate if adequately safeguarded, must obviously be held to be of unclear, derivative and indirect significance. It may also lead people to imagine that the abstract 'cuts' which can be artificially erected into the content of a sensation or an image, are things com-plete and concrete in their own right, concerning which the very

THE LOGIC OF 'BEWUSSTSEINSLAGEN'

same questions may be asked that it is proper to ask in regard to material objects.

Now it seems to me that the same objections that could be raised against our whole procedure in trying to turn our intercourse with solid objects into a mere intercourse with sensory phantasms, could also be raised against the doctrine that we never have experiences of deciding, of understanding or of hating, but that we can at best have experiences of the waxing or the waning of pains, or of certain immediate simple throbs, pangs and shudders. The same inadmissible diremption of the immediate from the non-immediate occurs in both cases: we perpetrate the same fantastic abuse whether we say that a man talking about physical objects is really putting interpretations upon his sense-data, or whether we say that a man reporting on his emotions is putting a diagnosis upon his throbs and pangs. Nothing can in fact be plainer or more easily shown than that things—even pangs, throbs and flashes—alter their look or 'feel' profoundly different according as they occur in one context or another: it is as obvious and as demonstrable that they sometimes show such a characteristic and appropriate look or feel, even though the context appropriate to it has not yet come into being, or even when this context has already passed away. *Bewusstseinslagen* are therefore things of the most common occurrence and the most ready ostensibility, and while they may be inseparably associated with dispositions, it is not at all possible to give an adequate analysis of them in purely dispositional terms.

My last reason for favouring talk in terms of *Bewusstseinslagen* is that I cannot help feeling that it represents something *categorial* in our language, something at once so deeply rooted and so widely ramifying, that the attempt to eliminate it, or to find substitutes for it, will simply throw the whole machinery of our speech out of gear. Just as I should feel profoundly dissatisfied with a proposed linguistic reform which attempted to do away with the distinction between individuals and their characteristics, or between the characteristics of things and their relations to other things, or between things and events, or between the tenses which are our best expression of the passage of time, so I should feel profoundly doubtful of the value of a linguistic reform which overrode the deep distinction between what I may call the extensive and the intensive, between that hard, spread-out form of reality which is best exemplified in tables and chairs, and that dissolved, fluid, concentrated form of existence which is best

LANGUAGE, MIND AND VALUE

exemplified in *Bewusstseinslagen*. I seem myself to be well acquainted with both these modes of being; I seem to myself to understand how they are related to one another, and also how the one passes into the other through a large number of transitional steps and phases. I am also disposed to say that they fulfil complementary roles in the cosmos, and that they should therefore be granted complementary roles in our talk and thought. And I should like, at this point, to borrow a leaf from the Wittgenstein of the *Tractatus*, who held that the objects entering into his ultimate States of Affairs might be said to be of different logical forms, or to possess different logical properties, inasmuch as it would be nonsense to say of one of them what could be said of the other. It appears to me that physical things and *Bewusstseinslagen* are in this sense things of different logical form, in that what one can appropriately say of the one, cannot properly be said of the other. But I also think that there are many formal relations among the things said of each of them, which should be reflected in any adequate symbolism.

XI

REVIEW OF WITTGENSTEIN'S
PHILOSOPHICAL INVESTIGATIONS
(1955)

I

THIS review is strictly limited in scope. We shall take it for granted that Wittgenstein was responsible for a major revolution in philosophical thought, a revolution that has affected that thought at all points, even if we may not go so far as to regard it as having been *more* fundamental and *more* final than the Copernican Revolution of Kant, than Locke's New Way of Ideas, or than any other large change in the direction of thought. We shall also assume that the general character of that revolution is sufficiently known. Our aim will be merely to consider some of the points specially stressed in this posthumous work of Wittgenstein's, and to see how they fit in with the points raised in his other published work and his informal teachings.

If we compare this book with Wittgenstein's previously published work, the *Tractatus Logico-Philosophicus*, we may have at first a somewhat disappointing impression. It is unfinished, whereas his previous book was superlatively finished. It is somewhat rambling and loosely put together, whereas the *Tractatus* reveals itself, upon careful examination, as a veritable exemplar of close-knit unity. It seems, further, to revolve about a comparatively narrow range of problems, whereas the *Tractatus* has something to say on almost every philosophical issue. On further consideration it will, however, become clear that the work before us makes a major contribution to an all-important, central set of philosophical issues, to the question of what may be involved in the acts and orientations of our mind, to the question of how these may be related to the outer acts and

LANGUAGE, MIND AND VALUE

words that are said to 'manifest' them, to the question of the manner
in which they refer or point to objects, as well as of the manner in
which we refer or point to *them*. If many of Wittgenstein's views on
these topics have become familiar through the writings of others,
they are none the less indefeasibly and characteristically his own.

The work before us consists of a loose series of sections, generally
longer and less aphoristic than those of the *Tractatus*, in which (as
Wittgenstein remarks) 'the same or almost the same points were
constantly being approached afresh from different directions', so as
to afford ever new views of the same philosophical landscapes. These
landscapes come into ever better focus as the work proceeds. The
first 150 sections are a bit condensed and hard to read: they seem,
in fact, to be a summary of doctrines more vividly and more con-
versationally presented in some of Wittgenstein's unpublished
lectures. The sections from § 138 to § 693 are the heart of the book:
they range penetratingly over a number of problems of philosophical
psychology, which they show to be most variously and intimately
related. At the end of the book there are a set of unnumbered sections,
which Miss Anscombe tells us were written since 1945, and which
consist of material not as yet sufficiently worked up to be incorporated
in the book. Some of these sections show the beginnings of entirely
new approaches to problems raised in earlier parts of the work. It is
plain that Wittgenstein's thought went on developing and deepening
up to the end, and that, had he lived longer, he might have had very
much more to offer us.

The opening sections of the book might seem somewhat obscure
and pointless to many, since their main concern is to effect a complete
clearance of views put forward in the *Tractatus Logico-Philosophicus*,
positions which have only ever been fully intelligible to a few, and
fully acceptable to an even smaller number. These positions are that
'the world' is composed of the numberless unions of certain colourless
simples, whose whole intrinsic nature consists in their sheer capacity
for the unions in question, and that the task of language is merely
to 'show forth' the manner of such unions, both by devising names
to stand for the simples, and by arranging parallel marriages among
these names. Wittgenstein is concerned to show how unsatisfactory
all this really is, and to repudiate the whole primitive picture of
shadowy correlates corresponding to the significant words in our
language, let alone the fiction of ultimate simple correlates corresponding to the words that lack an analysis in that language (see particularly

198

WITTGENSTEIN'S 'PHILOSOPHICAL INVESTIGATIONS'

§§ 9–51). He then puts forward as a profitable account of *one* meaning of the word 'meaning'—he does not by any means claim that it is *the* meaning of the word—that the meaning of a word consists in its *use* in the language (§ 43), to which he adds, as a further principle, that the uses of different words in our language are as various as are the uses of the different tools in a carpenter's tool-box, a variety much too wide to be brought under a single formula. It is we who are tricked by the unvarying, discrete, thinglike aspect of the words in our language into thinking that they all must stand for unvarying, discrete, thinglike entities of some sort (§§ 11, 12).

Wittgenstein then introduces, as a valuable expository and illustrative device, certain simplified models of linguistic usage which are known to him as 'language-games'. In these we see symbols functioning in a manner too simple to occasion any mystery: we can then, by contrast, achieve a better understanding of the complex workings of our actual language. One such language-game may be illustrated by the performance of a shopkeeper who interprets the word 'five' in the order 'Five apples!', by reciting the numerals one after another up to five, and by taking a fresh apple from a drawer as he utters each numeral (§ 1). The doctrine of language-games is slightly and confusingly sketched in this book: it was much more tellingly and completely worked out in some of Wittgenstein's unpublished lectures (which it may be hoped will be allowed to see the light of day, if only to throw light on the present passages). There is little to criticize in what Wittgenstein says in this part: the writing, too, is often of considerable beauty. (See, e.g., the fine comparison in § 18 of our language to an ancient city, with a central tangle of twisted streets and much added-to buildings, surrounded by suburbs where the streets are regular and the houses uniform.)

In the §§ 109–33 Wittgenstein puts forward many pregnant and beautiful expressions of his well-known doctrine of philosophical puzzlement, of the view that our philosophical difficulties arise from a misunderstanding of the forms and rules of our language, a misunderstanding which always has a character of depth, since the forms which it misinterprets are so basic and all-pervasive. (Wittgenstein, it may be noted, never equates the verbal with the unimportant.) He puts forward his view of philosophy as a cathartic or exorcistic discipline, one that endeavours to do battle against 'the bewitchment of our understanding through the instruments of our language' (§ 109), and one which seeks to free us from our various deep-set puzzlements by giving us a synoptic *oversight* over the multitudinously interweaving, mutually interfering tendencies in that language (§ 132). Some of Wittgenstein's utterances at this point are so finely aphoristic and so memorably phrased as to deserve a finer rendering than Miss Anscombe has been able to give them.

Wittgenstein in these sections acknowledges the cathartic and the synoptic functions of philosophy, but he finds no place for a reconstructive or creative function. 'Philosophy', he tells us (§ 124), 'must in no way interfere with the actual use of language: it can in the end only describe it.' He emphasizes the point that, since the words in ordinary speech have a sense and a use, each sentence that employs them conventionally must be 'in order as it is' (§ 98). It is the task of philosophy to discover what that order is, and to bring words back from a mistaken metaphysical to an everyday usage (§ 116). All this seems dogmatic and a trifling sweeping. For the fact that our ordinary expressions have a sense and a use, and are to that extent 'in order as they are', would not seem to preclude us from developing alternative forms of speech, all every whit as much 'in order as they are', which will none the less express their sense in a manner more pointed, more unified, more perspicuous or more deeply satisfactory than does ordinary diction (a point elsewhere conceded by Wittgenstein, though not in this book). It would appear that Wittgenstein's condemnation of an attempt to *deepen* our ordinary accounts of things arises out of his repudiation of his own previous attempts to construct an ideal language which should accurately mirror the structure of fact. But one may have other reasons for preferring a philosophical form of speaking than its supposed conformity to the relationships of ultimate simples.

In the sections from § 138 onwards Wittgenstein develops his analysis of a number of mental states, of their relations to their objects, as well as to their verbal and behavioural expressions. He deals also with the epistemological and semantic problems which attend on our knowledge of, and our talk about, our own and other people's experiences. His immensely complex, varied treatments seem to hinge on a small number of fundamental theses (if one may speak of 'theses' where so much is tentative and a matter of deliberate emphasis).

The first of these theses may be called that of the impossibility of a purely private language, of a form of speech in which one talks to oneself about the inner quality or make-up of one's own

WITTGENSTEIN'S 'PHILOSOPHICAL INVESTIGATIONS'

experiences, without troubling to link what one says with anything that is, or might be, accessible to others. Wittgenstein's reason for objecting to such a private language is that it would lack an acceptable standard of *correctness*. If I wrote the letter 'E' in my diary every time I had a certain private sensation, there could be no further criterion of my correctness in so writing, than that I felt *inclined* to do so on the occasions in question. This, says Wittgenstein, is a standard so different from an ordinary public standard of correctness as not properly to count as a standard of correctness at all (see §§ 257, 258, 260). We can indeed make use of a sign like 'E' to *evince* the quality of our inner experience, but it will then not refer to or describe that quality: it will merely serve as an artificial substitute for the many natural expressions of some state of mind (§ 244). The inner quality of experience can in fact play no part in linguistic intercourse among persons: it resembles something which each man keeps in a box of his own, and which he never scans but in secret. Though all should agree to connect the same sound 'Beetle' with their secret object, this sound would still not function as a genuine name, since there would be no criterion for the identity, the constancy or even for the existence of what it stood for (§ 293).

On this thesis a second thesis depends: that in so far as the expressions applicable to mental states have a use at all, this use must be tied up with something showable, i.e. with behavioural criteria. It is 'only of a living human being, or of what is like or behaves like such a being, that one can say: This has sensations, this sees or is blind, this hears or is deaf, is conscious or unconscious' (§ 251). Wittgenstein dwells amusingly on a variety of fantastic and fairy-tale cases in which thoughts and feelings are attributed to such things as pots, pans and articles of furniture. He points out that such talk either lacks all clear sense, or that it depends on an assimilation of the form or behaviour of such objects to those of the human body (see, e.g., § 361). Of a disembodied existence we can form only a variety of images or pictures, not anything that amounts to a genuine or meaningful reference.

To these two theses Wittgenstein adds a third: that it is impossible for an attitude or an orientation of mind to declare itself in a *single* performance or on a *single* occasion. It is necessarily a *practice*, a *manner* of responding, and as such can only reveal itself in a long series of performances or occasions. If we thought to find it in what happened on a single occasion, we should really ourselves be looking

201

LANGUAGE, MIND AND VALUE

forward to what *might* happen, or to what *would* happen on other occasions. Such anticipations would of course always be open to correction or regulation. And not only is this so, but there is no sense at all in trying to set bounds *in advance* to the whole range of acts and expressions characteristic of some mental attitude, nor yet of our own expectations in regard to this range. This is obviously so where our attitude is indefinite or vague, but it is just as much so where our attitude involves obedience to some rigorous rule. For a rule can be neither so expressed nor so exemplified as to exclude all variety of interpretation: however far its exemplification or expression may have gone, there will still always remain an indefinite number of deviant possibilities as to its *further* exemplification or expression (see, e.g., §§ 85, 86, 189, 222–6, 229, 239).

To these theses a fourth may be added: that the forms of our language promote in us a certain deep-seated illusion, through which a thing absurd in itself would seem to become a matter of direct observation. We imagine that a pattern which can at best declare itself (and that always with incompleteness) in an endless series of situations, can be somehow 'queerly present' in a single experience, and that it can, as so present, *give rise* to that very infinite series of applications and expressions, which 'flow from it' as from some inexhaustible source. Wittgenstein shows how we cherish such an illusion in regard to the understanding of principles. We think that we can grasp them in a flash, and that this grasp will then extend itself to an infinite series of applications and interpretations. To hold this is very much like holding that we understand because we have understood (§§ 154, 188). We cherish a like illusion in regard to the meaning of expressions: we think that their use can be illuminated by a lightning flash of understanding, and that it can thereafter hang about them like some sort of atmosphere (§§ 177, 195). We yield to this illusion when we say of a tune that we know, that we feel as if it were there in its entirety (§ 144). We are subject to its spell in the case of reading, when we think that the sound of read words must come up in consciousness 'in some special manner', and that we experience the 'guidance' or the 'influence' of the seen word in a manner foreign to cases of rote-repetition. Whereas reading, being nothing but the *practice* of connecting one sort of mark or sign with another, could not possibly be compressed into a single performance or experience. We are subject to the same illusion in the case of thinking, when we think of it as of some incorporeal process which

WITTGENSTEIN'S 'PHILOSOPHICAL INVESTIGATIONS'

precedes and inspires our speaking (§ 425). And we are subject to it in the case of expecting, wishing, willing, hoping, believing, imagining or hating (§§ 144, 572, 611, 642). In many cases, too, we not only locate a whole mode of proceeding in an act or experience: we imagine that the *object* of such an act or experience can be encapsulated within it. We are thereby led to populate the world with such novel entities as images, projects, propositions and the like, whose intro-duction means no more than a rearrangement of the grammar of our psychological expressions (§§ 367, 368, 400, 401, 437, 442, 445).

That this multiform illusion really *is* an illusion becomes clear, Wittgenstein thinks, when we reflect that, even if there *were* a peculiar inner feeling that invariably presaged or invariably accompanied the unfolding of a mental attitude, its connection with that attitude would be an empirical and contingent matter: we could have no guarantee that it would obtain in all persons, nor could it matter whether it did so obtain or not (§ 153). Wittgenstein recommends, in fact, that we should so speak of a 'mental process' that it would cease to make sense to speak either of understanding or of willing as mental pro-cesses: 'a pain's growing more or less, the hearing of a tune or a sentence: these are mental processes' (§ 154). It will be plain that Wittgenstein's recommended way of speaking is not very different from the 'existential' programme of Titchener: for him too, mental processes must be considered 'for what they are, and not for what they mean'. And Wittgenstein is led on into many fine-drawn accounts of the varied settings, adjustments, etc., characteristic of certain mental attitudes, accounts highly reminiscent of the best work done by Titchener's pupils at Cornell (see, e.g., §§ 33–5, 596, 602). In all these treatments it has become practically an axiom that there is never *one*, but always *a vast number of alternative experiences* which are characteristic of a given attitude or performance.

We may now permit ourselves a few words of criticism and appraisal in regard to the four 'theses' extracted from Wittgenstein's imprecise and unassertive utterances. In regard to his denial of the possibility of a private language, it is plain that he bases himself on grounds of linguistic propriety: his doctrine is in fact no more than a linguistic decision. Wittgenstein is unwilling to *call* anything a 'language' from which a public standard of correctness is absent. There are, however, grounds that might have led someone else to a contrary decision. There would seem, in fact, not to be any fun-damental difference between a standard of correctness depending upon

LANGUAGE, MIND AND VALUE

the presence of a number of mutually confirming tendencies in *one and the same person*—all prompting him to use words in certain ways in certain circumstances—and a standard of correctness depending on the very same tendencies when distributed among a *number of persons*. And Wittgenstein himself has made plain that talk about the absolute privacy of experience, or about the absolute privacy of the inner quality of such experience, has a grammatical rather than a factual basis. We could, if we wished, have given a sense to the having of another person's pain, or to the entering into the quality of another person's experience (see, e.g., §§ 251, 253, 275). All this means that it is only a conventional, and therefore modifiable, barrier which shuts out the inner quality of experience from linguistic intercourse among persons. (A barrier, we may note, which is non-existent for the non-philosophical.)

It may, however, be freely admitted, in regard to what we have called Wittgenstein's second thesis, that he is right in holding that we do in fact pin down the senses of expressions in our mental vocabulary, by connecting them with ostensible and observable behaviour, and that other uses of such expressions do in fact grow out of, and are in fact dependent upon, such a primary use. Our talk about the so-called inner life is throughout *parasitic* upon talk about the so-called outer life: Wittgenstein is the first to have made us *fully* aware of the many all-important implications of this readily forgotten fact.

As regards what we have described as Wittgenstein's third thesis, the view that it is impossible for rules or patterns to be laid down in advance, but that they can at best declare themselves, with endless imperfection, in the actual elaboration of practice, this too seems an insight as simple as it is incalculably important, which could only have been grasped and stated by a mind of the highest genius.[1]

In regard to Wittgenstein's fourth thesis—that we are mistaken or misguided in speaking as if a mental process could contain 'as in a nutshell' whatever can be elicited from it in practice or application—our attitude must be somewhat more critical. Wittgenstein is here counselling us not to speak in terms of those Non-imaginal Awarenesses which were brought into psychology by the Würzburg psychologists: he is applying to their reported existence the kind of

---

[1] I now regard this third thesis as completely mistaken. See my 'Use, Usage and Meaning' in the Aristotelian Society Supplementary Volume 1961, or in the book of reprinted articles *Clarity is Not Enough*.

204

WITTGENSTEIN'S 'PHILOSOPHICAL INVESTIGATIONS'

sensationalistic reduction that they also received at the hands of Titchener and the school of Cornell. It is, however, clear, as Wittgenstein himself admits (see §§ 316, 436), but as he does not always obey in his practice, that our problem here is not one of describing refined or elusive phenomena, but of making up our minds *how to speak* about the inner quality of experience. We may refuse to do so on principle, but if we decide (as Wittgenstein himself has decided) to engage in such an enterprise, then it is hard to see how we can adopt any other standard of correctness than one which bases itself on what those who engage in the enterprise feel themselves pressingly, persistently and generally (or nigh-generally) prompted to say. And if talk in terms of 'nutshell containment' should commend itself to wide bodies of people, who are all engaged in the task of describing their insights, decisions and the like, and if they can't help feeling that something is 'left out' by alternative manners of speaking, then it becomes correct to speak of such experiences in terms of nutshell containment, and statements framed in this idiom will often be true.

It is in fact hard to imagine that Ach or Külpe or Watt or anyone trained in the rewarding but difficult 'Systematic Introspection' of the Würzburg school, would have been in the least degree moved by Wittgenstein's recommendations. These are, in fact, subject to a more fundamental objection: that they commit the fault also committed by attempts to reduce statements about material objects to statements about sensory contents. If it is proper and correct to say of a pot or a pan that it can be there 'all at once' on a single occasion, then it is proper and correct to say the same about our felt insight into a situation or our felt grasp of a rule or pattern, or a felt surge of hate or anger or a felt decision to embark on a certain course of action. What was *in* such experiences can no doubt only be made plain in the laborious process of unpacking them, but this will not make it wrong or senseless to say that what is thus elicited from them was *in* them all along. This in fact is how we feel it right to speak in certain circumstances.

If we turn to the second part of Wittgenstein's book, where numbered sections give place to reflections not as yet definitely placed or ordered, we shall find that practically all our last objections have been fully countered. Wittgenstein no longer feels it undesirable to say that our words often carry with them an atmosphere, 'a corona of lightly indicated uses',[1] or that certain passages may give us 'a

[1] P. 181.

205

LANGUAGE, MIND AND VALUE

quite special feeling'.[1] He only emphasizes (with entire correctness) that these special feelings or atmospheres are in no sense necessarily or universally present in our references to objects, and that they also are not *explanatory*[2] of the latter. An atmosphere may fit in with a set of applications or developments, but it is not to be regarded as their source.

Wittgenstein points out, further, how we frequently find it natural to transfer words having a well-established use in common contexts to the characterization of such feelings or atmospheres. We thereby confer a *secondary* meaning on such words, which is wholly distinct from their primary ordinary meaning. Thus the words 'lean' and 'fat' which have a primary application to Mahatma Gandhi and Marshal Tito respectively, may be felt by some to have a secondary appropriateness in expressing the atmosphere of the words 'Tuesday' and 'Wednesday'. Wittgenstein points out that there is nothing 'metaphorical' in this secondary use of expressions. It is the only way in which feeling and atmosphere can be verbally conveyed, and we cannot therefore oppose it to some more straightforward or unmetaphorical style of speaking.[3] Wittgenstein also has a great number of interesting things to say about the perceptual groupings studied by the Gestalt psychologists. He seems to me here to show some traces of a queer sensationalistic bias, but as I am far from clear as to the full import of all that he says, I shall abstain from detailed comment.

I shall end this review by remarking that my criticisms of Wittgenstein's methods and principles are to this extent unimportant: that they all rest, to an overwhelming degree, on those methods and principles themselves. It is by the principles of Wittgenstein that one can be led to develop what one may call his philosophical film-negative, so as to invert its annihilating emphasis, and so as to make better sense of traditional philosophizing. And if one feels that, like the Pied Piper of Hamelin, he has rid one of a plague of rats only to deprive one of one's own dearest children, one may, if one wishes, have those children back again, though one now has to look for them in another country. The greatness[4] of this book will be apparent to

[1] P. 182.

[2] I should now believe in their explanatory power. This is in fact a perfect example of one sort of explanation.

[3] Pp. 215 and 216.

[4] 'Greatness' now seems to me not applicable to this book, though it is applicable to the *Tractatus* and to Wittgenstein himself.

WITTGENSTEIN'S 'PHILOSOPHICAL INVESTIGATIONS'

anyone who will use it as a basis for systematic discussion: it is a greatness of provocation and inspiration, not of definite outcome. Miss Anscombe's translation seems to me both adequate and honest: it only fails to do justice to some of the more memorable, splendidly rhythmic passages.

XII

SOME REFLECTIONS ON MEANING[1]

(1959)

I

I PROPOSE in this paper to examine the relations between three important concepts: those of Meaning, Fulfilment and Validation. The first and third are extremely familiar, being a constant theme of philosophical discourse over the past two decades: the word 'validation' is meant to cover all procedures that establish, or that help to establish, the *truth* of a statement or proposition. It covers both Verification, on the one hand, and Confirmation, on the other. The second concept, that of Fulfilment (*Erfüllung*) is taken from Husserl's final study in the *Logische Untersuchungen*, an essay not much studied at any time, but which I have always regarded as one of the supreme masterpieces of philosophical analysis. The fact that the territory I am to cover has been repeatedly tilled in the very recent past has both advantages and disadvantages. It makes some of the issues stale and tedious to reopen; on the other hand, it enables one to make certain rapid, overall recommendations, and to leave many issues unopened, since one knows precisely to what interesting vistas or to what blind alleys they will lead.

On the concept of Meaning I do not propose to expatiate very profoundly, but to deliver myself in somewhat brief and dogmatic fashion. This dogmatism will have the justification that what I say will be comparatively close to accepted usage. We have lived through a period in which 'meaning' has been made to mean all sorts of things that it does not normally mean: Use, Range, Content, Operational Approach, Manner of Verification, Inscriptional Design,

---

[1] Some points in the present paper were presented, in more condensed form, in a paper read at the International Conference of Philosophy, Venice, September 1958. Published in the *Indian Journal of Philosophy*, August 1959.

SOME REFLECTIONS ON MEANING

etc., etc. These new usages have given currency to concepts which have illuminated countless dark corners in the philosophy of language, and which would never have gained an *entrée* had they not first masqueraded as 'meanings'. They have none the less overlaid and confused the indispensable, ordinary sense of the word, though this has lingered on amusingly in the interstices of discussions embodying the new usages. I myself would wish these illuminating new concepts to continue to illuminate us, but to do so in their own clothes, and to allow the old, shivering, commonplace concept to resume its needed garments. What this concept is I shall now attempt briefly to explain.

We have been taught recently that there is something peculiarly heinous in regarding the meaning of an expression as an *object* connected with it or corresponding to it: this is, however, in a sense, precisely what it is. It would have been natural to use the word 'meaning', on the analogy of other gerundival words, to stand for the act or process or function of using words in a meaningful manner. It is not, however, used in this way: it stands for *what* a word or expression means, i.e. for the 'object' of the function of meaning. We give the meaning of an expression—either alone or in a completing context—by enclosing that expression (with context) in quotation marks, or using some other indication to show that we are now talking about a *mere* expression—following our quoted expression by the verb 'means', and then following this verb by an expression which may be said to *give* the meaning of the subject-expression, this latter expression being of necessity *interpreted* or *understood*, since it could not otherwise give the meaning of the other. Thus I might say that 'a grandfather of someone' means a father of a father of someone. This giving of a meaning need not be a formal definition, nor need it involve the use of a precise synonym.

It is natural to speak of the meaning as an *object* in this connection, since the expression which 'gives' it is a grammatical object, and might, by a turn of phrase, have been made a grammatical subject. It is also natural to treat it as an object, since the expression which gives meaning is an *interpreted* expression, one that stands for something: one would not get a statement of meaning, except *per accidens*, by merely relating expressions to other expressions. And it is also natural to treat it as an object, since the meaning of an expression can itself be referred to by countless other significant expressions, and can thereby itself satisfy second-order meanings. It can, e.g., satisfy the meaning of being what is meant by a certain expression, of being distinct from certain other meanings, etc., etc. But, from another point of view, the expression that gives a meaning does *not* correspond to an object, since it may be as incomplete and as synsemantic as the expression whose meaning it states. ' "Identical with" means same as' may not be elegant English, but it is entirely idiomatic and intelligible. It is in fact preferable to ' "Identical with" means the relationship of being the same as', since the abstract nominal expression, though innocuous if rightly employed, has confusing syntactical and meta-physical suggestions.

Even where an expression, as normally used, *does* correspond to an object, it does not really so correspond when used to give the sense of another expression. The expression 'the father of the father of *A*' certainly fulfils a different role when used to state the sense of the expression 'the grandfather of *A*' than when it is used to refer to a particular person. What this difference of role is, it is amazingly hard to say: Frege devised an elaborate theory of a hierarchy of senses each of which enables an expression to refer to its own previous sense. The expression 'a father of a father of someone' is on this account capable of being used 'obliquely' to stand for its own original sense, in which use its sense would be better expressed by the phrase 'the sense of the expression "a father of a father of someone" ', which sense can in its turn be referred to by an expression whose sense could be best expressed by the phrase 'The sense of the expression "the sense of the expression ""a father of a father of someone""" ', and so on. Instead of using the *same* phrase to refer to any one out of an infinite hierarchy of senses, we should be better advised, on some views, to use totally *different* names or phrases to stand for each of these senses, and it is a mere weakness of our language that we do not do so.

As opposed to this view, I should take up the position that while an expression used to state meaning may not mean *exactly* what it ordinarily means, it none the less represents a normal transformation of its ordinary meaning, in which transformation that original meaning is in some sense contained or preserved. And if asked what this transformation is, then I should say that an expression used to give meaning is in some sense 'sealed off' from further developments, much as Hegel taught that the 'understanding' froze our conceptual mean-ings, so as to prevent them from passing over into their normal complements. The meaning of 'a father of a father of someone' is, in its ordinary use, essentially *open*, it permits *supplementation* by the meanings of countless other expressions, all of which have a common point of intersection, and may be said to describe the same object. Thus we may say that a father of a father of someone is also called James and is fair. These supplementations would, however, be quite improper if we were using the expression to give the meaning of another expression. When we use an expression to give the meaning of another expression it would not even always be right to supplement or replace an expression by an expression *logically* equivalent. But though sealed off from its normal supplements, and wrapped up like a mummy in its semantic casing, the meaning of the expression remains, I should hold, alive, and not only alive, but able to wriggle some of its more essential semantic toes. There are *some* logical transformations of an expression, that are still possible even when it is being used to give a meaning. This 'sealing off' is further signalized by such devices as writing the meaningful expression in capitals or in italics, rephrasing it in abstract nominal form, or enclosing it in quotation marks. This last device differs *toto caelo* from the use of quotation marks to indicate that we are talking about a mere expression.

There is, further, despite much wanton obfuscation on the part of recent philosophers, no particular difficulty or obscurity in the way in which we manage to make meanings objects of special references. We are not necessarily involved in the issues of synonymy, with which recent discussion has clouded the whole issue. For an expression is like many other instruments, e.g. a telescope; it can be used to reveal matters alien to itself, and it can also be used to reveal just those features of itself which enable it to deal with such matters. A telescope can be used to survey the heavens, but it can also be used to discover the peculiarities of its own *field of view*. In the same way we can make use of words in a special, arrested, semantic manner to elucidate their own intension or semantic scope, or that of other more or less synonymous expressions.

To talk about 'meanings' need not, further, commit us to regarding meanings as entities in any other sense than that they enter into the analysis or description of a meaningful reference. The meaning of an expression is like the reach of an arm: that an arm's reach is an object 2 feet 6 inches away does not imply that there actually is anything 2 feet 6 inches away that the arm reaches, and in the same way the fact that an expression means something as being 2 feet 6 inches away does not imply that anything actually satisfies or even

LANGUAGE, MIND AND VALUE

is this meaning. I leave the construction of a really satisfactory logic of oblique reference to those best fitted to carry it out. I do not, however, think that it presents the hopeless difficulty that it has frequently been held to involve.

II

From the consideration of Meaning I turn to my second concept, that of Fulfilment. This is borrowed from Husserl, and I shall, to some extent, follow him in expounding it. The fulfilment of a meaning is a state in which that meaning may be said to be (wholly or partially) carried out, exhibited, illustrated, embodied or actually given. These phrases are largely metaphorical, but it is not hard to see what they aim at. Such fulfilment is in some sense a necessary correlative of meaning: a meaningful use of terms must in some sense prepare for, do duty for, look or strive towards a state in which *what* it means will be completely shown or worked out. This is true even in the case of self-contradictory or not finitely exhaustible meanings: it is in *attempting* to carry them out that we become aware of their self-contradictory or not finitely exhaustible character.

Mere meaning, therefore, *presses* towards an appropriate fulfilment, and is incomplete till that fulfilment is achieved. To use meaningful phrases is, of course, not literally to expect, not literally to yearn, not literally to operate with a *faute de mieux*: it is often more expeditious and satisfactory than to press on to final fulfilment. But there is plainly some sense in which a fulfilled meaning has a prerogative over one that occurs 'emptily': this is shown by the redundant, honorific use of the words 'self', 'very', 'actual' in situations of fulfilment. We employ exactly the same words, and understand them as fully, whether we express some meaning emptily, or apply it to some actual object or situation. But in the latter case we say that the thing *itself* is present to us, that we have the *very* thing before us, that this is the *very* situation we were meaning, etc. etc.

The obvious paradigmatic case of such fulfilment is of course the simple case of sense-perception, to which Husserl has devoted such incomparably acute analyses. The meaningful use of the phrases 'my inkpot', or 'my inkpot on this table', are fulfilled by actually seeing my inkpot, or by seeing it on this table. It is important to realize that there are vast differences in the degree or the extent of such perceptual

212

SOME REFLECTIONS ON MEANING

fulfilment. To examine an inkpot from several angles and at close range is obviously a *better* fulfilment of what we mean by calling it an inkpot than to see it remotely and from a single angle. It is also important to realize how the fulfilment of meaning may be piecemeal, and brought together in a synthesis which never achieves complete fulfilment: thus we may fulfil the meaning of a complex description of St Paul's Cathedral by having countless imperfect views of the church, each involving as much loss in fulfilment as it also involves gain. We must emphasize, further, that there are an infinity of less adequate forms of fulfilment. My meaningful reference to my inkpot is genuinely though less adequately fulfilled by merely seeing a *picture* of my inkpot, or by seeing *another* inkpot of similar type, or by merely *imagining* my inkpot. It is important to realize that in the case of wholly general meanings an imaginative fulfilment is as satisfying as one that involves the additional luxury of the actual. There will also be cases where we fulfil meanings by means of maps, diagrams and charts, which have the special merit of avoiding redundancies. Even beyond this schematic type of fulfilment there are possibilities of more remote fulfilment, as where we merely explicate a reference by translating it into one involving a longer and more analysed series of expressions.

Husserl has further widened the application of the notion of Fulfilment to cover the case of introspective meanings: whether or not we like his notion of 'inner perception', we must, I think, admit that it is by actually *being* in certain inner states, or in something like them, that we can give concreteness to our references to certain inner life conditions. And Husserl further extends the use of the concept to the case of purely formal or logical expressions, e.g. logical constants, numerical expressions: there is said to be a purely 'categorial intuition' which fulfils these. This mode of speaking is enough to send a chill up a modern philosophical spine, but is none the less really innocuous. Husserl intends no more than a linguistic recommendation: we should extend the use of 'seeing', 'intuiting' to the special case of the logical expressions, since there is a sense in which we can be said to *fulfil* our use of these. Thus it is our being permitted to fulfil *two* distinct meanings by one presentation, e.g. the meanings of 'sitting next to me' and 'having a pock-marked face', which also fulfils our use of the copula, of the constant 'and' and of the sign of identity: we can say such things as that the man sitting next to me has a pock-marked face, or that the man sitting next to me is the same as the man with the pock-marked face, or that a man is sitting next to me and also has a pock-marked face. In the same way it is the frustrating *non*-fulfilment of a meaning by some present situation which itself fulfils the higher-order meaning of negation. Our use of numerals and numeration may, likewise, reflect procedures of classification and counting, but it also *articulates* the given: we can, e.g., *see* the fourfold fourfoldness of some grouped assemblage before us. It is not fashionable to want to fulfil mathematical and logical symbols in the fashion suggested by Husserl, but I myself believe that such 'intuitivization' is in the last resort indispensable if such symbols are to have meaning.

The notion of Fulfilment seems to me to have the further merit of bringing out the extreme *intimacy* of the relation between a meaning and what illustrates or realizes it. This disposes of the suggestions of adventitiousness and externality encouraged by such terms as 'application' or 'use'. When one talks of *applying* a word to a thing or situation, the thing or situation seems unconcerned in such application: one wonders why one cannot apply *any* word to any situation whatever. In the same way the constant harping on *use* obscures the fact that it is things as well as ourselves which provoke the use of words on certain occasions, and that whether the use is acceptable depends, at least partially, on what the things are.

III

We may now turn to the third of the concepts we wish to consider: that of Validation. Of this Strict Verification and Partial Confirmation may be reckoned as the subspecies. Such Validation applies, of course, only to propositional meanings, while Fulfilment applies also to the meaning of names, adjectives and synsemantic particles. This apart, there is a strong temptation to feel that there is the same intimate *liaison* between Validation and Meaning which obtains between Fulfilment and Meaning: one may even confuse the two notions, and say that for a situation to fulfil a meaning is for it to validate the corresponding assertion, and *vice versa*. This immense confusion has bedevilled thought for the last half-century, and has turned semantics into a branch of epistemology and the theory of science, yet it is not at all easy to avoid, nor resting on a very obvious mistake.

The difficulty, of course, is that the same situations which very

SOME REFLECTIONS ON MEANING

often serve to fulfil the meaning of an assertion also serve to validate it, and vice versa, so that the two roles seem to be the same. Thus if I see my cat reposing tranquilly on the mat, this may show what it *means* for a cat to be so reposing: equally it may serve to establish that my cat *really* is so reposing. The use of the situation in these two manners is, however, profoundly different. One could fulfil the meaning of 'my cat sleeping on the mat' more or less adequately by a picture or a model or a mental image, though this would contribute absolutely nothing to validation. It is even possible that the cat before me is hallucinatory: here the fairly adequate fulfilment provided coincides with a total failure to validate.

It is clear, further, that Validation necessarily brings in features extrinsic to Meaning: to validate a statement it is not enough to have something before one that exemplifies one's meaning. It is also necessary to be able to *fit* what one means and asserts into a vast tissue of *other* assertions and assumptions, and to subject it to critical tests, which not only lie outside of its content, but whose precise nature is not even definite when the assertion is entertained. The meaning of the words 'red' or 'square' is readily fulfilled, but the question as to whether certain things really are, or are not red or square involves all sorts of complex issues which we do not and should not seek to crowd into the relatively clear-cut meaning of these adjectives.

Validation, moreover, depends on factors which have nothing to do with the bestowal or clarification of meaning: the *experimentum crucis* which establishes one alternative at the expense of others, the precise, singular instance, utterly improbable in itself, which none the less yields the highest confirmation to the theory not framed *ad hoc* to meet it: all these are the stock-in-trade of Validation, though they have little or nothing to do with Meaning. The meaning of being in heaven might be fairly well fulfilled by a rather short sojourn in what *looked* like that medium, whereas the proof that one *really* was in heaven would involve applying all sorts of *experimenta crucis*, designed to uncover chinks in the celestial armour, which would certainly not be appropriate to the celestial condition. Husserl himself, we may hold, went wrong in this regard, when he held that a completely adequate fulfilment of a propositional meaning would involve also the evident establishment of the proposition as true. This view rests on a confusion between seeing and knowing which runs through the whole of philosophy.

LANGUAGE, MIND AND VALUE

It is clear, further, that so far are processes of Validation from throwing light on Meaning, that we may go quite a long way towards validating an assertion whose meaning we do not understand at all. We do this whenever we pin faith to an assertion that we do not understand, but which has been made by some expert or reliable person. Thomist theologians thus assert the truth of many propositions, of whose full sense, as known to the angels, they claim only an analogical inkling, and physicists likewise assert and make use of many sentences to which they have not as yet given a satisfactory sense. One of the main uses of the word 'true' seems in fact just to enable us to lend assent to assertions with whose precise content we are not for some reason conversant. Far from being one of the most noble words in our language, the word 'true' has one of the most menial and surrogative of functions. We know little or nothing of anything when we know it to be true.

We may hold, lastly, that the attempt to connect Meaning too closely with Validation has resulted in a large number of gratuitous quandaries which have haunted thought in the past decades, and whose ghost is not even now fully exorcised. These quandaries arise since a speaker's actual position in space and time, and the severance of his experiences from certain other experiences, affect his capacity to validate assertions much more seriously than they affect his capacity to understand them. It is essential, therefore, that we should learn to separate the investigation of the techniques by means of which sense is given to our expressions, and is connected with appropriate fulfilments, from the investigation of the techniques by means of which our assertions are validated.

XIII

THE CONTEMPORARY
RELEVANCE OF HEGEL

(1959)

I WISH this evening[1] to defend the proposition that Hegel is an extremely important philosopher, well deserving the closest of contemporary study, and not at all belonging to what some have called the 'palaeontology' of philosophical thought. To defend this proposition in the present climate of opinion still requires a certain expenditure of energy and personal authority, though much less than it did a little while ago. There has been, as you know, ever since the beginning of the century, a Hegel-renaissance in Germany, which has increased rather than declined in strength: it is now culminating in a really authoritative edition of Hegel's work, with a correct, unjumbled use made of the invaluable notes of his various students. There has also been a Hegel-renaissance in France ever since M. Hyppolite produced his excellent translation of the *Phenomenology of Spirit*, and Sartre's philosophical production is as much influenced by what I regard as the healthy philosophizing of Hegel as by the somewhat morbid, if interesting, philosophizing of the German existentialists. In Anglo-Saxon countries a Hegel-renaissance has been made more difficult by the comparative recency of a period in which Hegel's prestige was immense, though his doctrine and method were very imperfectly understood. Hegel is a philosopher whose misfortune it has been to fascinate philosophers of a wholly different and much less subtle cast of mind, who have then created a one-sided image of his thought to fit their rather limited horizons, and who have involved Hegel in the discrediting reaction which their own views ultimately provoked. No one probably now wants to revive the Spinozistic

[1] Lecture first given at a Colloquium on Contemporary British Philosophy in London, September 1959.

217

absolutism of Bradley, the time-denying monadism of McTaggart, the febrile subjectivism of Croce and Gentile, even the optimistic rationalism of Royce: what is not realized is how very remote all these philosophers are from the toughness, the empirical richness, the logical brilliance and the astonishing self-subversive movement of Hegel's dialectical thought. Whatever these thinkers may have learnt from him, most of them never learnt to think dialectically at all. What they hold has always a final definiteness of assertion, a systematic stability and clarity, an elimination rather than living suspension of conflict, which stamps it as a 'still', a product of 'understanding', rather than of what Hegel understood by 'dialectic' or 'reason'. Had Hegel known of these thinkers, he would have disposed of each of them in a few paragraphs of his system.

A Hegel-renaissance has also been made difficult in the Anglo-Saxon world by the immense prestige of mathematical logic: since 1911 one may say that we have all lived in the noble shadow of *Principia Mathematica*. Hegel is, however, believed, chiefly by those who have not read him, to have been grievously contumacious as against that sort of logic, and in particular against the logical law of non-contradiction, and by such contumacy to have corrupted all clear thinking at its source. It was in this connection, probably, that Ryle said, on some occasion in the past, that Hegel did not deserve study, even as error. Ryle was, however, completely misguided, since few philosophers have so well understood, and so eloquently admired, the peculiar genius of the mathematicizing understanding, when at work on its own tasks and at its own level, and the indispensability of its clarifying, fixing, separating, equational activities, its moves that really serve to maintain immobility, from the point of view of exposing the limitations of each thought-position and of making it possible to progress to the next. The fact, further, that Hegel uses superficially self-contradictory language in an illuminating manner, simply shows that Hegelian contradiction, like Hegelian identity, is not the nugatory, self-stultifying notion of the mathematical logician, but has an entirely different, valuable role. Hegelian dialectic has, in fact, a function complementary to the thought of *Principia Mathematica* and similar systems: it is the thought of the *interstices* between clear-cut notions, fixed axioms and rigorous deductive chains, the interstices where we are as yet unclear as to what our notions cover and what they do not, where we constantly stretch or retract them as we try them out on new material, where we are concerned to look at them

THE CONTEMPORARY RELEVANCE OF HEGEL

from the outside, and see how well or how ill they do certain conceptual work, where we are concerned with innumerable loose, inexact, sliding, shading relations of notions to one another which are not less important for being loose. Hegel's dialectic corresponds to the sort of informal, non-formalizable passages of comment and discussion in a book like *Principia Mathematica*, rather than its systematic text, and it has the immense importance of that interstitial comment. The decisions and moves of thought that precede formal statement, and that lead us to discard one formal statement for another, are in fact the only part of a mathematicized system that has genuine philosophical interest, and all these are certainly dialectical in the Hegelian sense.

Having said so much in mitigation of initial prejudice, I wish to range my remarks on Hegel under three distinct heads: I wish to discuss dialectic as a feasible philosophical method which we might to some extent use on our modern problems, I wish to say something about the Hegelian use of the notions of internality and totality which differs so utterly from the not very useful employment of these notions by Bradley and the British Idealists, and I wish lastly to say something about the remarkable general perspective in which Hegel sees experience and the world, a perspective much more closely adjusted to the tough and tender aspects of experience, much less inclined to soar over them to some non-empirical beyond, than almost any other philosophical system, and a perspective which is, moveover, utterly misrepresented by what is generally thought to be the connotation of its name, i.e. 'absolute idealism'. In the sense in which other philosophers are idealists and absolutists, Hegel is not one at all: a perspectival rationalist or spiritualist, with a strong realist, empiricist and even materialist infusion might describe him better.

I shall now attempt to say what I think are the basic characteristics of Hegel's dialectical method, as actually evinced in his philosophical practice. The textbook accounts of thesis, antithesis and synthesis are descriptive nullities idly repeated by people who have for the most part no real acquaintance with the actual writings of Hegel or the real workings of his thought. I should say that the basic characteristic of the dialectical method is that it always involves *higher-order comment* on a thought position previously achieved. What one does in dialectic is first to operate at a given level of thought, to accept its basic assumptions, and to go to the limit in its terms, and then to proceed to stand outside of it, to become conscious of it, to become clear as to what it really has achieved, and how far these achievements

219

do or do not square with its actual professions. In dialectic one sees what can be said *about* a certain thought-position that one cannot actually say *in* it. And the sort of comment made in dialectic is not a comment on the correctness or truth of what is said in a certain manner or in terms of certain concepts, but a comment on the adequacy or logical satisfactoriness of the conceptual approaches or instruments one has been employing. In dialectic one criticizes one's mode of conceiving things, rather than the actual matter of fact that one has conceived. One is, if one likes to use Moorean terms, giving a series of deepening analyses of ordinary matters of fact, whose 'truth' in the common-or-garden sense is never questioned, or one is, if one likes, putting forward a series of 'linguistic recommendations' each of which illuminates matters of fact more intensively and more widely. Hegel would of course never have expressed himself in either of these ways, but with his uncanny prescience for later philosophical developments, he very often comes close to it. His official description of what he is doing is that he is giving a series of improving definitions of the Absolute.

What Hegel does is in fact extraordinarily like what is done in modern syntactics or semantics or similar formal studies, when we pass from discourse *in* a language to discourse *about* that language, when we make a language an object-language *for* a meta-language. It includes of course the further willingness to make what is brought out in this manner itself part of a widened object-language, but this is likewise something regularly done in many metalinguistic exercises. What is further important to realize is that such metalinguistic dialectical comment always involves the possible emergence of definite novelties of principle, things not formally entailed by what one has done at the lower level. Sometimes these novelties are slight, mere reaffirmations or endorsements or particularly stressed versions of what one had previously thought: sometimes, however, they involve an ironical swing-over to what is totally contrary, the assertion *about X* of something which is just the opposite of what *X* itself intends or asserts, as when we assert from a higher level the complete nullity of a distinction which a lower level vehemently makes: sometimes again they involve the making clear of a conceptual inadequacy, and the concealed need for some sense-making, saving complement. Sometimes, still more remarkably, they involve a reversal of perspective which turns a problem into an explanation: we come to see in certain very difficult contrasts and oppositions the 'very nature' of something

THE CONTEMPORARY RELEVANCE OF HEGEL

which requires just these contrasts and oppositions and so renders them acceptable. This last step resembles the falling in love with a woman for the very features which at first made her unattractive. The central nerve of Hegel's dialectic is in fact of this sort: it consists in finding absoluteness, finality and infinity *precisely* in what at first promised *never* to be so.

The building set up by thought's perpetual self-transcendence is in fact not an erect but a tapering structure: it is a widening, top-heavy building in which the higher storeys extend farther and farther beyond their base. *More* entities, *more* concepts and principles are in fact always needed to cope with the entities, concepts at a given level than are to be found at that level, a fact well known to those who construct formal systems, but strangely ignored by all those nominalists, reductionists, phenomenalists, etc., who think it incumbent on them to keep the higher storeys of the conceptual building well *within* its supporting base. Fortunately the principles of logical stability are not those of architecture, since there is not in their case any overwhelming urge towards the ground.

Two of the greatest logico-mathematical discoveries of fairly recent times may in fact be cited as excellent and beautiful examples of Hegelian dialectic: I refer to Cantor's generation of transfinite numbers, and to Goedel's theorem concerning undecidable sentences. In the case of Cantor we first work out the logic of the indefinitely extending series of inductive, natural numbers, none of which transcends finitude or is the last in the series. We now pass to contemplate this series from without, as it were, and raise the new question as to how many of these finite, natural numbers we have. To answer this we must form the concept of the first transfinite number, the number which is the number *of* all these finite numbers, but is nowhere found *in* them or among them, which exists, to use Hegelian language, *an sich* in the inductive finite numbers, but becomes *für sich* only for higher-order comment. And Cantor's generation of the other transfinite numbers, into whose validity I shall not here enter, are all of exactly the same dialectical type. Goedel's theorem is also through and through dialectical, though not normally recognized as being so. It establishes in a mathematicized mirror of a certain syntax-language that a sentence declaring itself, through a devious mathematicized circuit, to be unproveable in a certain language system, is itself unproveable in that system, thereby setting strange bounds to the power of logical analysis and transformation. But the unproveable sentence at the same time soars out of this logico-mathematical tangle since the proof of its unproveability in *one* language is itself a proof of the same sentence in *another* language of higher level, a situation than which it is not possible to imagine anything more Hegelian.

There are countless other good examples of such a dialectical swing-over in the history of philosophy: Descartes's Cogito which turns universal first-order doubt into absolute higher-level certainty, Anselm's similar transformation of the God doubted by the fool into a being that even the philosopher cannot doubt, Hume's ironic claim that the hideous pantheism of Spinoza was in fact indistinguishable from the belief in an underlying substantial soul, Wittgenstein's solipsism which by eliminating the possibility of talking about another person's experiences ends by making it impossible to speak of one's own, etc. etc. We perform similar dialectical moves when we recognize concreteness to be an extraordinarily abstract notion, the idea of beauty to be profoundly unbeautiful in its non-sensuous remoteness, the militancy of the 'free world' to be in danger of becoming tyrannical, the null-class or class devoid of members to be itself a perfectly good member of a class of higher order, the absence of the *doux printemps d'autrefois* to be itself lamentably present, the wonderful abstractness and gratuitous purity of a behaviourist theory to testify unwittingly and unwillingly to the existence of what can never be fully evinced in behaviour, etc. etc. I am not, however, concerned to make dialectic reputable, but to make plain what it is. It is a method in which step 2 is a true and inevitable and sometimes ironic comment on what has been present at step 1, step 3 a true and inevitable comment on what has been present at step 2, and so on. If at any stage in this proceeding, a step is not a true and inevitable comment on what went before, wrung from it by reflection, then the step in question is not valid. Hegel's dialectic is not an amusing or boring parlour game of setting up arbitrary oppositions among notions, and then arbitrarily 'overcoming' them. The emergence of the oppositions and their overcoming must be the inevitable fruit of reflection on what the notions are, if it is to be valid at all: it must, as Hegel says, be the *Erfahrung*, the experience of a previous phase, or, more radically, it must be simply what is involved in the conscious view that the previous phase *has* gone before, much as, on a plausible analysis of time, the content of the present simply *is* the pastness of whatever has gone before it.

You will no doubt now feel that I should to some extent illustrate

THE CONTEMPORARY RELEVANCE OF HEGEL

all these sweeping assertions regarding Hegel's dialectic, the fruit, I may say, not of pondering over commentaries, nor of armchair reconstruction, but of reading and repeated reading of Hegel's actual text, over a large number of years, and of repeated dissections of his arguments with several seminars of intelligent students. I do not shrink, as some commentators shrink, from this sort of test, but the extent to which I can submit myself to it this evening is unfortunately (or perhaps fortunately) very limited. I shall therefore refer to, rather than actually expound, a few of Hegel's dialectical sequences, so that you can see how the pattern works in practice. Let us begin with the famous beginning of the Logic, where we start with the mere notion of 'being', the sort of notion we have when we collide with an object in the dark without making out what it is, when we face the world after a swoon without as yet construing it, or when we have a vague 'objectless' affect directed merely to 'something'. This notion gives itself out to be positive and rich in content, and the most opposed to the mere absence of anything. Seen from a higher point of view it reveals itself, however, as utterly empty and abstract, and as not really differing in content from the total absence it excludes. To think merely of *some* object, one knows not what, does not differ significantly from thinking of *no* object at all. The 'truth' of the indeterminate first something is therefore nothing, in Hegel's intriguing language, and the 'truth' of this *last* affirmation is simply the impossibility of keeping emptily abstract notions apart, their tendency to lose their would-be distinctness and to flow over into one another. Logical instability, marginal fluidity, notional becoming is in short the 'truth' of hard-and-fast abstractness carried to extremes. The whole phantasmagoric flux points, however, inexorably to definite being, the being of an object united with a determining feature, which is a being-this or a being-such or a being-there rather than a *mere* being. The dialectic here grasps at the differentiatedness from which it is possible to abstract, and apart from which references to an *a* and a *b*, to something and something else, such as we make in pure mathematics, make no sense at all.

I have now shown you the working of the dialectic in Hegel's famous first triad, that through being, nothing and becoming to determinate being, which has been so much misunderstood and abused. Let me now take a flying leap to the beginning of the Doctrine of Essence where Hegel dwells on the notion of identity and shows it to be senseless unless connected with essential difference: it only

223

LANGUAGE, MIND AND VALUE

makes sense to say that A, e.g. the Buddhist religion, is one and the same, if A is also differentiated into co-ordinate forms A_1, A_2, A_3, A_4, Theravada Buddhism, Mahayana Buddhism, Zen Buddhism, etc., *in* which it can be identical. Hegel is here recalling the strayed sheep of formal logic, which try to be so independent and self-sufficient, to the fold of ordinary usage and understanding. This essential difference is at first mere difference, the diversity of things in the world which have nothing to do with one another: it is plain, however, on unblinkered reflection, that each different form only is what it is by virtue of what it excludes, and this makes the hidden 'truth' of mere difference lie in polar opposition. Polar opposition brings to a focus what all difference less obviously illustrates. Opposition, however, reveals itself, on deeper examination, as not so 'head-on', so crass, as it superficially gives itself out to be. Opposites depend wholly for their being on their contrast, as is brought out saliently in opposites like east and west, and this means, if we reflect on it, that each opposite really has *its* opposite built into itself, has its whole being in opposing that opposite. This leads, on a profounder examination, to the insight that all opposition is in a sense veiled equivalence, the A of a B facing the B of an A, a proposition whose import modern psycho-analysis has used to the full in its studies of sexual permutations.

A last flying leap will now take us to the very different final triad of the Logic where the idea of life, as the passing on of an organic type or pattern through a variety of individuals is shown to involve the possible separation of that type in and for a mind. The natural world is essentially a petrified, externalized version of an order which science internalizes and abstracts and makes its notional own. One cannot understand the natural world, and certainly not its highest organic phases, except as a series of universals sunk in matter which must be lifted into full consciousness in the medium of science. Science, however, shows us mind in the ever unfinished endeavour of subordinating the natural world to rational explanatory patterns of various sorts, but always finding the fathomless individuality of things eluding the net of its patterns. What intelligent activity aims at, however, practical activity achieves, i.e. the complete mastery of *individual* natural reality by rational pattern. The 'truth' of theory, as Marx was afterwards plagiaristically to repeat, lies in practice. Practice, however, also is unable to complete the rationalization of an alien order—to do so would lead to its own destruction—and needs the help of a final injection of theory, the view of the world in all its

THE CONTEMPORARY RELEVANCE OF HEGEL

theoretical and practical imperfection as the eternal foil or battle-ground required by rationality in order to deploy itself fully and become fully conscious of itself. In all these dialectical transitions there is no entailment in the formal logical sense, and yet no stringing together of random observations. At each stage we see the sense or the truth of the previous stage, what it did not try to be yet was, or what it was not but tried to be, and by so seeing things we see them in an ever changing and enriched perspective. Some of Hegel's transitions are no doubt much more far-fetched and questionable than others: sometimes they are so far-fetched as to seem arbitrary and irrational. Dialectical movement, however, is not inference, but notional deepening of what has gone before, and deepening may have many varying grades of relevance and illumination. On the whole, however, the experienced Hegelian finds profound illumination even in the most far-fetched of Hegel's transitions: it is illuminating, e.g., to see the profound analogy between a syllogism, which attaches a universal to an individual by way of some suitable middle term, with a scientific object, which is merely a syllogism turned on its head, an individual illustrating various specific and generic concepts. Likewise to find in historical and other changes a gross carrying out of the self-criticism present in dialectical thought is by no means unhelpful and absurd. The fact, further, that we can question or criticize Hegel's transitions shows that there is something in his method. A purely arbitrary, illogical stringing together of ideas would not be open to criticism.

I wish now to lay some stress on the use throughout Hegel's system of an appeal to implications, internal relations among concepts, which are not the entailment-relations dominant in formal logic. Hegel assumes throughout that, while we can and must blinker our gaze in using each limited concept—we must think in terms of abstract identity when we are doing formal logic, in terms of mere quantity when we are doing mathematics, in terms of pushes and pulls and weights when we are doing mechanics, in terms of mere realism when we are studying nature, in terms of abstract rights when we are studying jurisprudence, etc. etc.—that our notions are none the less not without a profound and necessary relevance to other notions not included in their purview, that they require these other notions to make sense, and that this requirement reveals itself in dialectic as soon as we examine each notion from above or from without. We can see, for instance, that the abstractions of logic and mathematics

LANGUAGE, MIND AND VALUE

are nothing without a qualitatively variegated world, that mechanics is an imperfect illustration of connections more clearly exhibited at the organic and teleological levels, that the natural order ultimately needs the scientific intelligence to interpret it, that abstract rights can only obtain in a much more closely knit, not merely juridical unity, etc. etc.

The internal relations I am citing must be carefully distinguished from the internal relations appealed to by writers of the school of Bradley, and I shall try to indicate the main ways in which they are different. In the first place, the internality appealed to by a writer like Bradley is universal, and of equal intimacy throughout: it is more a reflection of Spinozism and of nineteenth-century determinism than of Hegelianism. For Bradley, etc., there are no external relations, no irrelevances, nothing could have been different without disrupting the whole: the most trivial fact of experience is as closely linked with other similar facts as are the most fundamental features of experience. In Bradley, we may say, the universal sway of internal relations reduces them all to non-significance, it does not differ from the sway of the most absolute externality. It is like the situation aptly put in Gilbert and Sullivan, where when everybody's somebody then no one's anybody. In Hegel there is nothing of this sort. It is held that there are vast reaches of experience where contingency ranges unchecked, where the philosopher must strenuously avoid the temptation of trying to prove that things *must* be so and not otherwise. And even at the level where rational implication obtains, the connections studied are still open to empirical exception, even on a large scale. They represent norms, paradigms, completely rounded out cases needed to make full sense of everything, but not necessarily realized everywhere and always. Thus Hegel's idealism, which holds that the natural world has an inner affinity for mind, and that it necessarily produces minds to which it will, after a struggle (like the sea-god Proteus) deliver its secrets and reveal itself in its true notional form— this idealism is compatible with the view that mind was the last thing in time to appear on the world-stage, and that there were long ages of past existence when there were *no minds at all*. Hegel as an idealist is infinitely far from both Berkeley and Kant, and he is more nearly a dialectical materialist than most Hegelians have realized.

The inner connections which link one notion to another are therefore rather carried out in limiting or fully perfected cases than in any and every instance: they are goals towards which cases move, rather

226

THE CONTEMPORARY RELEVANCE OF HEGEL

than concomitances they always satisfy. And Hegel believes like Aristotle that one cannot understand the richer, more developed case from the more meagre and less developed: the developed, fully rounded case has the priority in explanation. If Hegel's view of internality differs from Bradley's in being liable to much empirical exception, and being much more limited in scope, it differs from it also in laying no stress on an all-embracing *whole*. The word 'universe' is hardly ever mentioned in Hegel, and then only at some definite phase of thought such as that of the 'object'. What is infinite and absolute in Hegel is always the individual concrete reality, pinned down in time and space, especially when it is conscious of itself. It is infinite and absolute not by losing itself in the 'whole', but by concentrating the whole in itself, by demoting the 'universe' with its trivial, dispersed being to a condition of its own self-conscious, rational life. For Bradley philosophy is a dumb grasping at the Absolute, for Hegel philosophy is the Absolute. It is in and for the rational activities of conscious human individuals that everything 'cosmic' may be held ultimately to exist.

If you now ask me whether I actually believe in all this mild internality, the answer is that I do believe it, and that I believe that a philosopher should look for it everywhere. Philosophy should not be an experimental playing about with logical possibilities and a seeking to make them more numerous than they at first seem to be: it should aim at a judicious reduction of them, at finding them much less numerous than they at first seem to be. I am encouraged in this attitude by the extent to which even modern logical empiricism or analytic philosophy has deferred to it in practice, if not always in theory. For modern logical empiricism and analysis, as for Hegelianism, it is not merely an accident that our sense-experience exemplifies regularly recurrent patterns: without it there would be no identifiable objects, and objectively oriented discourse would not be possible. The occasional loose sense-experience exists, and radical looseness is not logically self-contradictory, but it is implied by all our discourse that it will not obtain. In the same manner logical empiricism like Hegelianism admits the non-accidental character of the existence of persons other than the speaker: all our standards of truth and significance are implicitly public. Wittgenstein, throughout his life a prey to dialectical *Umschwünge*, after dallying long with solipsism passed over to what may be called radical publicism, the doctrine that it is impossible to talk purely to oneself in a language

227

LANGUAGE, MIND AND VALUE

framed only for one's private use. I do not myself accept this extreme swing of dialectic—I believe that in a world where publicity exists privacy also has its possibility and its legitimacy—but I mention it to indicate the degree to which modern philosophy covertly admits non-analytic connections. Personally, as I have said, I believe them to exist everywhere, and to penetrate far down into the detail of experience: practically everywhere one finds, if one seeks for them, extraordinary analogies, affinities and relations of mutual complementarity among the most seemingly disparate, disconnected things.

I now wish, in the limited time at my disposal, to say something about Hegel's central affirmation, his so-called absolute idealism. This is not the belief that all things exist only in and for a consciousness, but that all things must be seen either as necessary conditions of, or as stages towards, self-conscious rationality, towards the conscious rational use of universals, or, as Hegel calls it, *Geist* or Spirit. What does Hegel mean by saying that Geist is the truth of everything, and is such an affirmation in any way valid or acceptable? The whole of our study of Hegel's dialectic shows that this assertion is not to be metaphysically understood: it does not go beyond the facts of human experience, its sense lies in the daylight of our conscious rational life. Geist is in fact exemplified in the three forms of Art, Religion and Philosophy: it is there and nowhere else that Hegel's Absolute is to be found. And that Geist is the truth of everything does not mean that Geist engineered the world, or was causally responsible for it: Geist makes its appearance at a comparatively late stage in the world's history, its supreme stage, philosophy, is even said to arrive in the world when the shades of night are falling. Clearly the sense in which Geist is the truth of everything in the world is a perspectival sense: it is an *Ansicht*, a peculiar view of the facts of experience—Hegel sometimes characterizes it as the removal of an illusion—not something which underlies the universe or is causally responsible for it.

The precise way in which this *Ansicht*, this crowning perspective, arises, is not left obscure by Hegel. When we fully realize that the various unspiritual things in the world are *necessary conditions* for the emergence of Geist, of rational conscious activity, their apparent unspirituality vanishes: they become mere adjuncts and aspects of rational subjectivity, things built into it and inseparable from it. This insight is again and again achieved in relation to different kinds of material. We start, for instance, by treating the material of sense-experience as something alien and external to our minds: we painfully

228

THE CONTEMPORARY RELEVANCE OF HEGEL

struggle to impose on it the rational pattern of perception or scientific law. This venture succeeds continuously, but is never finally successful: each triumph of scientific explanation creates new problems for the scientist. But on the endless approximations of science a mystical insight supervenes: we realize that the struggle with recalcitrant sensory materials is *necessary* to the being of science, that if all nature could be reduced to a tautology, without irreducible elements of sense-given individuality, rational science would wither away and die. In this insight lies also the way to the absolute: we realize that the recalcitrance of sense is only (as it were) a sham recalcitrance, a recalcitrance presupposed by and necessary to science, the shadow cast by its own abundant life. It will be always there, because science will always be there—perhaps with some cosmic intermissions—but to realize its merely shadow-character is to overcome its alienness, to see it as a mere adjunct of rational science.

In the same way, our practical life starts in a welter of instincts and personal interests of which no rational deduction is possible. Practical life consists in subjecting these instincts and interests to individual and social discipline, in weaving them into great, ordered projects, a task which again can never be finally completed. On this welter of passion, and on this everlasting approximation of practice, a mystical vision supervenes: we see the passions as the mere raw stuff for rational control and planning, as being there to be organized and subjected, as themselves rational *because* they are the necessary conditions, the raw material of reason. In much the same manner, our social life starts in a brutal struggle with other individuals, which at first tends to the enslavement of individuals or classes of individuals by other individuals or classes of individuals, at a later stage to the co-ordination of persons in various social unities. This co-ordination, too, can never be carried to completion: there will always perhaps be excluded individuals and repressed classes. But on the broken arcs of the social unity and the class-struggle a higher vision supervenes: we see that the deep gulf between persons and classes of persons is a necessary condition of their emergent rationality. Only because people are rent apart in atomic privacy can the rational life of science bridge their differences of insight and experience, only because they live immured in selfish interests, can morality and social obligation arise among them. The distinctness of persons is therefore a *necessary condition* of the rational life common to them all, and is therefore a *part* of that life. If it did not exist, it would have to be imagined or invented. In

229

LANGUAGE, MIND AND VALUE

the same way, lastly, we begin to see the whole material world, with its ladder of forms rising from the inert and mechanical to the purposively organized and organic, as a mere hieroglyph of the order found in conscious rationality, as a mere preparation for that rationality itself. In this crowning vision all discrepancies, frustrations, resistances, conflicts are seen as necessary conditions of the final rational outcome, as in fact already part of it. Can we accept this Hegelian *Ansicht*, and is it in some sense the ultimately *right* perspective in which to view life and the world?

I shall here merely say that I think there are several strong grounds for being an Hegelian, and that I doubt whether there are equally strong grounds for being anything else. One *should* be an Hegelian because, as a rational being, one *must* be one anyway, because one must at least *act* as if all theoretical discrepancies could be removed, all irrational impulses controlled, all differences of personal insight and interest adjusted, the natural world deprived of its alienation and remoulded to serve the rational purposes of man. There is, I think, a good practical ground for being an Hegelian, and for those who believe in the unity of thought and practice, this should be sufficient. There is, however, also a good theoretical ground for preferring Hegel's perspective to any other, and this lies in the fact that rational subjectivity alone demands, requires, presupposes all the other toward and untoward factors in life and experience, whereas they do not seem to demand, require, presuppose rational activity. It explains them as they do not explain it. Rational activity is in a sense the most dependent of all things in the world: not only the stresses of Hitler's concentration camps, but a mere breakdown in the central heating may suffice temporarily to disrupt it. But its dependence on everything can be seen, by a rational change of perspective, to be a dependence of everything on it: the world either has no explanation at all, or is explained only by it. Either the world is merely a bad tragedy, a series of episodes, everything which is the case, or it has its 'sense' in Spirit.

What shall I recommend you to believe? And what do I myself believe? In my not infrequent moods of exaltation I am certainly an Hegelian. When I do hard theoretical work and succeed in communicating its results to others, I feel that the whole sense of the world lies in endeavours such as mine, that this is the whole justification of its countless atrocious irritants. I feel clear too that the world *has* a sense, and that no other philosophy expresses this sense

THE CONTEMPORARY RELEVANCE OF HEGEL

satisfactorily. But in my more frequent mood of mild depression I am not an Hegelian, I regress to a materialism which is not, I fear, at all dialectical. I see the world as bereft of sense, and I submit masochistically to its senselessness, even taking more comfort in its cold credibility than in the rational desirability of Hegelianism. I am not even convinced that there is one best or right perspective in which the world should be viewed: it seems a provocative staircase figure always idly altering its perspective. Being myself uncertain, I shall not try to turn you into Hegelians. But what I shall insist on is the need of keeping Hegel, despite all his difficulty and the difficulty of getting anyone to teach him properly, in our philosophical curriculum, for to miss his illumination is to miss one of the greatest pleasures and treasures of civilized life.

XIV

SOME NEGLECTED ISSUES IN
THE PHILOSOPHY OF G. E. MOORE[1]

(1960)

I PROPOSE to speak to you this evening on some neglected sides of
the thought of G. E. Moore. It might seem strange that one can find
anything neglected in a philosopher so much admired and so frequently cited as G. E. Moore. The fact is, however, that, as in the
case of a great philosopher like Leibniz, whose fame among his contemporaries was vast, Moore's general 'image', even among philosophers, is very far from doing justice to the actual thinker: in some
respects, I should say that he really is the unknown philosopher.
The people who read him, teachers and pupils alike, generally read
him by the way, as leading up to or throwing light on other people:
he is rather like Padua or Verona, with their incomparable art-
treasures, in which people spend a few hours on their journey to
Venice. There is, if you will read some recent writing on Moore—
I shall refer particularly to Professor Wisdom's Foreword to *Some
Main Problems of Philosophy* and to Mr. Alan White's in many ways
excellent book—a note of faint patronage, of historical relegation,
in the way people speak of Moore: he is spoken of much as the Ger-
mans used to talk of *der gute Locke*. I wish to suggest this evening
that Moore is undoubtedly the greatest British philosopher of the
present century, and that he stands with perhaps William of Ockham
and David Hume among the three greatest philosophers we have
ever produced. No one has at all approached him in dialectical
accuracy, or in the ability to talk with unfailing clearness on the most
difficult of philosophical issues. Even as a stylist I should hold him

[1] A paper given at the Cambridge Moral Sciences Club and the Royal Institute
of Philosophy.

unsurpassed. Why then is it the case that he is so comparatively unappreciated?

The reason for such under-valuation lies, I think, in the fact that Moore, like some immense central peak in a mountain range, always managed to be partially occluded or overshadowed by less eminent but nearer peaks, as a background to which he was invariably seen. For the first quarter of the century we have the period of his occlusion by Russell, an immensely dazzling philosopher, whose greatness at that period, though inferior to Moore's, I should not wish to abate in the least. For the second quarter of the century we have the period of his occlusion by Wittgenstein, a man whose wonderful but somewhat confusing genius was assisted to immense influence by his unique personal magic, an influence which has declined steadily since his death. Why did Moore, whom I think more penetrating and more responsively constructive than either of these thinkers, allow himself to be thus occluded? The answer lies in his incredible personal modesty which was not, as perhaps in the case of Socrates, at all ironic: in other ways, however, he was more like Socrates than any philosopher that has ever lived. Socrates you may remember—we may for the moment pretend that the *Phaedo* is history—spent a lot of his time in youth studying the books and attending the lectures of the philosophers, and wondering why on earth they said the queer things they said, and this study was the stimulus which led him on to his own inquiries: Moore in much the same way was jolted into philosophy by the queer statements of McTaggart, Bradley and other idealist philosophers, and without their stimulus would never have developed his profound analysis of common sense. Moore was essentially a man who required prodding, a great lazy genius, who would produce a masterpiece if asked to give a lecture to some quite unimportant body of amateurs, but who, if not asked, preferred to take refuge in the dream world of *Redgauntlet* or Mr Pickwick. Moore, like Cézanne, thought little of his work: his remarkable book *Some Main Problems of Philosophy*, which he gave as extension lectures to Morley College, was never published at all. I am immensely glad that Professor Lewis has rescued it from oblivion, and that I urged him to go and look for the treasures that Moore might have in store. A great deal of Moore's most valuable thought is, I believe, still contained in lecture notes, and will be published by Dr Lewy.

With this really small opinion of his own performance went a

LANGUAGE, MIND AND VALUE

great and generous admiration for the intellectual performance of others: being slow and infinitely cautious, he admired the meteoric swiftness of Russell, the wonderful mental versatility of Ramsey, the brilliant queerness of Wittgenstein. Moore liked to be a commentator on other people's work: 'Russell has said, Broad thinks, I know Wittgenstein maintains though I am not quite sure that I understand it', etc. etc. I shall not pretend, of course, that he admired everyone's intellectual performance, and where he did not admire it, he either showed or said it. But the generosity of his spirit meant that he constantly let himself be silenced by others: while he was starting to construct one of his incomparable, scrupulous sentences, others less scrupulous had already leapt into the breach, and Moore readily deferred to them. All this was a little unfortunate, since his utterances, when he developed them fully, had a quality that no one else's could approach.

Another reason for Moore's general overshadowing is that his most brilliant philosophical work, like that of Russell, was early: it extends to about 1925. In that period Cambridge thought as a whole was overshadowed by Oxford idealism: at Oxford, if one referred to Cambridge thinkers at all, it was only to utter epigrams. When Cambridge thought began to gain on that of Oxford in the 'thirties, Moore's genius was in decline: he made few fundamental innovations, and became more and more absorbed in the minutiae of correct expression, which led the historical or legendary Chinese student to remark that while Moore might have taught him little about the universe, he had certainly taught him much about the English language. It also led to the monumental misinterpretation of Moore by Malcolm—a misinterpretation whose interest I do not deny—which made Moore refute philosophical errors merely by showing them to be stated in bad English. I have, I think, said enough of the reasons why Moore has not been properly appreciated. I hope that some people here who knew Moore better than I did and over a longer period, will be able to resolve some of my perplexities, and perhaps also criticize some of my interpretations and assessments.

What now are the aspects of G. E. Moore that I think particularly worth stressing? I think that by far the most interesting, characteristic thing about G. E. Moore is not his ordinariness, his common sense, but the *gnostic* character of his philosophical approach. Moore claims that we know certain truths, e.g. that this is a pencil or that a human hand, and that we know independently that we have knowledge of

NEGLECTED ISSUES IN THE PHILOSOPHY OF G. E. MOORE

them, and that this knowledge, though its existence and detailed content may be mysterious, is incomparably firmer than any premiss dragged up to confute it, or any argument used to subvert it. What I think it important to stress is that Moore means his claim to know certain things to be a remarkable, *substantive* claim, something it would not be at all senseless or contrary to usage to deny. This is shown, first of all, by the fact that Moore says that we are incomparably *more* sure of what we know than of any premiss or argument that could be used to show it false, or that could be used to show it true. There are certainly passages where Moore suggests that we cannot, in some sense of 'cannot', be wrong about what we know, but I do not think that his claims to knowledge make any use of the infallibilism thus merely written into the notion of knowledge. What he in effect means by knowledge is just what he says: it is for something to be much more certain than any premiss used to prove it false, and also much more certain than any premiss used to prove it true. It is to occupy a supreme, an unchallengeable place on the ladder of certainty, not a place differing wholly from any other place. And of course what we know need not be logically necessary, and does not in this way differ from what we merely believe.

I think, further, that the substantive character of Moore's claim to knowledge comes out in the fact that he uses it most impressively in the case of *singular* certainties, in regard to which there is what may be called an *immediate* element. I do not primarily know *general* propositions about material realities and their relation to sense-experience, dreams, etc., about other minds and their relation to behaviour, about the past and its relation to memory, etc. etc. What I primarily know is that *this* pencil exists, that *this* is a human hand and so is *that*, that the name 'Moore' was uttered by myself a few moments ago, that Professor Stace whom I now see has thoughts and that I am not dreaming that I see him, however much it may be the case that I often have dreams in which I seem to meet intelligent people. The *singularity* of the Moorean gnosis is all-important, and it is here that Moore is quite at variance with Malcolm who thinks that one produces human hands, etc., merely to show that certain expressions have a use, and that provided one knows they have a use, one might dispense with the particular illustrations. Moore does not think that one can dispense with the particular examples, nor does he regard them as mere illustrations: they yield the necessary premisses on which our more general knowledge reposes. It is quite possible

LANGUAGE, MIND AND VALUE

in general that I might be dreaming when I seem to confront someone like Professor Stace, and there may be no living person of that name at all: when I confront Professor Stace in the lecture room, however, I cannot doubt that I am face to face with a living person, with thoughts as well as with a body, etc. etc.

I think it important to stress, further, that my knowledge of all these singular matters of fact does not merely mean that the situation is appropriate to my making certain utterances, that it is the sort of situation in which such utterances have a use. Moore thinks that the gnosis involved in such situations goes beyond anything palpably contained in them, and that it would therefore not be inappropriate or stupid to refuse to make my gnostic statements: only I should then know them to be false. 'Where therefore I differ from Russell', Moore says, 'is in supposing that I do know certain things that I do not know immediately, and which also do not follow from anything which I do know immediately.' The message of the somewhat confused *Proof of an External World*—Moore was right in not thinking it one of his best writings—has been widely misconceived, by myself among others: it may be taken to mean that, since I can correctly say 'This is a human hand and that is also', therefore it is certain that two human hands, and therefore two material objects, exist. What it is all-important to note is that Moore only thinks the proof valid because he thinks that he *knows* the premisses, and the knowledge involved in those premisses is for him immense and substantial, and goes far beyond the immediate situation. It is in fact amazing that we have such knowledge, though the fact is that we undoubtedly do have it. It includes the knowledge that one is not dreaming, that what one is seeing could have existed even if no one had experiences, etc. etc. At no point does Moore think that it would not make sense to say that one was dreaming: he merely thinks that one sometimes knows that this is not the case, and that the unwary statements of philosophers who say that all is a dream, show that they really all know that this is not the case. I therefore come to my second major puzzle regarding Moore: why, since his views are plainly not those of Malcolm, did Moore never repudiate Malcolm's account of his views? Why did he never correct Malcolm when he put forward these views as Moore's own? Why did he allow Malcolm to persuade many people to think that Malcolm's linguistic-use interpretation of Moore's gnosis was Moore's view? Malcolm has of course admitted that his whole interpretation was a 'theory', based, it seems clear, on a conflation of Moore

236

with Wittgenstein? Why did Moore permit all this? I leave it to those better acquainted with Moore to provide a full answer.

Moore's gnosis may seem to be attenuated by the comparatively commonplace character of what he claims to know: it covers what he calls the *common-sense* view of the world. It is worth emphasizing, however, that what Moore puts into this common-sense view is not anything and everything that men are disposed to believe, but matters concerning instances of what may be called the *main categories* of existent things and their essential properties and relationships, matters whose acknowledgement is so wrought into, so presupposed by, organized discourse that such discourse is largely disrupted by their denial. What he knows of is the existence of many material bodies occupying space and standing in spatial relations to one another, that have existed in long ages of the past and will presumably exist in the future; he likewise knows of the existence of acts of consciousness in connection with the body he calls *his* own, and of parallel acts of consciousness in connection with other similar living bodies: he also knows about the knowledge he has of various facts and about the precisely parallel knowledge of other persons of other corresponding facts, etc. etc. What the gnosis reveals are the existence of the main types of furnishings of the experienced world and their essential interrelations, and though it may reveal them primarily in the immediate, individual case, yet it would not seem to arrive at its total world-picture through a process of piecemeal extension. There is in fact something very Kantian about the world professedly open to common-sense, an impression strengthened by the use of transcendental arguments to buttress its main certainties, arguments which show these certainties to be presupposed by all our arguments, even by such as seek to undermine them. But however much the structure and main contents of the common-sense world may be basic to discourse, Moore still thinks that they may with some effort be questioned. We may speak as if they did not exist or obtain, without committing absurdity in doing so, but we shall *know* that we are not then speaking truly.

The substantive character of the Moorean gnosis is of course plainer when we turn to his views on analysis. Moore plainly treated his analyses with the greatest of seriousness. There is even a sense in which one might say that his common-sense certainties are ambiguous: they might mean A, they might mean B, they might mean C, etc. etc. In making common-sense assertions, we are for Moore committing ourselves to *one* out of a number of queer alternatives, and the whole task of philosophical analysis consists in finding *which* of the queer alternatives is the true one. This is fortunately a point on which Moore *has* committed himself to a definite assertion. In reply to the suggestion of Lazerowitz that his various revolutionary analyses are merely linguistic recommendations, proposals to alter the language ordinarily used in certain situations, Moore tells us that he definitely does not think this was all he was trying to do, that he certainly holds that analysis is of concepts, not of verbal usages, etc. etc. I think therefore that Moore is positively misrepresented as a philosopher of what most people understand by 'common-sense', even though he may himself have adopted the designation. For Moore thinks there are abysses of incomprehension even in our most commonplace certainties. And many of the queer things that other philosophers assert in controversion of commonplace certainties Moore asserts in analysing commonplace certainties. The views of Moore are in fact *more* queer than those of the metaphysicians he attacks, for while they say that certain commonplace beliefs are false, and other queer things true, Moore says that certain commonplace beliefs are really the *same in content* as certain wildly strange beliefs. So far from really holding that 'Everything is what it is and not some other thing', Moore may be said to have held that everything when scratched shows itself to be something quite unsuspected.

I think we must not forget the immense substance Moore packs into his analyses: he is so sure that this pencil exists, that he knows it exists, that he is prepared to think that he may know that something exists which he has never observed and never will observe, and that it stands in a relation he also has not observed nor will observe to what the senses reveal of the pencil. And he is prepared, if nothing else will do, to refute Hume and Hume's principles by this drastic piece of gnosis. And he is prepared to maintain, in the face of all immediate appearances, that when I say 'That is a door', the ultimate subject of my judgement is not a door, but something, a 'sense-datum', of which most people have never heard at all, and which is in fact introduced just to *be* the real subject of this sort of judgement. It is worth emphasizing, too, that while Moore thought the analysis of commonplace certainties more likely to end in failure than success, he was still gnostic about analysis. We can certainly, if we reflect, know that we *don't* include certain things in certain of our concepts, that certain analyses *won't* work at all. Thus Moore never falters in repudiating idealistic accounts of material-object statements, though surprisingly he is not unwilling to accept phenomenalist accounts, perhaps because a possibility of sensation has something objective about it. Propositions as entities are likewise very decisively rejected because we see that the relation of a mind to a proposition *cannot* be what obtains when we consider cases of false belief, and this in the face of the fact that Moore admits, both early and late, that a perfectly good sense can be given to the statement that there are propositions. That statements can be given a perfectly good sense, and have a use, does not therefore make them correct as analyses.

What is now the role of ordinary language in this queer analytic *approfondissement?* Ordinary language we may say is the net in which we catch the fish (or the dolphin or mermaid) which we then get to perform in our analytic aquarium: alternatively it is the press gang that captures the man of whom we then proceed to make an able seaman. The role of ordinary language is to ensure that we have a *genuine* notion before us for analysis, that we are not merely playing with words and saying nothing at all. Let me take a case of Moore's use of ordinary language from the brilliant but forgotten article 'The Subject Matter of Psychology' published in 1909. Moore says: 'I wish here to define as clearly as I can those kinds of entities which seem to me to be undoubtedly mental and to consider how they differ from those which are not mental. To begin with then: I see, I hear, I smell, I taste, etc., I sometimes feel pain; I sometimes remember entities which I have formerly seen or heard, I sometimes imagine and I sometimes dream; I think of all sorts of different entities; I believe some propositions, and think of others without believing them; I take pleasure in certain events and am displeased at others; and I sometimes resolve that certain actions shall be done. All these things I do, and there is nothing more certain to me than that I do them all. And because, in a wide sense, they are all of them things which I do, I propose to call them all "mental acts". By calling them acts I do not mean to imply that I am always particularly active when I do them. No doubt I must be active in a sense, whenever I do any of them. But certainly when I do some of them I am sometimes very passive. Now I think we may say that, whenever I do any of these things, I am always "conscious of" something or other. Each of these mental acts consists, at least in part, in my being conscious of something. I do not mean to say that in the case of each of them I am conscious of something in one and the same sense. For instance when

I actually see a colour I am certainly conscious of that colour in a very different sense from that in which I am conscious of it when I remember it half an hour afterwards and do not any longer see it. And I am not sure that there is anything whatever in common to these two senses of "consciousness". But still I think the name can certainly be rightly applied to what occurs in both these cases, and that similarly we are, in *some* proper sense of the word, conscious of something whenever we do any of the acts I have named."[1]

The above is a marvellous piece of Moorean concept-trapping. We trap a concept by taking a number of ordinary phrases in regard to which we are sure that they have an application, and we introduce various other phrases, e.g. 'mental act', by connecting them precisely with some of these. Even here Moore does not teach that the mere fact that we use a word in certain circumstances shows that there is a clear and consistent concept behind that use: in certain cases, however, we do know this, and the ground is now prepared for further analysis. It may be noted how Moore is willing to gather together concepts under a new concept which may never have previously existed, e.g. mental act, and how he also allows that a word which appears to have one sense may be found to cover a number of quite distinct concepts, e.g. 'consciousness'. What is remarkable in the whole process is how firmly it secures the existence of its subject-matter by using ordinary words that we *know* have an application, and how resolutely it then moves from that ordinary starting-point towards goals more and more extraordinary. There is in Moore no great respect for the suggestions made to philosophers by ordinary language: he thinks in fact, as a famous passage testifies, that it is sometimes so constructed as systematically to mislead them.

We must in philosophy get our concept away from the net in which we have trapped it; we must make it *perform* in our analytical aquarium, in which special environment we may find it doing astonishing things that it never did in ordinary contexts. The kind of tests we put it through consist in trying to detect affinities and differences not ordinarily noted, and using in this connection the now standard method of conceptual experiment. Moore asks, e.g., if we can conceive a case in which there might be an act of consciousness which had not that relation to other acts of consciousness which is ordinarily expressed by the phrase 'belonging to the same mind', and decides that he *can* conceive of it, or at least that he isn't clear that he cannot.

[1] *Aristotelian Society Proceedings,* 1909–10.

This experiment reveals the independence and distinctness of two concepts: mentality in the sense of being an act of consciousness, and mentality in the sense of belonging to a mind, which are not normally kept apart at all. Only last week I heard the same method elaborately applied at Oxford: we had to deal with people who couldn't move their own limbs directly, but who could move remote objects directly, and their own limbs indirectly by them, etc. etc. I do not myself think the method of conceptual experiment a safe one in philosophy, tending as it does to cut off the vague penumbra which is implied by, rather than included in, a concept, but it remains a conceptual technique which has *some* importance even now, as it had in the time of Descartes and again of Moore. In all this procedure Moore makes us think of Plato's procedure as described in the Seventh Epistle. In philosophical thought we don't deal with mere words, definitions, illustrations, etc., we have to rub them all together in the mind until reason flashes forth. We may start with the routines of ordinary usage, but we may end with our thought and language utterly transformed.

I have given you two aspects of Moore not sufficiently regarded: his profound gnosticism, and his use of ordinary language to make sure that we *have* a substantial gnosis and not a mere verbal appearance of one. I now wish to consider a number of other aspects I regard as very fundamental. The first is Moore's assertion of the unique nature of consciousness, its complete categorial difference from anything attributive. In this respect he brought to full clearness in England a perception which Brentano and Husserl clarified on the Continent, that being conscious is not at all like being blue, that the one is *of* things in a way in which the other is not. Moore possibly got this idea from a reading of Brentano who also influenced his ethics profoundly, but his main interest in it was of course as a tool to combat epistemological idealism and to put epistemological realism in its place. The source of this interest explains why Moore's analysis of consciousness remains rather rudimentary and in fact ends in failure: Moore is unable to give more than a very partial analysis of the thought of the non-existent, and never worked out a complete map of the forms of consciousness as was done by Husserl. The very faulty 'Refutation of Idealism' has, however, as its main merit, the insistence on the unique character of consciousness, and also the insistence on its accessibility. Consciousness represents something of which, though it may be retiring and evanescent, we can in some circumstances be directly

LANGUAGE, MIND AND VALUE

aware. I think it clear that Moore never gave up his belief in the reality and seizable character of what he called 'conscious acts', that for him such words as 'apprehension' and 'knowledge' meant more than peculiar series of sense-contents or of considered and correct speech and action: they meant something interior and episodic, realizable in an instant and fitly described by way of metaphors derived from illumination and light. In apprehension and knowledge something appeared to, was before the mind, and this appearing or being before the mind was itself something that could be taken note of or apprehended. At the time when Russell was trying to get away from intentionalism in the *Analysis of Mind*, Moore was unable to go the whole way with him. He pointed out that in mental contexts we never merely have loud sounds, red patches, etc., but sounds heard *as* loud, patches seen *as* red, etc., that more or less disengaged universals play a part in mental contexts that they do not in physical ones, and that one cannot in consequence adopt Russell's oversimple picture of two modes or arrangement of sense-contents giving rise to the mental and physical worlds. Hints of these views are to be found in the paper 'Are the materials of sense affections of the mind?' published in 1920.

I must confess, however, that I do not understand what Moore meant by his strange statements in the 'Defence of Commonsense' (1925) that he feels 'doubtful whether there is any intrinsic property expressed by the words "I am conscious now" ', and 'that the proposition that he has had experiences does not necessarily entail the proposition that there have been any events which were experiences, and that he cannot satisfy himself that he is acquainted with any events of the supposed kind'. It is really very obscure how one can have experiences without there being events, things which happen to one, which *are* experiences. I should have said the one was entirely tantamount to the other. Perhaps the stress is on the word 'intrinsic', and Moore means to hold some view of consciousness as a *relation* among a number of entities. If this is so, I think it wholly obscure what he thought this relation was. Perhaps he was at this time in a genuine wobble about consciousness, as he was at a later time in a wobble about the predicate 'good', as where he remarks amusingly that he is inclined to think that the predicate 'good' is not the name of a characteristic, that it has merely 'emotive' and not cognitive meaning, but that he is also inclined to think that this is *not* the case, and that he cannot say in which way he is inclined more strongly. I have heard

242

it said that Moore in his later years definitely came out of this particular wobble, and *was* more inclined to believe once more in the unique non-natural character of goodness, and on the only occasion on which I discussed consciousness with Moore his remarks suggested that he had come out of his 1925 wobble also, and that he again believed consciousness to be something unique, irreducible and well known.

Moore then had something valuable and important to say about consciousness: I think he also had something valuable and important to say about universals and other *entia rationis*. Moore assumed in his early writings that we are asking substantial questions if we ask whether or not such *entia rationis* have being, if they have being in the same or a different sense from concrete particulars, and into how many distinct sub-varieties they fall. The Morley Lectures, chapters xvi–xx, contain in my view one of the most brilliant, interestingly argued ontologies or sorting out of categories with which I have any acquaintance. On reading them one feels that what I may call the peculiar treachery of *entia rationis*, their proneness to antinomy, of which Plato had such disillusioning experience when he wrote the *Parmenides*, has been dispelled: it is really possible, it would seem, to talk clearly and without contradiction about entities of reason. In this ontology, whose details I recommend to you for study, Moore maintains that there are at least three basic categories all of which have being univocally: there are particulars, there are truths or facts, and there are universals or general ideas which are in no sense mental. What is interesting about Moore's treatment of universals is his cold attitude to qualitative universals, such as salmon-pink and whiteness. He readily admits that there are relations and relational properties, but of qualitative universals all sorts of elaborate relational reductions are attempted. In the end colour is admitted to the rank of genuine entities while salmon-pink is not. I should not wish anyone to accept these opinions—I am quite unpersuaded myself—but they afford a unique piece of philosophical discussion of which I seem the only student and admirer. What should be noted is that Moore's loyalty to his *entia rationis* was not changed by the nominalistic climate through which he lived: for him the being of facts and universals never became a mere question of how one chooses to speak. This is shown by the remarkable Appendix to *Some Main Problems to Philosophy*, written in 1952, where Moore makes various corrections to his 1909 views, and discovers some 'gross mistakes' in them. What is important, however, is that Moore proposes no fundamental revision of these earlier views: they are broadly endorsed once the 'gross mistakes' have been discounted.

I shall not say anything about the peculiar contributions of Moore to ethics since, whatever else they may have been, they have not been neglected. Perhaps, however, it is worth calling attention to the remarkable degree to which Moore appeals to synthetic *a priori* connections in his ethics, connections held to be necessary and not empirical, and yet not tautological. I should also have said that the system of values set up in *Principia Ethica* represents a far more daring flight of *a priori* moralizing than any found in the idealist moralists: what is for Moore good or right has nothing to do with what is ordinarily thought so, nor with the ordinary use of ethical words.

I have now created what I feel to be a reasonably true image of Moore as a philosopher, laying my main emphasis on his neglected aspects. I wish to stress that these neglected sides were never discarded by Moore, and that without them it is not possible to appraise him properly. I now wish to say something about the philosophical importance of these peculiar Moorean aspects. Are they of contemporary interest, or do they perhaps belong wholly to the past, to the 'philosophical palaeontology' into which contemporary thinkers so readily relegate what they do not regard with sympathy?

I should like first of all to stress the immense, permanent value of the *gnostic* element in G. E. Moore, the doctrine that there are things of which we are much more sure than of any premiss or argument devoted to their overthrow, and of the Moorean extension to this view to the effect that there are interpretations of the gnosis which the gnosis itself rejects, or which at least cannot readily be squared with it. It does seem to me that the presence of this gnostic element is an essential element in a philosophy, and that it differentiates what I should call a responsible philosophy from one which, though brilliant, is also irresponsible. A responsible philosopher seems to me one who, when certain assumptions and methods lead to plainly preposterous conclusions, will begin to suspect something invalid in the assumptions and methods he has been employing, not draw the preposterous conclusions, and who will never accept *any* mode of argument, however persuasive, which makes nonsense of *too* much of what he knows very much better. This is not to say that a philosopher who is sound will not be prepared to try out assumptions and methods as far as they will go, and to see whether their results will

244

square with what he knows very much better, but only that he will remain possessed of what he fundamentally knows, and will judge all assumptions and methods in terms of this. Now it seems to me that the main fault of three brilliant philosophies of meaning successively launched upon the world—I shall speak here of the philosophy of meaning as mirroring, of meaning as verification and of meaning as use—is their grave lack of a regulative gnosis. They have been remarkable schizoid fantasies irresponsibly launched in the void without regard to the preposterous character of their outcome. I do not need to particularize elaborately, but the kind of thought which at one stage teaches us that we cannot talk about our friends' experience without talking about the possible movements of their bodies, and which at a later stage teaches that we cannot identify or distinguish our own experiences except to the extent that there is a public check on what we say of them, obviously lacks all gnostic regulation. For we certainly do understand what it is for experiences to belong to different minds, and what it is for such experiences to be similar or different, and that their similarities or differences are not similarities in anything bodily and linguistic, and we not only understand all this, but we know that we understand it, and we know it to express truth, and we are much more sure of all this than we can ever be of any theory of meaning. If a theory of meaning, therefore, makes it seem dubious or impossible that we should understand or know any of these things, or if it forces us to interpret them in a fashion that we know not to accord with their meaning, then it is the theory of meaning that must be sacrificed or altered, not the certainties in question. In the same way we understand what it is for one thing to be better than another, or to be something that we absolutely ought to do, and we likewise *know* that there are some things better than others, and some things that we ought absolutely to do, and we know further that these things, though discerned with difficulty, do not differ from one man or society to another. We have now various theories of the use of ethical terms which do not readily accord with this claim, or which do so only with a great deal of subtle trimming. What must one do? Must one discard philosophical ethics as the systematic study of absolute values and norms, or reduce it to a meta-ethical branch of linguistics? Not at all. One must question the theories which fail to make sense of a fundamental enterprise, which we know to be feasible, even if we are then left with the hard task of finding out just how it is 'feasible' and where the opposing theories are mistaken.

LANGUAGE, MIND AND VALUE

Does this all mean that I am proposing a new movement of 'Back to Moore'? By no means. The movement in question has, I think, been going on covertly for a long time. Contemporary philosophy has, in my view, considerable elements of the saving gnosis. Professor Ayer, e.g., has long shed his early behaviouristic analyses of other people's experiences, simply because he found he could not believe them, i.e. he knew them to be false, and he has had much to say in criticism of the dogmatic thesis of the impossibility of a private language. No one would likewise accuse a contemporary thinker like Austin of being prone to preposterous theses: he is in fact an analyst after the manner of Moore, except that he conducts his analysis largely by considering the use of words, which is from a Moorean point of view legitimate, since the content of a concept certainly comes out in our verbal usages. Nor is a philosopher like Austin a mere worshipper of ordinary speech, though his occasional tidying up of our usage certainly does not go as far as the analyses of Moore.

What I should myself like to complain of in Moore is not that he was a gnostic, but that he did not carry his gnosticism far enough. To me it seems that in addition to the hard core of certainties rightly defended by Moore—certainties about material objects, other minds, time and space, knowledge, etc.—we have an immense number of softer near-certainties, things of which we are not indeed more sure than of *any* premiss or argument brought in to confound them, but of which we are certainly more sure than of *many* such premisses and arguments. I am, I fear, a philosopher who thinks the air positively thick with the synthetic *a priori*, that there is hardly a sphere of experience or knowledge in which we do not have important advance intimations of various sorts, even though these intimations may at times prove delusive, and even though their content is often only probabilistic, and permits of empirical exceptions. It is not, however, my business to give you *my* gnosis nor to oppose it to Moore's, but only to insist that to have a gnosis in philosophy is quite essential if one's thinking is not to be vain and sterile.

I should like, in closing, to criticize another aspect of Moore: the precise form taken by his analyses of common-sense certainties. I believe Moore right in thinking that the accounts one ultimately arrives at in thinking over and rethinking ordinary certainties will be startlingly different from the accounts one starts with, that philosophical assertions can't be a mere reassertion of what one ordinarily says. But I should gravely object to the form in which Moore often

246

NEGLECTED ISSUES IN THE PHILOSOPHY OF G. E. MOORE

tried to cast his analyses, and I believe it largely responsible for his inability to reach satisfactory results. I should say that Moore was unduly obsessed by a misleading model of *whole and parts*: whenever one has a many-sided reality to deal with, one must resolve it into a set of *constituents* put together in a certain way. Thus if one is analysing the consciousness of blue, one must split it up into two elements, consciousness pure and simple, and blue pure and simple, or if one is analysing a good thing like personal affection one must split it up into a natural psychological activity, on the one hand, and a non-natural value-predicate, on the other. Now I think this whole-part type of analysis completely mistaken, and that whole and part is a category simply not applicable to most of the facts that have interest for philosophy. For I think it plain that in some sense our notions have other notions 'built into' them, that they are *of* this or of that, or are oriented to this or to that, without having this or that as a part or constituent, and I think that a notion can only be philosophically grasped when it is seen in its place in a total notional economy, each of whose members realizes the living paradox of doing little more than take in the others' washing. Now it is plain why Moore avoided this built-in, internal analysis: he thought too readily that it was logically absurd, and he was also reacting to the exaggerations of Bradley's *Appearance and Reality*. But his determination 'to chop everything up into little bits' resulted in the failure of his philosophical psychology, the failure of his theory of perception, the failure of his theory of our knowledge of the physical world and the failure of his ethics. And from that failure has sprung the slow nihilism that has sapped British philosophy for so long, but which is now, I hope, at its dying gasp. I am sorry to end on a critical note, but I do not wish to diminish the greatness of Moore. Moore, like Socrates, was a great philosophical watershed. Socrates produced Cynics, Cyrenaics and logic-chopping Megarians as well as the great synthetic thought of Plato. Moore likewise has been the father of much triviality and of much valuable thought. Of the advent of his Plato, however, there is as yet no sign.

XV

THE METHODOLOGY OF NORMATIVE ETHICS[1]

(1961)

THE aim of this paper is to discuss certain peculiarities of ethical reasoning and, in particular, of the procedures by means of which a *normative* ethics may be established, an ethics that can, with some show of justification, claim to set up standards holding for everyone. These peculiar reasonings have not, I think, been sufficiently studied, and, with the sole exception of some points raised by Mr Toulmin in his writings on logic and ethics, nothing at all like them has been systematically considered. The reason for this neglect of what are, *par excellence*, the reasoning forms of ethics and axiology, lies in the overwhelming prestige, the appalling dominance, of the logic of strict entailment, which has been the bane of our age. Wittgenstein in his early writings bifurcated all true utterances into the brutally empirical, on the one hand, and the emptily tautological, on the other; by implication, he divided our thought-shifts into those justified by tautological transformation, on the one hand, and by augmented experience, on the other. Though we are now far from endorsing such positions, their ghost lingers on as part of the fog left behind him by a great but somewhat stupefying genius. Dimly we feel, though we are perhaps not willing to avow it, that a conclusion, to be respectable, must be capable of being made to follow incontestably from a set of premisses themselves incontestable, that it must represent a tautological transformation of such premisses. Such an approach excises almost all that is worth while in philosophy, to which the tautologically evident and the empirically true represent the two poles of

[1] A paper delivered on May 5, 1961, at the meeting of the Western Division of the American Philosophical Association at St Louis.

THE METHODOLOGY OF NORMATIVE ETHICS

utter uninterest, and it certainly excises all that is worth while and characteristic in ethics, in which practically every statement represents an uneasy compromise of different styles of diction, every notion stretches subtly as we use it, and each reasoning involves a subtle and at times a large shift of ground. The typical arguments of ethics are not those which deduce trivial applications from principles of firm validity and of clear sense and scope; they are arguments in which a notion is stretched and developed to cover new types of case, in which application is retracted from cases to which a notion formerly applied, in which a notion constantly passes over into sister notions or doubles itself by gemmation or fission. Typically ethical are such reasonings or rational asseverations as 'What is sauce for the goose is sauce for the gander', 'Who wills the end must will the means', 'All the world necessarily loves a lover', 'I like this, so others should like it too', 'I like fishing, you like fishing, so I can't help liking you', 'You don't admire this, so perhaps I was wrong in thinking it so very admirable', 'You have done to me what I personally don't like, therefore you should suffer what you personally don't like', 'You have done what no one can tolerate, therefore you should suffer what you personally cannot tolerate', etc. etc. All these arguments are not only good arguments, having considerable persuasive force; they are also, I should like to maintain, the very paradigm of the logical. Too long we have been hypnotized by the virtuosity of reasonings which, with a vast expenditure of energy, manage to hover stationary over some spot, illuminating it perhaps from a variety of angles, but not bringing to vision anything fundamentally new. They have made us forget that the task of worth-while inference is to go farther, to cover new ground, and that inferences that fail to do so, though including in their scope the unimagined wealth of mathematics, are in reality degenerate cases, inferences only by courtesy.

The kind of reasoning I propose to study is, further, a sort of reasoning which transforms not merely our persuasions but our interests, and with our interests our emotional overflows, our coolly expressed valuations, and also our practice. It is similar to the sorts of reasoning studied by Stevenson in *Ethics and Language*, though differing from these in that its natural movement is from the personal to the impersonal, from the merely actual to the normative, from a speech that only *tries* to be for all to one that more and more succeeds in being so. A fixed firmament of values, we may hold, necessarily arises out of the crass turbulence of human interest, much as a fixed

LANGUAGE, MIND AND VALUE

calculus of probabilities, with which it has in fact a fundamental analogy, arises out of the crude variety of human credulity. To believe in this emergence of the normative out of the non-normative is, in a sense, to commit the naturalistic fallacy, in a sense not to commit it. It is to commit it inasmuch as one refuses to see any ultimate gulf between what we *do* like, and what we *must* and what we *should* like; it is not to commit it inasmuch as one recognizes the gulf between description and prescription, between taking up a stance or attitude and saying that one has done so, though one recognizes, too, that the two ways of speaking are inextricably blended, even in the use of the same word. That the normative emerges smoothly out of the non-normative is a well-known doctrine of idealism, which finds it absurd to criticize a performance in terms of a standard extrinsic to itself.

The most basic moves of ethical, or rather pre-ethical, reasoning, are in no sense remarkable; they are moves dominated by *analogy*, which, here as elsewhere, plays a part so central in reasoning as to be practically identifiable with reasonableness itself. To like something, even personally, in some character in which we see it, is, by a logical but not formally logical transition, to like something else like it in this respect; '*That* such-and-such is good' and '*This* also is a such-and-such' potently if not cogently mediate the conclusion: 'This is good also.' It is by a more openly radiating extension of the same type that one proceeds from the liking of this so-and-so to the liking of anything like it in being so-and-so, and, by a more sophisticated retraction, possible only to those whom language has taught to splinter things into 'features', that one proceeds from all these likings to the pin-pointed liking of being-so-and-so as such, to an attribution of goodness, even if only for oneself, to card-playing or French millinery or mountain scenery. The processes I am describing are anything but novel; what is perhaps novel is the characterization of them as 'rational'. They have, however, all the traits of corresponding extensions of expectation in the realm of theory, to which we do not hesitate to apply the word 'rational', and the same tendency which leads us to embark on either sort of process also leads us to *endorse* either from higher levels, to say, in the ethical case, for instance, that a man *should* like ϕ-ness or should think ϕ-ness good if he likes this or that ϕ, or that he should think ϕ-ness good (or like it) in *this* case if he does so in *that*. (The same tendency also endorses the approval of, or the view that, one should have all these likings.) This higher-order endorsement of primary liking is itself a move deeply charac-

250

THE METHODOLOGY OF NORMATIVE ETHICS

teristic of ethical reasoning, perhaps the most fundamental of such moves. If one likes X, one will and should like one's liking of X, and should find it 'suitable' and 'right', and one should like one's liking of anything like X. By a subtle sophistication, one may then learn to like X, not merely because it is X, but because it is liked by or pleasing to oneself, a sophistication of great importance, in which shameless voluptuousness and rational prudence alike have their source. By an equally rational extension, if one likes X, one should like not only one's own liking of X but also that others should like it. Not only art, morality, religion, and other 'higher interests' are inveterately propagandist, but any interest whatever. To be fond even of trout fishing is to desire all men, in the absence of special hindrances, to share one's fondness, to approve of those who do share it, and to reprove those who do not.

All these rational extensions of interest are rational just because they are *not* inevitable. They admit of possible exceptions; they have, in fact, many actual exceptions. Few philosophically interesting connections are in any other case. Their rationality means that they *ought to* or *should* obtain, not that they infallibly will. But this 'should' or 'ought' is not without *some* relation to a 'will'; it is, as the shifting use of the auxiliaries 'should' and 'ought' abundantly indicates, incredible that what should happen does not happen at all, or happens only with the greatest rarity, that it is not in some sense 'normal', that its non-occurrence does not require special explanation, as its occurrence requires none. Special impediments, physical hindrances, personal conflicts, etc., must explain why a man who likes something cannot bear others to like it, whereas no special explanation is required in the contrary case.

Interest will also rationally extend from an object to its necessary conditions, and the rationality of its extension to means and instruments has been recognized in Kant's hypothetical imperatives. But it is important to stress the process by which, with predictable regularity, the interests called by Butler 'particular passions' almost inevitably bring to birth those new, higher-order interests called by him 'self-love' and 'benevolence'. A man moved by particular passions is a man interested in X as X, Y as Y, etc.; a man moved by self-love is a man interested in X only as interesting or satisfactory to himself, an interest which, on our principles, develops naturally and rationally out of his primary interests and which, by the variety of sources that feed it, can persist and act even when primary interest is lacking. Few

LANGUAGE, MIND AND VALUE

philosophers have to my mind commented sufficiently on the remarkable fact that men are able, as animals are not, to plan meals when they are not hungry, to contract marriages when they are not sexually excited, to buy pictures when they are not aesthetically stirred, etc. etc. Men are, in fact, capable of being moved not merely by certain primary objects of interest, the succulence of cherries, the curve of limbs, etc., but by the interesting or satisfying power of such objects; primary motivation becomes itself a source of secondary motivation, and this at times when the former is merely thought of and not actual, and it is in this power to be moved by the mere thought of movingness that practical rationality mainly consists. For when our interest is directed to the interesting as such, interests necessarily are set on a level and co-ordinated, and no mechanical mystery is required to account for the fact that we do what will please us *on the whole*. Cool calculation decides the issue rather than a synergy of motives. Nor is it obscure why the cool calculative interest thus generated should extend itself to others, and should beget a family of benevolences ranged around their prime parent, self-love. There is, in fact, *more* of a logical leap from the interest in X to the interest in X's interestingness than from the interest in X's interestingness to *me* to X's interestingness to *you*; both are remote, rational, detached from primary impulsion. Nor is it obscure, lastly, why a move should take place in a direction of further generality, and why men should become interested in the fact that something is interesting or satisfactory to *someone*, regardless who that someone is, and that, at this new level of interest, the primary interests of different persons should be alike co-ordinated in a pattern of over-all benevolence. Benthamite generosity and generality, which seeks to extend the minimum of satisfyingness and the minimum of dissatisfyingness to the widest body of persons, is, in fact, as inevitable a first fruit of the operation of reason on human interest as the rules of probability and the primary generalizations of science are an operation of rationality on human belief and the data of experience. To make generalized benevolence a special product of Christianity or of bourgeois society or of our personal decisions is like attributing the calculus of probabilities to the gaming habits of the eighteenth century.

Benthamite benevolence is, however, a small mouse for our dialectical mountain to have brought forth; we must do better. To be interested in interestingness as such, regardless whose interest is concerned, is a kind of interest impartial among individuals and indifferent

252

THE METHODOLOGY OF NORMATIVE ETHICS

to their differences. To have a certain sort of interest leads, however, by a natural or logical transition, to a higher-order approval of that kind of interest and of its special objects. In so far as we start being impartially or undiscriminatingly interested in objects of interest, this kind of interest creates its own zest, and becomes interesting to itself; a Butlerian conscience or Adam Smithian impartial spectator is a necessary outcome, given time and social peace. How *strong* this higher-order product will be will, of course, depend on many factors, many fortuitous and not all admirable, but, once established, we may expect it to increase in strength, being fed from so many sources. But the *authority* of the higher disinterestedness rests on what it is: it endeavours to speak for all, and to express only what all must feel, in so far as they are interested in the interesting as such, and this aim it can achieve, and can approve of its own success in achieving it, in a manner leaving no further scope for revision. This disinterested omni-interestedness must, moreover, tend to buttress itself with a defensive dislike of whatever tends against itself, a dislike of the *arbitrary* endorsement of one interest at the cost of another. While not hostile to particular interests as such, since it grows out of them and presupposes them, it must be hostile to any one-sided or biassed endorsement of them. To be interested in the interesting as such leads naturally to aversion from exclusive absorption in single interests. No notion, however, behaves more tantalizingly under analysis than the notion of impartiality, and we cannot hope to have eliminated all its squirmings here.

What we may call disinterest or omni-interest can, however, not be rigidly undifferentiated; it will ramify into fundamental species of interest, each arising in an inevitable manner. Here my exposition is lamed by the limits of my time; there is room only for suggestive dogmatism. Let me say, therefore, that our interest in the particular characters of things, a side of all our primary interests, must, by processes not here to be dealt with, become separately interesting to itself, and so lead to that detached respect for *character* as such, and for its due presentation, that is usually called 'aesthetic'. In the same manner, our interest in what is *matter of fact* and *truth*, which is necessarily a side of all our primary interests, is such as, by processes not here to be sketched, to detach itself and become interesting to itself, leading thereby to a higher-order interest in and respect for truth and fact as such, and to a balanced respect for the varied alternatives that *may* be true, and to a defensive dislike of all that obstructs the way to truth, or limits

LANGUAGE, MIND AND VALUE

the fields in which we shall seek it, etc. etc., to the interests in short that are scientific or cognitive. In the same manner, our persistent involvement with *other persons*, which has not (it may be argued) a merely contingent relation to our other concerns, which entails at once the conquest of new spheres by sympathy and the relegation of their contents to the transcendently alien, a situation as straightforwardly plain to ordinary thought and speech as it has been teasing and bemusing to philosophers—this persistent involvement with persons, I say, is necessarily such as to detach itself and become interesting to itself, thereby leading to that higher-order interest in and respect for persons as such, and the immensity of their distinctness, by which Benthamite arithmetic may be mitigated, and on which all justice is founded. We develop, in short, a special set of higher-order interests that may be called 'ethical'. In the same manner, finally, our *practical* interests—and our primary interests must all be practical—lead inevitably to a detached interest in practice or conscious causality as such, and in such causality as directed to ends themselves having an impersonal sanction and savour; we reach, in short, the special interests called 'moral', those concerned with the good will and with good practice as such, regardless of what they succeed in achieving.

All these higher-order interests have their own style of impartiality: there is the detachment of art, which does not care what it presents nor whether what it presents is true or otherwise satisfactory, but only if it is *well* presented; there is the detachment of science concerned only with what is *true*, or with what *may* be true, regardless of its precise content or any special satisfaction it may give; there is the detachment of justice, which abhors arbitrary discrimination and privilege among persons (each as much a world on its own as are the creations of art, or the alternatives studied in probability); there is, finally, the detachment of morality concerned only with integrity and purity of intention, regardless of the particular projects this turns itself to, or of its success in executing these. All these forms of detachment, or rather of undiscriminating omni-attachment, form a *family*; they may be said to carry out analogous tasks on different materials—justice does with persons what probability does with alternatives, etc. etc.—and as a family they must be moved by strong family feeling and affinity. Except as hindered by extraneous circumstances, each must endorse and approve the others. And the desire for detached, general objects of satisfaction which, as we held, necessarily grows out of our primary interests, cannot help finding satisfaction in

THE METHODOLOGY OF NORMATIVE ETHICS

attitudes sharing its *own* detachment and in their appropriate objects. Impersonally or impartially, therefore, we must not merely be interested in the satisfactory or hedonic as such, the backbone of welfare; we must also be interested in our several styles of disinterest, and the aesthetic, the scientific, the ethical and the moral must take their place beside the merely satisfactory as 'values' having no merely contingent or personal sanction. The firmament of values begins to wear a familiar face, and it is only confusion and the spell of a false logic that could have led men to think otherwise.

It is clear, of course, that my sketch of the value-firmament leaves much to be decided. I have left obscure the precise application of the various vague rubrics I have mentioned to the concrete objects of primary interest, an application never mechanically definite and yet never merely arbitrary. Here I believe there is indefinite room for 'decision' and personal choice. I have also left obscure the grading and ordering of various ethically relevant considerations, of varying types of interest and disinterest and their objects, believing that here, too, the radical disparateness of the reasoned 'cases' to be made out for different types of value leaves indefinite room for personal preference and choice. I believe, however, that the arbitrariness of such decisions is never radical, and that it must also involve an impersonal legitimation. Just as we can detachedly endorse the liking of a particular object, but only *because* someone personally likes it, because it seems good to *him*, so we can and must endorse the personal applications and orderings of the value-firmament just because they *are* someone's personal applications and orderings. They are endorsed as *for him*, but the endorsement for him is *by all*. Conscience, as Hegel stressed in the *Phenomenology*, and as is clear to all who have operated tribunals for conscientious objectors, is a faculty not leading to detailed agreement but rather to disagreement. What is uniform and mandatory is the need for respecting this personal faculty, without which all morals would be void through vagueness. Not even here, therefore, is there a place for radical arbitrariness; those who defend it must, I fear, be cast forth from the ranks of sound moralists as poets were from the Platonic Republic.

I have now completed my inadequate exposition and illustration of what I hold to be the reasoning forms of ethics and axiology. They embody, I think, a logic of *family relations*, in a sense somewhat like that given to the term by Wittgenstein: different axiological principles lead up to and introduce one another by a kind of loose, rambling affinity, which is not less important and inescapable by virtue of being loose. (Moral philosophers, and philosophers generally, should be men open to influence even by the most far-fetched and loose connections, rather than men moved only by the most rigorous and, therefore, most trivial bonds.) That I have, in my time, been intelligible and persuasive is too much to hope; at best I may have made you receptive to the kind of loose dialectic necessary in ethical discourse.

INDEX

Ach, N. 182–3, 205
Aesthetic experiences 112, 253
Alexander, S. 104
Analogy 120–1, 250
Analysis 237–9, 246–7
Animals 20–1
Anscombe, E. 198, 207
Anselm, St. 103, 156, 222
Aristotle 16, 94, 126, 149, 153–4, 227
Attitudes 167–71, 173–81
Augustine, St. 44–50, 118
Austin, J. L. 246
Ayer, A. J. 246

Bentham, J. 252–4
Berkeley, G. 226
Bewusstseinslagen 20–1, 182–5, 187–96
Bolzano, B. 150–1
Bosanquet, B. 125
Bradley, F. H. 126, 218–19, 226–7, 233, 247
Brain 142–4
Brentano, F. 109, 166, 241
Broad, C. D. 130, 169, 234
Brownies 140–1
Butler, J. 176–7, 251
Butlerian attitudes 176–81, 253

Cantor, G. 146, 150–5, 162, 164, 221
Carnap, R. 57n
Cognitive interests 254
Common-sense 237–8
Communication 27–8
Confirmation 117, 208, 214
Conscience 255
Consciousness 241–3
Consistency 48
Corrigibility 33
Courage, logical 122
Croce, B. 218

Definiteness (value) 113–15
Descartes, R. 33, 222, 241

Developed ethical responses 75–6
Dialectic (in Hegel) 219–28
Disembodied existence 142–3, 201
Doubt 27, 34
Driesch, H. 120

Economy 115–16, 120
Edification 95
Ejaculation 71
Emotions 73, 107–10, 165
Erigena 104
Ewing, A. C. 173
Expression (of attitude) 16, 19–20, 67, 70

Family relations (conceptual) 74, 110, 254
Fichte, J. G. 104
Frege, G. 158, 210
Fulfilment 189, 208, 212–15

Galton, F. 170
Gentile, G. 218
Ghostly element 16–18, 22, 129, 139–40
Gnosis (in Moore) 234–8, 244–6
Goedel, K. 57–8, 221
Goedelian Sentences 58–65
Goodman, N. 153

Heeding 131–2
Hegel, G. W. F. 65n., 114–15, 125, 150, 156, 210, 217–31, 255
Hempel, C. G. 117n.
Heraclitus 32, 37, 115, 124
Higher well-being 89–92, 253–5
Hume, D. 67n., 70–1, 164, 186, 222, 232, 238
Humphrey, G. 184, 188
Husserl, E. 18, 74, 208, 212–15, 241
Hyppolite, J. 217

257

LANGUAGE, MIND AND VALUE

I 16, 55–6
Idealists 17, 219, 226
Identity 29–33, 223–4
Imagination (in ethics) 83
Impartiality 86–7, 112, 177–8, 253–5
Impersonality 110–11
Induction 121–2
Infinity 146–64, 221
Inner experiences 25, 73, 98*n.*, 187–8
Introspection 73–4, 119–20, 167–8, 205
Ionians 147

James, W. 185
Judgement 17, 71–2
Justification (of attitudes) 72–3, 98–9, 109–10, 165–81
Justice 93–4, 254

Kant, I. 86, 96*n.*, 102–3, 104*n.*, 118, 121, 149, 177, 197, 226, 237, 251
Keynes, J. M. 122

Language 14–16, 23;—(ordinary) 15, 40, 53–4, 239–41; —game 23, 199
'Lead-up' and 'lead-down' 137–40
Leibniz, G. W. 150, 232
Lewis, H. D. 233
Lewy, C. 142, 233
Locke, J. 149, 197
Logic, Formal 248
Logical values 105, 112–13, 124

Mace, C. A. 188
McTaggart, J. M. E. 53, 55, 126, 218, 233
Malcolm, N. 234, 236–7
Marx, K. 114, 224
Meaning 16, 18, 22, 26–7, 208–16, 245
Meinong, A. 18, 166
Mental acts 36, 239–40
Metaphysics 24, 123–7, 129–30
Mill, J. S. 90
Mind-body relation 37, 139–40
Misology 126
Modality 54*n.*, 157
Moods of Soul (*Bewusstseinslagen*) 20–1

Moore, G. E. 40*n.*, 69–70, 142, 232–47
Multiplicative Axiom 164

Names 17–18, 59–61, 198
Naturalistic fallacy, 69–70, 250
Ness, A. 42*n.*
Nietzsche, F. 86, 179–81

Ockham, Wm. of 232
Ontological Proof 96*n.*, 102
Pascal, B. 166
Philosophy 28–9, 36–8, 199–200, 227
'Pictures' 134–5
Plato 74, 110, 126, 148–9, 161, 241, 243
Positivists 67
Present tense 43–5, 53–6, 125–6
Presuppositions (of attitudes) 170–1
Price, H. H. 120*n*, 186
Principia Mathematica 218–19
Prior, A. N. 54*n.*
Private language 24–6, 200–1, 227–8, 246
Private states 19, 21, 204
Probability 122, 252, 254
Proselytism 84, 251
Publicity 24–5, 134, 187, 203–4, 227–8

Quine, W. V. 149, 153–4, 158, 162

Ramsey, F. P. 234
Religion 97–104
Richness (value) 116–17
Royce, J. 218
Russell, B. 115, 151–2, 155–6, 233–4, 242
Ryle, G. 131–2, 139, 141, 186, 192–3, 218

Sartre, J. P. 217
Scepticism 34–6
Scheler, M. 166
Schlick, M. 142
Scholasticism 101–2
Sense-datum 238
Sidgwick, H. 86
Smith, Adam 86, 111*n.*, 177, 253
Space 121

258

INDEX

Spinoza, B. 102, 150, 217, 222, 226
Stevenson, C. S. 110*n.*, 171–2, 175, 249
Stout, G. F. 186
Sympathy 83

Tarski, A. 160
Teaching of use 16
Tenses 54
Thoughts 16–22, 187, 189, 191, 202–3
Time 39–56, 121
Titchener, E. B. 108, 182–4, 188, 192–4,
   203, 205
Toulmin, S. 248
Truth 71, 106, 145, 216, 223

Unconscious, The 140–1
Use 15

Validation 208, 214–16
Values 80, 110, 255
Verification 26, 118, 152, 208, 214
Voluntary acts 78–9

Welfare 81–2, 88–94
White, A. 232
Whitehead, A. N. 47*n.*, 51–2, 124
Wisdom, J. 75*n.*, 237
Wittgenstein, L. 13, 46*n.*, 75*n.*, 115,
   134, 184, 186–7, 192–3, 196–206,
   222, 227, 233–4, 237, 248, 255
Würzburg School 182, 186, 189, 192,
   204–5

Zeno 37, 50–1, 163